Beethoven's Immortal Beloved

Solving the Mystery

Edward Walden

Introduction by William Meredith

THE SCARECROW PRESS, INC.
Lanham • Toronto • Plymouth, UK
2011

Published by Scarecrow Press, Inc.
A wholly owned subsidary of The Rowman & Littlefield Publishing Group, Inc.
4501 Forbes Boulevard, Suite 200, Lanham, Maryland 20706
http://www.scarecrowpress.com

Estover Road, Plymouth PL6 7PY, United Kingdom

British Library Cataloguing in Publication Information Available

Library of Congress Cataloging-in-Publication Data

Walden, Edward, 1933–
Beethoven's Immortal Beloved : solving the mystery / Edward Walden ; introduction by
William Meredith.
  p. cm.
Includes bibliographical references and index.
ISBN 978-0-8108-7773-3 (cloth : alk. paper) — ISBN 978-0-8108-7774-0 (ebook)
1. Beethoven, Ludwig van, 1770-1827—Relations with women. 2. Arnim, Bettina von,
1785-1859. 3. Beethoven, Ludwig van, 1770-1827—Correspondence. I. Title.
ML410.B4W217 2011
780.92—dc22
[B]   2010039075

∞™ The paper used in this publication meets the minimum requirements of
American National Standard for Information Sciences—Permanence of Paper
for Printed Library Materials, ANSI/NISO Z39.48-1992.

Printed in the United States of America

To the memories of Mrs. Hedwig Salzer of New York City,
Professor Hans Eichner of Rockwood, Ontario,
and Konstanze Baumer of Syracuse, New York,
all of whom provided inspiration and support in the author's quest.

Contents

Acknowledgments

$\mathcal{I}$ would like to express my thanks and gratitude to the many people who gave me guidance and help during my quest. Some but not all of them are noted and briefly described below, in alphabetical order.

Peter Anton (Tony) von Arnim (Brandenburg, Germany), Bettina's great-great grandson, provided invaluable assistance to me before his death in the summer of 2009.

Dr. Wolfgang Bunzel (Frankfurt, Germany), a German scholar and specialist in areas of literature that include Bettina, is co-editor of the *Internationales Jahrbuch der Bettina von Arnim Gesellschaft*, which published my paper on the 1812 Teplitz Letter described in chapter 5. Although he does not share my views on the truthfulness of Bettina, he has been consistently helpful and dispassionate, providing me with sources that supported my views when he encountered them. I have tried to be equally magnanimous whenever I came across material that would support his views.

Bram Costin (Toronto, Ontario) is a former legal colleague who read my manuscripts and provided moral support. In particular, he acted as my guarantor to gain access to Bettina's extremely valuable papers in the Morgan Library in New York.

Dr. Hans Eichner (Rockwood, Ontario) was, before his death in 2009, one of the world's leading scholars of Romantic German literature, and a poet and novelist as well. He provided me with translations of key German passages, analyzed and supported the authenticity of Beethoven's sonnet, and assisted me in responding to a particularly acerbic academic attack on one of my published papers in the *Beethoven Journal*. His wife, Kari, a former professor of German, collaborated with him on the especially difficult German passages.

Freundeskreis Schloss Wiepersdorf gave their kind permission to use the painting of Bettina reproduced in this book. This and other paintings and correspondence of Bettina and her family may be found in the Bettina und Achim von Arnim Museum at Schloss Wiepersdorf, which is near the little village of Wiepersdorf, Germany, approximately 50 miles south of Berlin.

Sylvi Goode, B.A. (Salzburg, Austria), supported my project from the very beginning and helped me with the translation of difficult passages of German sources.

Dr. Stanley Hamilton (Vancouver, B.C.), a professor of business and commerce, took the time to read my manuscripts and give me advice on the expectations of academia in the technical portions of the papers reprinted in the *Beethoven Journal*.

Dr. Michael Ladenburger and his assistants at the Beethoven-Haus in Bonn spent several days helping me in my research there.

Chisholm Lyons, Q.C. (Ajijic, Mexico), a former legal colleague who reads all sorts of literature voraciously, spent many hours reading my manuscripts, recommending corrections, and pointing out gaps in sequential narrative and argument.

Mag. Lukas Mayerhofer (Vienna, Austria) is a skilled academician whose research helped me considerably, especially his sorting through old handwritten Imperial Austrian Protocols and discovering what I was seeking but in a form I had never envisaged.

Dr. William Meredith and Patricia Stroh of the Ira F. Brilliant Center for Beethoven Studies in San José, California, provided me with encouraging words at the very beginning and continued to help me in my research throughout the past two decades.

Gordon Sato (Toronto) is a former legal colleague and voracious reader, extremely knowledgeable about literary formalities, who took the time to read my drafts and provide me with critical comments.

Patrick Saunderson (Toronto) is a friend who acted as my sounding board throughout, giving me moral and literary support and comments.

Bruce Thomas, Q.C. (Toronto), a former legal colleague, provided sage, realistic advice in developing the structure of my theory.

Jennifer Walden, my eldest daughter, read through my final manuscript, gave invaluable suggestions, and accompanied me to visit Mrs. Felix Salzer in New York.

Brian Young (Toronto) graciously took the time to read my manuscripts and cut out frequent repetitions, for which I am somewhat notorious.

Introduction

William Meredith, Director
Ira F. Brilliant Center for Beethoven Studies
San José State University

BETTINA BRENTANO, THE IMMORTAL BELOVED, AND BEETHOVEN HISTORIOGRAPHY

$\mathcal{T}$o enter, or reenter, consideration of the identity of the woman Beethoven called his "Unsterbliche Geliebte" (Immortal Beloved) is to come face to face with one of the most disputed topics in Beethoven historiography. Just as biographies often reveal as many—if not more—insights into their writers as their subjects, so the most commonly accepted theories about the identity of the Immortal Beloved reveal a great deal about their authors and the field of Beethoven research in general. As well, a close examination of the topic exposes the widely divergent and heated opinions on the importance of biography in musicology as a broad topic, as well as the complex interplay between biography and music. Though many Beethoven scholars—especially those who were trained in and subsequently adopted essentially positivist/modernist frameworks—regard the question of the identity of the Immortal Beloved as a subgenre of lightweight scholarship that cannot result in new insights into the "music itself," other Beethoven scholars, including myself, regard the subject to be extremely revealing—a sort of Rorschach music-biography test.

As editor of *The Beethoven Newsletter/Journal* published by the Ira F. Brilliant Center for Beethoven Studies at San José State University and the American Beethoven Society since 1986, I have been drawn—sometimes willingly, at other times somewhat unwillingly by virtue of my position and the consequences of peer review decisions about articles submitted to the journal—into the passionate debates over the identity of the Immortal Beloved.[1] Because we established at its founding that the newsletter should be an open forum to publish both new information about Beethoven as well as new interpretations of subjects, it contained a significant number of substantive articles either on or related to the Immortal Beloved topic by Virginia Beahrs (1986, 1990), Maynard Solomon (1987), Marie-Elisabeth Tellenbach (1987, 1993–94), Susan Lund (1988, 1991), and Christopher Reynolds (1988) during the nine years the publication was titled the *Beethoven Newsletter*.[2] These included not only challenges to Maynard Solomon's popular theory that the Immortal Beloved was Antonie Brentano from Virginia Beahrs and Marie-Elisabeth Tellenbach (both of whom supported the candidacy of Josephine Brunswick), but also endorsement of his theory from Susan Lund, who built on it with her own hypothesis that Antonie's son born on March 8, 1813, was Beethoven's own child. (Solomon had not included the information that Antonie had borne a son in either the article in which he first put forth his theory or in the subsequent chapter on his theory in his biography.)[3] The decision to publish articles on Beethoven's biography in the newsletter drew praise from esteemed English Beethoven scholar Alan Tyson, who wrote to me on October 3, 1987, "The ordinary musicological journals usually contain very little information about Beethoven's personal life; it's very good for us to have today a place for comments on his personality, his letters, etc."

For an editor trained in the traditional Beethoven topic of sketch studies, however, I quickly learned that dealing with such articles was a plunge into hot water. Solomon, for example, did not believe that the newsletter should have published Lund's theory because it was "sensationalistic," as he told me at a national meeting of the American Musicological Society in 1988. Some of the articles were less controversial, such as the literal scholarly translation in English that Virginia Beahrs made of the letter to the Immortal Beloved, which we published in 1990 and which still remains the most accurate translation.

I also had to accept early on that my own opinion on the identity of the Immortal Beloved, speaking in my role as director of the only Beethoven center in the United States, was of interest to some people. As I revisited Maynard Solomon's theory and argument, became more familiar with the competing theories, discovered the weak points in the arguments for every candidate, and realized that uncontested confirmatory evidence does not exist, I officially adopted the position that the matter remains contested but that there may well be evidence that has yet to come to light that will help solve the problem, and that it is best to keep an open mind on the issue. Indeed, instead of the matter becoming clearer over the past two decades, it now appears to be fraught with complexities that have obscured what I naively once imagined to be a purely scholarly matter whose solution would eventually succumb to the normal tools and methodologies of musicological inquiry. Before turning to Bettina Brentano's musicality and other facts that make her an attractive candidate, let me elucidate some of these complexities.

THE RELATIONSHIP BETWEEN BIOGRAPHY AND MUSIC

The complexity that plays a decisive role in the Immortal Beloved debate is the matter of the relationship of a composer's biography to his or her music. The ways in which we answer the straightforward question "Did the circumstances of Beethoven's life affect his music?" have profound implications. Every Beethoven article, monograph, and biography answers the question either by replying to it directly or by ignoring it. Let me give an example that may seem at first unfair. In 1961, the eminent modernist Schenkerian theorist Allen Forte published an elegant, well-written study on the sketches for Beethoven's Piano Sonata in E Major, Opus 109. The monograph was published by the Music Teachers National Association.[4] In the book's 12 chapters, Forte surveyed the "traditional bases of Beethoven's compositional technique," analyzed the three movements of the sonata, and discussed the sketches for each movement. In a remarkably concise, Webern-like conclusion (all of seven sentences!), Forte wrote:

> The nature of Beethoven's original musical idea for Op. 109 remains concealed. However, the sketches and autograph revisions suggest that he had in mind a plan for the entire work, a plan which during the composition process was amplified and refined until all elements had been coordinated to form a cogent tonality. . . . In Example 38 we see that the thirds of the variation's theme bass (Example 38c) are implicit in the tetrachords of the second movement (Example 38b, mm. 4 and 8), while both tetrachords and thirds are given by the bass line in the first movement (Example 38a). The intervallic basis of this extended relationship also enables us to understand more fully the significance of detail, for we see that the first four notes of the composition constitute a microcosm, a concise linear statement of the two intervals which are to control the whole work.[5]

As elegant and valuable as Forte's analysis is, at the same time it is as clear an example as possible of a methodology of interpreting music that divorces the notes not only from the generally accepted sphere of "meaning" that was articulated by Classical period writers on aesthetics but even further from the realm of a composer's biography. In such writings, the value of Opus 109 appears not to lie in its immensely rich depiction of human emotions but in its "cogent tonality" and the microcosm of the first four notes that "control the whole work."[6]

Contrast this position with the words of one of the most important aestheticians of the second half of the 18th century, Johann Georg Sulzer: "We have seen that music is essentially a succession of sounds that *originates* in a passionate emotion, and which has the power to depict, arouse, and strengthen such emotions" (italics mine).[7] Or, in the words of Heinrich Christoph Koch from 1782–93, "the proper aim of music is to awaken feelings. Accepting this a given, we now wish to consider more closely the principal aspect of this art, that is, compositions and the works arising therefrom."[8] Such conclusions from writers of Beethoven's lifetime would seem to imply that music analysis and criticism have as their most important task the unveiling of emotions in music and how those emotions are depicted and symbolized: in other words, the origins of the music.

To be fair, Forte did not set out to explicate the "passionate emotion" that was the origin of Opus 109 or the manner in which the sonata communicates meaning. And what he did set out to do, he accomplished with a finesse and skill I deeply admire. But his 20th-century view of the "compositional matrix" of the origins of the sonata demonstrates how distant his approach was from that of Beethoven's own time.

If we adopt the opposite approach and proceed from the Classical period framework that this sonata was designed to "depict, arouse, and strengthen" emotions, are there any connections between the sonata and the composer's biography in general and also specifically to the identity of the Immortal Beloved in particular? In the latter case, the answer is clearly yes. We need only consider the moving letter that Beethoven wrote to the dedicatee of the sonata, Maximiliane Brentano (1802–61), one of the daughters of Antonie Brentano, who remains the leading candidate for the Immortal Beloved in the United States. On December 6, 1821, the composer explained the rationale for his dedication to "Maxi," directly linking it back to the years 1810–12 when he had been accepted into the intimate circle of the entire family:

> A dedication!!!—now it is not one [of those dedications] that are misused by a great many—It is the spirit that unites the noble and better people on this earth, and which <u>time</u> can <u>never</u> destroy, this is the spirit of which I speak to you now, and which makes me see you still in your childhood years, likewise your beloved parents [geliebte Eltern], your excellent and gifted mother, your father inspired by truthful, good, and noble qualities, always thinking about the well-being of his children, and so I am in this moment [again] in the Landstrasse—and see you before me, and when I think on the excellent qualities of your parents, I have not the slightest doubt that you will have been and are daily inspired to be a noble imitation of them—never can the memory of such a noble family fade in me, may you sometimes remember me fondly—my heartfelt wishes, may heaven bless you your life and the loves of those around you forever.—Affectionately and always your friend Beethoven.[9]

The backstory of the letter begins with Antonie's father, Johann Melchior von Birkenstock, who owned a large house on the Landstrasse (destroyed today) that contained his immense collection of art, books, and scientific objects. After his death in late October 1809, his daughter Antonie, along with her family, moved from Frankfurt to handle the sale of many of these objects, a sale that took place in 1812. Though she may have met Beethoven already in the 1790s (according to two sources), it was during the period 1810–12 that Beethoven became close to the family. According to family lore, the children brought the composer flowers and fruit, and the composer returned the favor with chocolates. In addition, in June 1812 he dedicated the Piano Trio in E-flat Major, WoO 38, to Maxi "to encourage her in her fortepiano playing." Beethoven is supposed to have visited the family often, attended chamber music concerts at the Landstrasse house, and improvised for Antonie when she was indisposed. In August 1812, in the aftermath of what appears to be some catastrophe regarding the Immortal Beloved, perhaps in Teplitz, Beethoven traveled to Karlsbad and Franzensbad with the family, immersing himself once more in their family life.

Any interpretation of Beethoven's dedication letter for Opus 109—one of the most personal dedications of his entire career—must, it seems to me, take into account the riddle of the Immortal Beloved. If, as Yayoi Aoki and Maynard Solomon have argued,[10] Antonie was the Immortal Beloved, Beethoven's poignant remembering of what the entire family meant to him must somehow be reconciled with the fact that the composer and Antonie, during those very same years of 1809–12, were not only in love with each other but writing to each other about their love (not to mention the possibility that Antonie's child, Karl Joseph, born on March 8, 1813, may have been Beethoven's son). If Antonie were the Immortal Beloved, it is difficult for me not to interpret the dedication letter as disingenuous if not deliberately deceitful. How could Antonie be one of the "noble and better people on this earth" if, as Maynard Solomon suggests, she "may well have asserted that the conditions of her existence were not an insuperable bar to their union, and advised Beethoven that she was willing to leave her husband and remain in Vienna, rather than return to Frankfurt"?[11]

On the other hand, it is difficult to know what to make of the fact of Beethoven's attempted and successful dedications of three of his most important piano works to Antonie in 1823. Antonie herself was the intended dedicatee of the English editions of Beethoven's last two sonatas, Opuses 110 and 111. In an undated letter probably from February 1823, Beethoven instructed Ferdinand Ries, "The dedications of the two sonatas in A-flat and in c minor are to Mrs. ~~von~~ [?] Brentano born von Birkenstock."[12] For some reason, Beethoven's directions were not followed exactly: the English first edition of Opus 110 bore no dedicatee, but the English first edition of Opus 111 was indeed dedicated to "Antonia Brentano." (The continental first edition of Opus 110 does not have a dedicatee; Opus 111 was dedicated to Archduke Rudolph, who was seemingly Beethoven's default dedicatee.) Antonie did receive the continental dedication of the Diabelli Variations, Opus 120, in June 1823. Was this flurry of dedications to Maximiliane and Antonie in 1821 and 1823 somehow related to the Immortal Beloved affair—or were they simply in reaction to the fact that Beethoven was involved in questionable financial dealings with Franz Brentano on the sale of the *Missa solemnis*, a complex matter far beyond the scope of this preface?

If one chooses to attribute these letters and dedications not to memories of the Immortal Beloved or to ongoing financial misdealing, it would be equally if not more reasonable, in my opinion, to interpret them as evidence of yet another example of Beethoven's deep attachment to a family that had meant much to him over the years. This is especially true because the last three sonatas have a striking nostalgic quality. In this regard, we can look not only at his first and most important "substitute" family, the Breunings from Bonn, who so "adopted" the young composer that their home became his second home, but also at families like the Malfattis, with whom Beethoven was extremely close for several months in the spring of 1810. Beethoven wrote to Baron Ignaz von Gleichenstein, who had introduced him to the family, "I am so happy when I am with them. I feel that they may be capable of healing the wounds with which wicked persons have torn my soul apart."[13] Beethoven's close relationship with the Giannastasio del Rio family in 1816 (through 1820)—as seen below, a relationship that resulted in important clues about the Immortal Beloved and Beethoven's views on romantic relationships—is yet another instance of intimate bonds with a substitute family. Fanny Giannastasio del Rio's diary clearly reveals that the composer turned to this family as a substitute as well.

If we, then, subscribe to the school of thought that allows for works to be connected to their composers' lives, the Sonata in E Major, Opus 109, had a deeper origin than mere tetrachords and intervals: the *Idee* (idea) that inspired the work, to use the word of Beethoven's pupil Carl Czerny,[14] may reside in a deeply felt nostalgia about what the relationship with the Immortal Beloved might have meant for the composer's life, in an attempt to curry favor with Franz Brentano indirectly through dedications to his daughter and wife, or to Beethoven being consumed by a desire to depict his remembering of what it felt like to be embraced and loved by an artistic noble family.

Of course, many if not most writers have refused to divorce music from biography. On the opposite end of the spectrum from Forte's works are studies where interpretations of the works depend to one degree or another on knowledge of some aspect of biography—either of specific events in the composer's life or of his personality or character. Many are not controversial: I don't recall a single study of the *Eroica* Symphony that does not somehow take into account Beethoven's relationship to Napoleon on one of several levels.

Other studies connecting biography and music have generated substantial opposition. Unfortunately, several of the most important and controversial studies about the Immortal Beloved have never appeared in English translation, which has substantially restricted their impact. The first is a monograph by Jean and Brigitte Massin, *Recherche de Beethoven*, that appeared in 1970. The first part of the work is titled "'L'unique bien-aimée' de Beethoven: Joséphine von Brunswick"; this part is divided into two sections. In the first, the Massins argue that Josephine was the Immortal Beloved, and in the second that the presence of Josephine in Beethoven's life left traces in his music. Over 65 pages, the Massins connect the opening rhythmic motive of the single movement piano work, the *Andante favori*—which Beethoven gave to Josephine with the words "here—your—your Andante"—to the reappearance of the same motive in a set of later works. From the standpoint of music theory, the connections make eminent sense. Among other works, they discussed the beginning of the Sonata in F Major, Opus 54; sections of *Fidelio*; the opening of the *Appassionata*; no. 6 of *To the Distant Beloved*, Opus 98; and the theme of the slow movement of the Sonata in E Major, Opus 109. As the Massins noted, the close similarity between Opus 109 and the song cycle had already been pointed out by Romain Rolland decades earlier in 1937. The melodic shape and rhythmic motives of the setting of the words "Und ein liebend Herz erreichet was ein lieben Herz geweiht" ("And a loving heart attains that which a loving heart consecrates") in the sixth song of *To the Distant Beloved* are strikingly similar to the melodic and rhythmic shape of the second phrase of the variation theme of Opus 109.[15] The sonata phrase appears to be an instrumental recomposition and rethinking of the song phrase:

An die ferne Geliebte, Opus 98, no. 6

Andante [molto cantabile ed espressivo], *Gesangvoll, mit innigster Empfindung*

Sonata, Opus 109

Seven years later, the Massins' work was elaborated on and extended by the Swiss/German musicologist Harry Goldschmidt in a lengthy monograph entitled *Um die Unsterbliche Geliebte: Eine Bestandsaufnahme* (Concerning the Immortal Beloved: A Stock-Taking).[16] It too has never been translated into English. The monograph is divided into five sections: a review of the topic, the Brentano family, the Brunswick family, consideration of the candidacies of Antonie versus Josephine, and "Music as Biographical Document." This last section is most important for my purposes here. In it, Goldschmidt argues that music can serve as a biographical document and that many works, Opus 109 again among them, contain musical encodings of the solution to the Immortal Beloved.

At first encounter, Goldschmidt's theory would suggest that Antonie Brentano was indeed the Immortal Beloved, since her daughter was the dedicatee of the sonata. However, he followed the Massins by connecting the music back to the *Andante favori*. Furthermore, Goldschmidt theorized that the opening is a musical encoding of Josephine's name, which makes sense in the light of the rhythmic settings of the name *Leonore* in the opera examples provided by the Massins:[17]

Goldschmidt's and the Massins' theories that the Immortal Beloved was Josephine Brunswick and that the music contained coded references to her found much broader circulation in German-speaking countries in a book from 1983 by Marie-Elisabeth Tellenbach titled—I give it here in English even though it too has unfortunately never appeared in English translation—*Beethoven and His "Immortal Beloved" Josephine Brunswick: Their Fate and Its Influence on Beethoven's Work*.[18] Trained in musicology, history, German history, and Latin, Tellenbach adopted many of the same works discussed by the Massins, including Opus 109, as her evidence while adding previously unknown documents from the Deym family archive. (Some of these are briefly discussed in the English-language synopsis article of Tellenbach's main points in 1987 and also in an essay by Virginia Beahrs that revisited the entire question; each appeared in the *Beethoven Newsletter*.)

Over time, Goldschmidt's preoccupation with the theory that many pieces of Beethoven's music contained coded references to Josephine seemed to become an obsession that threatened to derail his reputation as a—and I select this adjective carefully—sane Beethoven scholar. In the fall of 1985, at a conference organized by Beethoven scholar William Kinderman in Victoria, Goldschmidt gave an extended and bizarre presentation on the transformation of the *Andante favori* motive and its reappearance in later works. To those of us who were not then familiar with the Massins' work and Goldschmidt's own monograph, his obsession seemed not only excessive but also a clear demonstration of the perils of the approach.

It should not have surprised us, then, when the clearly exasperated Maynard Solomon vented his irritation in an essay from 1987. (It was not entirely clear if the source of the irritation was the continuing opposition to his own theory about the identity of the Immortal Beloved in English-language publications or to the connecting of music and autobiography.) In an essay that first appeared in the *Beethoven Newsletter* in 1987, he opined against Tellenbach, Goldschmidt, Beahrs, and the Massins. With learned sarcasm, Solomon closed his entire essay with these words:

> By elaborating the assumption that all music is concealed autobiography, Josephine Deym advocacy has become close kin to the more extreme speculations on the identity of the "onlie begetter" of Shakespeare's sonnets; and by resorting to the unriddling of secret codes and hidden texts in Beethoven's instrumental music, such advocates bid fair to become the new Baconians and Oxfordians. The pursuit of Josephine Deym threatens to convert the works of Beethoven into a new "Great Cryptogram," whose mysteries may be plumbed only by the initiate.[19]

Other Beethoven scholars had different reactions to Tellenbach's arguments as they appeared in 1987 in the English-language condensed synopsis of her book. Alan Tyson wrote Beethoven Center curator Patricia Stroh on January 7, 1988, to thank her for sending three copies of the issue containing the essay:

> It is very useful for me to have two extra copies of the Newsletter because of the especial value of Marie-Elisabeth Tellenbach's account of Beethoven and the Countess Josephine Brunswick—I shall want to show this very important article to lots of people (and I wouldn't like to risk the loss of my only copy!). Of course her point of view is in great opposition to Maynard Solomon's identification of the Immortal Beloved (which I accepted in the New Grove Beethoven); but I think it should at least be available to English-language folks who will not read her large German-language book on the subject. So I expect to see references to this Newsletter in a lot of footnotes!

Tellenbach herself generously wrote to me on February 6, 1988, "I perfectly understand Maynard Solomon's irony and can't blame him for this."

Stepping back from the fray and revisiting these competing theories, I was struck by the overlapping musical conclusions in two studies. The first I have already mentioned. In his Schenkerian analysis of Opus 109, Allen Forte made the following observations:

> 1. The possibility for interaction of [the third and fifth of the triad] and for their connection by means of the passing note A (or A#) is implicit. Indeed, it will become increasingly clear that to a considerable extent the melodic development of the [first] movement resides in the composing-out of relationships which are inherent in the upper third of the triad where A plays a primal role.[20]

> 2. [Codetta of the second movement:] Beginning on C in the upper voice of the third measure from the end we have a "diminutional" tetrachord which supports the more fundamental motion, B-A-G. . . . Clearly one of the main melodic considerations here is the descent from fifth to third. This may be regarded as a means of preparing the interval—the upper third of the tried—which is to be composed out in the subsequent movement.[21]

To pare down Forte's argument, in the sonata the interval of the third from B-G# (or B-G) and the notes A or A# and C (and C#) are "composed out" in each movement. What strikes me as particularly important about Forte's brilliant analysis is that, once transposed from E Major to E-flat Major, these are exactly the same notes and intervals that shape the phrase singled out by the Massins in the sixth song of *To the Distant Beloved*.

The second conclusion was put forward in 1988 by Christopher Reynolds in a sophisticated analysis of *To the Distant Beloved*. In it, he demonstrated

that "Beethoven remarkably, yet surreptitiously, depends on motivic transformation to derive songs 2 through 6 from individual phrases of song 1."[22]
Reynolds labeled the motive of the phrase quoted by the Massins "Motive 3";
he focused on it when he discussed the coda, remarking, "No other motive
compares." Near the end of his article, Reynolds suggested that "Beethoven
himself may have attached special significance to Motive 3, judging from its
appearance on at least three other occasions. He first used a strikingly similar
motive in his *Andante favori* of 1805. . . . Subsequently Beethoven used it in
the variation movement of the Pianoforte Sonata in E Major, Opus 109, in
the second phrase of the theme. And lastly it appeared again in 1825 when
George Smart heard Beethoven improvise 'for twenty minutes in a most extraordinary manner' on the motive."[23] Reynolds concluded his article with
a middle-ground position. After pointing out that scholars have "interpreted
the recurrences of its opening motive as evidence of Beethoven's unabated
love for the Countess" [Josephine], he ended: "While the possibility exists
that Beethoven—like Schumann, Brahms, and others afterwards—associated
particular motives with specific people and ideas, one cannot make such a
claim on the basis of the evidence now available. In any case, it is not necessary
to associate specific motives in *An die ferne Geliebte* with specific individuals
to show that the meaning of the text—and thus also of the music—parallel
Beethoven's life circumstances."[24]

The debate on whether music can—even should—be connected in a
general or specific way to a composer's biography is one that will assuredly
continue, even though postmodern theories that are still influential in musicology support analyses and arguments that contextualize music in the richest
ways possible.

BEETHOVEN SCHOLARSHIP AND THE
INFORMATIONAL CASCADE EFFECT

When I was a doctoral student at the University of North Carolina at Chapel
Hill, I was fortunate to study Beethoven's sketches in a graduate seminar with
visiting professor Douglas Johnson, then on the faculty of the University of
Virginia, Charlottesville. Johnson had written his dissertation on Beethoven's
early sketches, was completing what has become known as the "Sketch Bible"
with Alan Tyson and Robert Winter,[25] and was, as he mentioned in class one
afternoon, a self-confessed member of the "Beethoven mafia," as he labeled
it. Anyone familiar with Johnson's work knows both that he thinks critically
about every issue he visits and that he is not afraid to stir up matters, as he did
with an opinion essay published in 1978 that appears to have altered the course

of sketch studies.[26] His admittedly casual remark about a "Beethoven mafia" and its influences has made me question over the years whether the world of American Beethoven scholarship was indeed controlled by a relatively self-contained circle of scholars who were the go-to choices for vetting Beethoven articles and books for scholarly journals, arranged Beethoven conferences for each other at which members of the circle gave papers without issuing the standard scholarly "call for papers," and supported each other's work in very significant ways such as writing supportive letters for grants and promotions.

In two ways, Johnson's comment made sense. As the entire field of musicology became more and more responsive to postmodern theories about music, culture, and the arts in the 1980s and 1990s, the world of Beethoven scholarship appeared to remain, for the most part, stubbornly impervious to change. Even new subfields like sketch scholarship continued to be valued not for what the sketches could tell us about the meaning of the works (characterized in recent musicology as the field of "hermeneutics," which has proven to be especially fruitful in the writings of Lawrence Kramer),[27] but how they detailed the purely musical genesis of the themes and the formal construction of the pieces. Feminist work on Beethoven met with either outright ridicule or cool disinterest.

One possible example of the control of the field in journals intended primarily for musicologists is the absence of a single article about the Immortal Beloved in the 13 volumes of the prestigious journal *Beethoven Forum* that appeared from 1992 to 2006. I say *possible* because, while I was a member of the advisory board for the journal, I was never asked to vet an article, although I did on more than one occasion recommend that authors send their work to the editorial board. At one of the last annual meetings of the advisory board of the journal at the national conference of the American Musicological Society, one of the editors asked, after mentioning an article that had been submitted on the topic, if there was not an informal agreement in place to "embargo" any Immortal Beloved article. Perhaps the total absence of any articles on the subject simply reflects the fact that none substantive enough for publication were submitted.

It may also be true that something parallel to the "informational cascade effect" of behavioral economics has played a role in the belief that Maynard Solomon had solved the Immortal Beloved question once and for all, even though the cascade theory was developed based on actions and behavior more than information itself.[28] Briefly, an informational cascade "occurs when it is optimal for an individual, having observed the actions of those ahead of him, to follow the behavior of the preceding individual without regard to his own information. . . . Four primary mechanisms have been suggested for uniform social behavior: (1) sanctions of deviants, (2) positive payoff externalities, (3) conformity preference, and (4) communication. . . . These effects tend to bring about a rigid conformity that cannot be broken with small shocks. Indeed, the longer the bandwagon continues, the more robust it becomes.[29] . . . The fundamental reason the outcome with observable actions is so different from the observable-signals benchmark is that once a cascade starts, public information stops accumulating."[30] Cascades can, however, be broken: "in reality we do not expect a cascade to last forever. Several possible kinds of shocks could dislodge a cascade; for example, the arrival of better informed individuals, the release of new public information, and shifts in the underlying value of adoption versus rejection."[31]

The endorsement of Solomon's solution in the Beethoven entry by Joseph Kerman and Alan Tyson in the 20th edition of *The New Grove Dictionary of Music and Musicians* in 1980 did much to solidify support: "Of recent conjectures as to her identity the most plausible (by Maynard Solomon) is that she was Antonie Brentano. . . . Brentano fulfils all the chronological and topographical requirements for being the addressee of the famous letter." In the next sentence, however, Tyson and Kerman note: "Whether the psychological requirements are fulfilled depends on one's reading of her personality and of the letter's intended meaning."[32] Kerman and Tyson's endorsement of Solomon's theory as the "most plausible" became a point of fact in the revision of their article for *Grove Music Online* credited to Beethoven scholar Scott Burnham. Now the sentence reads: "Maynard Solomon showed in the 1970s that she [the Immortal Beloved] was Antonie Brentano, an aristocratic Viennese lady ten years younger than Beethoven who at 18 had married a Frankfurt businessman, Franz Brentano, Bettina Brentano's half-brother. (As there are no explicit letters from Antonie Brentano to Beethoven, some do not accept that the case is closed; but no plausible alternative has been presented.)" With the transformation of Solomon's "conjecture" (Kerman and Solomon's term) into *statement of fact* and the denial of the existence of at least one if not two plausible alternatives, Solomon's theory might seem confirmed.[33] Recently, a major American Beethoven scholar commented to me privately that those who refuse to accept the Antonie theory are "impervious" to the facts of the case.

Although I am old-fashioned enough to believe in "facts"—that is, discrete pieces of information that scholars and researchers use to construct their theories—my ears pricked up at the assertion that Solomon's case was indeed built of facts, even though the argument is masterfully constructed. The English Beethoven scholar Barry Cooper made two valuable observations about the case of the Immortal Beloved as it relates to facts at the end of an extended 1996 book review of Gail Altman's *Beethoven: A Man of His Word / Undisclosed*

Evidence for His Immortal Beloved.[34] First, Cooper wrote: "Frequently it happens that a hypothesis by one scholar becomes accepted as fact without proper scrutiny. . . . She demonstrates, as indeed Tellenbach has done, that much of the basis for the claims of Antonie's supporters consists of distortions, suppositions, opinions, and even plain inaccuracies."[35] He then goes on in blistering detail to elucidate Altman's many substantial errors and concludes, "The book is most useful, then, for reminding us how little we know for certain about Beethoven's personal life." Second, he states, "Although Antonie Brentano may seem completely unsuitable from a psychological angle (and not everyone is agreed about this), it begins to appear again that she must be the Immortal Beloved. The only other possibility is that Beethoven kept his relationship so guardedly that his connections to the woman in question are otherwise virtually undocumented. If that is the case, her name should be found on the Karlsbad arrival lists. Before there is any more speculation, a re-examination of these seems to be the next step."[36] Cooper's point, it seemed to me then, was well taken: the only "fact" of the case is that Beethoven believed the woman was in Karlsbad when he wrote the letter. As you will read in this monograph, however, another possibility must be considered: Beethoven only needed to have thought that the woman was in Karlsbad. If it can be demonstrated that any of the candidates intended to go to Karlsbad and may have communicated that information to Beethoven, she should be considered with an open mind.

Cascade theorists argue that the introduction of "new public information" has the potential to dislodge a cascade. In my opinion, Walden's research on Bettina Brentano has resulted in the injection of just such new information and arguments into the Immortal Beloved controversy. Whether or not his arguments succeed in displacing Antonie—and in the absence of any indisputable evidence in any candidate's favor—they surely warrant wider distribution and critical attention. I'll close with some of my own reactions to his theory.

BETTINA BRENTANO, THE MUSICIAN, AS THE IMMORTAL BELOVED

Having mulled over arguments in favor of Antonie Brentano, Josephine Brunsvik, Almeria Esterhazy, and Bettina Brentano over the past 25 years, I find three parts of the Bettina theory to be persuasive enough that I believe Walden's proposal merits unbiased consideration.

First, to the best of my knowledge there are only two extant Beethoven letters in which he unequivocally uses the informal "du" with a woman. The first three usages occur at the end of his letter of January 16, 1811, to Bettina

Brentano: "nun lebwohl liebe liebe B. ich küsse dich ~~so mit Schmerzen~~ auf deine Stirne, und drücke damit, wie mit einem Siegel, alle meine Gedanken für dich auf"[37] ("now best wishes dear dear B. I kiss you ~~thus with pain~~ on your brow, and impress thereby, as with a seal, all of my thoughts for you"; Beethoven crossed out "so with pain"). The second letter containing "du" is the letter to the unidentified woman now known as the Immortal Beloved written on July 6 and 7, 1812, 18 months after the first letter. Unlike the first letter, Beethoven uses the informal forms of *you* throughout the letter, even in the famous closing "ewig dein[,] ewig mein[,], ewig unß[.]" (It is difficult to translate the close into English with any assurance of accuracy as to Beethoven's meaning.[38]) Since the consistent use of "du" in the second letter occurs in what is clearly a love letter—even though one primarily of ambivalence, even rejection, as several writers have noted—such use makes logical sense. In the letter to Bettina, however, Beethoven began the letter, as he should have when writing to a married woman, using formal address (*sie, ihren, ihnen, seinen*) and continued with the formal *you* until he began the emotional close quoted above.

Is it really conceivable that Beethoven used the familiar *you* with the recently married Bettina in 1811, then used it again in 1812 with her married sister-in-law Antonie, and that these are the only two women whom Beethoven ever addressed with the familiar *you*? Besides the repeated use of "du" at the first letter's close, Beethoven also revealed in the 1811 letter, in my opinion, that he was at the least infatuated with Bettina and had been since his summer of 1810 in Baden: "I carried your first letter about with me the whole summer, and it often made me feel blissful[39] . . . yet in my thoughts I write you however 1,000 times thousand letters in my thoughts" (that is, a million letters!). Is it a coincidence that Beethoven begins the Immortal Beloved letter stating that he is writing "only a few words today, and to be sure in pencil (with yours)," meaning that he has been carrying around, again in the summer away from Vienna, a physical object that represented on some level the woman with whom he was in love?[40] Was it possible for Beethoven to be in love with Bettina and with her sister-in-law Antonie during the same months preceding the Immortal Beloved letter?

My second argument focuses on a single unusual word Beethoven used to describe the possibility of a life with the Immortal Beloved: "Chimäre." In the middle of September 1816, again spending the summer in Baden, Beethoven and the father of Fanny Giannastasio del Rio had a conversation that was later recorded by Fanny. According to Fanny, "er liebe unglücklich! Vor fünf Jahren hab er eine Dame kennen gelernt, mit welcher sich näher zu verbinden er für das höchste Glück seines Lebens gehalten hätte. Es sei nich daran zu denken, fast Unmöglichkeit, eine Chimäre" ("he loves unhappily!

Five years ago he made the acquaintance of a lady, whom to bind himself nearer to would have been the greatest happiness life could have afforded him. It was not to be thought of, almost an impossibility, a chimera"). Literally, a chimera was, according to Homer, "a thing of immortal make, not human, lion-fronted and snake behind, a goat in the middle, and snorting out the breath of the terrible flame of bright fire." Such a combination fire-breathing creature was of course an impossibility; as is clear from Beethoven's combination of the terms *impossibility* and *chimera* in his conversation with Giannastasio, he was remembering the possibility of binding himself to the Immortal Beloved as an almost impossible fantasy, a chimera. But why did Beethoven chose such a strange descriptor for this impossibility, one that would evoke—particularly for a learned teacher like Giannastasio—the weird Greek combination of creatures? Is it possible that the Immortal Beloved herself was chimera-like, that is, a combination of characters that do not belong together, a character with the potential to breathe fire?[41]

Viewed from the perspective of the 19th century (let alone the 21st), it is difficult for me not to view Bettina as a chimera: a beautiful woman who was famous for her ability to improvise songs, a woman composer, a feminist and intellectual, a writer, seducer of Goethe, a social reformer intensely interested in the political situation of the day and later in life an advocate for the oppressed Jewish community, a wife and mother, an early Romantic idealist, and a fiery figure on every level. By the end of her life, she had occupied at least three positions normally reserved for men: composer, published writer, and social reformer.

As feminist scholars have recently argued, Bettina rejected many societal models: she revolted "against any a priori limitations on particular biological entities" and sought to "dismantle the very categories on which notions of gender rest." According to Elke Frederiksen and Katherine Goodman,

> Unlike those of her contemporaries such as Goethe, Schiller, and Friedrich and August Wilhelm Schlegel, Brentano von Arnim's views on gender do not rely on Romantic understandings of the complemental nature of gender or on the realization or re-evaluation of virtues thought to be "feminine." Rather, she dismantles dichotomistic definitions of reality. . . . Brentano von Arnim's understanding of her own more complex identity obliges her to engage in activities traditionally thought to be the prerogative of men. That they are thought to be masculine, however, is shown to be the perspective of her culture and not her own.[42]

It is difficult not to add her dismantling of gender categories to the list of ways in which Bettina was chimera-like. In fact, in combination with her many activities, it is difficult to imagine how a life with her would have given

Beethoven the "stability and regularity" he said that he sought in the Immortal Beloved letter. I must note that many of Bettina's accomplishments mentioned above *postdate* her time with Beethoven. However, by the time she met him in the spring of 1810, Bettina had been fascinated and was immersed in three subjects that also preoccupied Beethoven: freedom and the ideals of the French Revolution (introduced to her by her grandmother), Goethe's writings,[43] and music.

It is this last item in my list of Bettina's accomplishments that leads to my third and final argument in favor of Walden's theory that she may be the Immortal Beloved. In my opinion, it is also the strongest. As mentioned above, some writers and scholars have opined that Antonie Brentano does not meet the "psychological requirements" for being the Immortal Beloved. Except for her "lack of regularity," Bettina seems to me to have been exactly the kind of woman to whom Beethoven would have been most attracted—most particularly because of her genius at improvisation. Her abilities in this regard and a serious assessment of her musical creativity are discussed in Ann Willison's excellent essay on Bettina's musical life, "Bettina Brentano von Arnim: The Unknown Musician."[44] The following survey of her musical biography is drawn entirely from Willison's work.

While attending the Ursuline school in Fritzlar in 1794–97, Bettina received her first music instruction. When she moved to Frankfurt, she studied piano and music theory with Philip Carl Hoffmann. At the age of 19, she described her musical activities to her brother-in-law: "I am taking [forte]piano lessons from Mr. Hoffmann again, despite the temptations that I am exposed to; I am also diligently learning to sing, and I am in the theater whenever operas are performed; music is now my only resource and refreshment."[45] In 1809, she traveled to Munich to study voice and composition with the opera composer Peter von Winter, whom Willison describes as her most important teacher. In February 1809, she wrote to Achim von Arnim and the Savignys that she had two 90-minute voice lessons a day in addition to piano and Italian lessons with other teachers. Upon her return to Landshut, she studied *Generalbaß* with Eixdorfer. In 1810, Bettina enlisted the assistance of a law student named Alois Bihler to help her transcribe her songs. Bihler helped her with harmony and the notation of rhythm and she returned the favor: "He gives rhythm to my music, I expand on his melodies, he writes a purer bass setting for me, I invent the instrumental countermelodies for him."[46] Her final formal voice lessons with Vincenzo Righini ended shortly after her marriage to Achim in 1811.

Beethoven must have been impressed with what Willison calls her "strongest musical talent, one for which she consistently received approbation": improvising music to poetry. Bihler enthused: "Irresistibly . . . Bettina ruled in the realm of song. Here she fully unfolded her wonderful individuality. . . . She seldom chose written songs—singing she created poetry and creating poetry she sang with a glorious voice in a kind of improvisation. For example, she knew how to pour a wealth of soulful emotion into the simple, slow scale as well as into the spontaneous improvisations welling up from within her, so that I listened enraptured by her creative genius."[47] Bihler was not alone in his praise; in 1806 the famous writer Ludwig Tieck was brought to tears by her improvisation. Clemens Brentano described the occasion: "she sang before him so wonderfully and beautifully, the wild cry of her soul, no *Aria brillante* like she used to sing. . . . As for her singing, her extemporaneous singing—I saw him shedding tears, and he assured me that he, the church musician, had never heard anything like it and he now knew how music originated."[48]

Though there are no records of Beethoven having heard Bettina improvise, if he did hear her on a similar occasion, it must have been a remarkable moment in the history of music: the most gifted instrumental improviser of his time, who was also famous for bringing music lovers to tears with his playing, listening to the spontaneous creation of music and words.

It may be that Bettina's genius at improvisation and deeply Romantic approach to the creative process held back her progress as a composer: in her own self-critiques, her technical musical skills remained far below her lofty inspirations. In 1810—the year she met Beethoven—she lamented: "I firmly believe that music would become my daily occupation, but more difficulties appear each day; for example, I have a true inclination to the most profound thoughts, but my technical ability does not match up to my imagination, which remains unfulfilled in consequence."[49] In later years, she expressed similar frustrations in her epistolary novels: "I am also exasperated with thoroughbass. I would like to blast this fraternity of tonalities into the air,"[50] and "I can invent a melody more easily than analyze it in terms of its origins. With music, everything must be grasped more deeply by introspection than by following the law; this law is so narrow that the musical spirit overflows it at every instant."[51]

The same disdain for pedantry reappears in her description of the seven songs published in 1842 in what is called the Spontini Songbook:

> I have kept my word to Spontini, by having seven songs engraved, together with their completely obstinate accompaniments. . . . As for the musical turnings, the craggy, uneven path of this product, I could not decide, even for the sakes of the foolish bigwigs who make laws governing an art which is much too powerful for their pedantic ears, to give up a single false fifth. . . . How many thousand times I repeated with rapture these tones that pleased only me, in whose place I never found any others, but only these, although they played for me such beautiful harmonic progression! Therefore ev-

erything had to remain as the true, original, stuttering conversation of my soul newly in love with music; and I could not bear that my bass—which dances with quick leaps and bounds around the melody like a deer, often chimes in and echoes more clearly in its feelings what the melody is unable to express—that they master its willful turning and spinning.[52]

Despite Bettina's statement that the songs will not make pedantic bigwigs happy, the set as a whole is remarkable. In fact, I think it is impossible to understand Bettina fully unless the music of this set is known and appreciated.[53] One of the most beautiful songs in the collection is "Aus dem *Wintergarten* von Arnim," no. 3 (see the music example).[54]

Achim von Arnim's *Der Wintergarten*, published in 1809 before he married Bettina, is a collection of short stories and novellas based on 17th-century German works of varying sorts. The stories are recounted by a group of people in a country house to pass the time during a long winter, a winter that is an explicit political metaphor for the French occupation of Germany.[55] The first of the four stanzas reads:

> The sluggish day is pursued by the moon,
> it breathes peace [Ruh] onto all living things,
> the sea is not accustomed to such peace,
> to unrest [Unruh] I am in this manner elected;
> my only happiness, the dream,
> I must foremost hate:
> in the highest bliss it will
> abandon me once more.[56]

In the second stanza, a wind from the east throws asunder the fruits and weaker blossoms of a fruit tree. In the last two stanzas, Achim writes about a secret love whose identity cannot be revealed because of "silent vows and virtue": "my completely hidden light of love must surely not reveal its flame."

Bettina's 15-measure strophic setting depicts, brilliantly and with sophistication, both the joyful subjects of the text (peace/fortune/dream, fruitfulness, love, Concordia) and their loss (hate, fruits and blossoms thrown asunder, the pain of secret love). Though set in the key of E-flat Major—a key associated by some writers with "love, devotion, of intimate conversation with God"[57]—Bettina blights the happiness traditional for this major key with a harmonic progression to F Minor—a key associated with sorrow, grief, and despair—on the word "Unruh" (unrest, agitation) in m. 7. In m. 9 she ironically tonicizes F Minor with its secondary dominant on the words "my highest happiness." When the music wants to turn to B-flat Major, a key associated with love, it stalls at F Minor.[58]

Aus dem *Wintergarten* von Arnim

Another important musical symbol in the setting is seen in Bettina's use of rhythmic suspensions. Just as the progression toward happiness, fruitfulness, and the dream of revelation is delayed by the long winter, so the progress of the melody is constantly impeded with suspensions across the beats and measures. The voice part contains suspensions in 13 of its 14 measures, and the piano part is laden throughout with single and double suspensions. Another "suspension" is the fact that the song begins not with its tonic chord but on the dominant—and resolves to the tonic midway through the first measure on the rhythmically weaker half of the measure.

Three more symbols stand out. The first involves the striking use of falling sixths in mm. 1 and 12. The melody begins on the fifth scale step, leaps up a fifth to the second scale step, and then descends a major sixth to the fourth scale step (the pitch A-flat, which she almost always harmonized as the third of the F-Minor triad). Falling major sixths are frequently used as symbols of incoming happiness, and indeed, in both measures, the sixth resolves with a suspension to the third degree of the scale, the note that most importantly signals the "major-ness" (happiness) of major keys. Thus, Bettina begins the song with a depiction of the happiness that eludes the singer throughout the poem, a happiness most clearly enunciated at its end: "O sweet last moment, there I will be able to speak, there will the stream of love break through my eyes and lips."

The desired happiness is also depicted masterfully in Bettina's construction of the melody. The melody rises again and again by step toward the goal of B-flat (the dominant note of the key) but never attains it. Such an ascent appears most clearly in mm. 3–4, but the stubborn withholding of the longed-for note returns three more times in this tiny jewel of a song.

The last symbol I will mention occurs in the last two measures. Just as the poet remains deprived of his dream, so the singer does not find musical completion: she stops singing on the weakest beat of the penultimate measure on a highly expressive diminished seventh chord on the note A-natural, and the piano completes the final cadence of the song in the only measure in which it plays alone. The singer's last note—on a weak beat and harmonized with a diminished chord—feels as unfinished as the poem in performance.

Willison suggests, though without supplying any evidence, that someone may have assisted Bettina with the accompaniments of the Spontini songs.[59] If she did indeed have assistance polishing the piano parts, such assistance would not contradict the fact that Bettina herself created the musical symbols discussed here. The use of key symbolism, melodic and harmonic suspensions, falling sixths, and the failure of the melody to reach the dominant note in its ascent are all aspects of the music that originated in the melody itself, and the creation of melody was—according to her contemporaries and this music—one of her greatest gifts and skills.

The fact that Bettina was a supremely gifted singer and very talented composer does not, of course, make her the Immortal Beloved. But the several completed songs that survive and her skill at improvisation document that she was indeed the kind of woman Beethoven found most compelling. It is surely no coincidence that Josephine Brunsvik, the only woman we know for a fact Beethoven loved, was a very gifted pianist and had a profound understanding of music.

Despite the opinions of some in the musicological world, uncovering the true identity of the Immortal Beloved remains an important goal for Beethoven biographical work. Walden's carefully drawn arguments and theories warrant our serious consideration. If they do not topple Antonie as a favored candidate in English-speaking countries, at the very least they will enrich our understanding of a brilliant and unique woman who meant a great deal to Beethoven in 1810 and 1811.[60]

NOTES

1. The most difficult series of events concerned the publication of an extended review article by Marie-Elisabeth Tellenbach titled "Psychoanalysis and the Historio-critical Method: On Maynard Solomon's Image of Beethoven," which was published in volumes 8 and 9 of *The Beethoven Newsletter* in 1993–94. Tellenbach had sent a manuscript of her critique of Solomon's work to Dr. Thomas Wendel, president of the executive board of the American Beethoven Society, who was a professor of history at San José State University. Wendel wrote her back that her critique "had to be" published, if I remember his conversation with me accurately; I foresaw—correctly—that there would be a significant backlash to its publication given the acceptance of Solomon's Immortal Beloved theory and the popularity of his work among Beethoven scholars and the public. The first half of the article, which does not concern the Immortal Beloved but Solomon's psychoanalytic interpretations of Beethoven's biography (the Family Romance, Beethoven's dreams, etc.), appeared in a double issue (Winter 1993–Spring 1994; vol. 8, no. 3, and vol. 9, no. 1). As with all such cases, I invited Solomon to write a response to Tellenbach's critique of the application of psychoanalysis to historical figures as opposed to traditional historiocritical approaches to the writing of biography. He declined the invitation to respond in the newsletter and subsequently resigned from the Center's advisory board, for this as well as other reasons. The resignation of one of the most popular Beethoven scholars in the United States from the Center's advisory board was hardly a fortuitous event in the history of the fledgling Center. The second half of Tellenbach's article critiques his Immortal Beloved theory.

2. For a list of the titles and citations, see the website of The Ira F. Brilliant Center for Beethoven Studies, www.sjsu.edu/beethoven.

3. Maynard Solomon, "Antonie Brentano and Beethoven," *Music & Letters* 58, no. 2 (1977): 153–89; and the chapter on the Immortal Beloved in his *Beethoven* (New York: Schirmer, 1977; rev. 1998).

4. Allen Forte, *Compositional Matrix*, vol. 1 of *Monographs in Theory and Composition* (New York: Music Teachers National Association, 1961).

5. Forte, 85.

6. In a famous complaint about Forte's book that appears in an essay criticizing analysis that does not include aesthetic criteria, Beethoven scholar Joseph Kerman argued that "the distinguished analyst Forte wrote an entire small book . . . from which all affective or valuational terms (such as 'nice' or 'good') are meticulously excluded." See Kerman, "How We Got into Analysis, and How to Get Out," *Write All These Down* (Berkeley: University of California Press, 1996), 14.

7. *Aesthetics and the Art of Musical Composition in the German Enlightenment: Selected Writings of Johann Georg Sulzer and Heinrich Christoph Koch*, ed. Nancy Kovaleff Baker and Thomas Christensen, no. 7 of *Cambridge Studies in Music Theory and Analysis*, ed. Ian Bent (Cambridge: University Press, 1995), 83.

8. *Aesthetics and the Art of Musical Composition*, 144.

9. The translation, which is my own, is based on the original German given in *Ludwig van Beethoven: Briefwechsel Gesamtausgabe*, ed. Sieghard Brandenburg, 7 vols. (Munich: Henle, 1996), 4:462, letter no. 1449. In Emily Anderson's edition, the letter is no. 1062: *The Letters of Beethoven*, 3 vols. (London: Macmillan, 1961), 3:932–3.

10. Yayoi Aoki's first article predates Solomon's by 18 years: "Ai no dsensetsu—Betoven to 'fumetsu no koibito'" ("Love-legends—Beethoven and the 'Immortal Beloved'"), *Philharmony* 31, no. 7 (1959): 8–21. (*Philharmony* is the magazine of the NHK Symphony Orchestra.) Her next study appeared in 1968: *Ai no densetsu—geijutsuka to joseitachi* (Love-legends—Artists and Women) (Tokyo: San'ichishobo, 1968). The most recent is *Beethoven: Die Entschlüsselung des Rätsels um die "unsterbliche Geliebte,"* trans. from the Japanese *Bētōven fumetsu no koibito no nazo o toku* by Annette Boronnia (Munich: ludicium, 2008). On the cover of this monograph, Aoki is credited with being "the first person to propose internationally that Antonie von Brentano was the Immortal Beloved." While this is true, the appearance of her theory in Japanese in a magazine of a symphony ensured that knowledge of it would hardly register in the West. It was not listed in the bibliography of new Beethoven literature of 1957–61 published by the Beethoven-Haus in its *Beethoven-Jahrbuch*.

11. Solomon, *Beethoven*, 2nd ed., 241. On the other hand, if Antonie was the Immortal Beloved and decided to remain with her family rather than leave them for Beethoven, that would have been evidence qualifying her as one of the "noble and better people on this earth."

12. My translation of Brandenburg no. 1592; Brandenburg expressed doubt on the struck-out "von"; the letter is no. 1118 in Anderson's edition. The first continental editions of Opuses 110 and 111 had already appeared with Maurice Schlesinger in July 1822.

13. Anderson no. 235; Brandenburg no. 436.

14. Carl Czerny, *On the Proper Performance of All Beethoven's Works for the Piano*, ed. Paul Badura-Skoda (Vienna: Universal Edition, 1970), 50.

15. Jean and Brigitte Massin, *Recherche de Beethoven* (Paris: Fayard, 1970), 134–36.

16. Harry Goldschmidt, *Um die Unsterbliche Geliebte: Eine Bestandsaufnahme*, vol. 2 of his *Beethoven-Studien* (Leipzig: VEB Deutscher Verlag für Musik, 1977), 551 pages. The monograph was also published in the West by Rogner and Bernhard (Berlin) in an undated edition.

17. Goldschmidt, 298.

18. Marie-Elisabeth Tellenbach, *Beethoven und seine "Unsterbliche Geliebte" Josephine Brunswick: Ihr Schicksal und der Einfluß auf Beethovens Werk* (Zurich: Atlantis Musikbuch Verlag, 1983), 340 pages.

19. Maynard Solomon, "Recherche de Josephine Deym," *Beethoven Newsletter* 2 (1987): 26.

20. Forte, 19.

21. Forte, 54.

22. Christopher Reynolds, "Separated Lovers and Separated Motives: The Musical Message of *An die ferne Geliebte*," *Beethoven Newsletter* 3, no. 3 (1988): 50.

23. Reynolds, 55.

24. Reynolds, 55.

25. *The Beethoven Sketchbooks* (Berkeley: University of California Press, 1985).

26. Douglas Johnson, "Beethoven Scholars and Beethoven Sketches," *19th-century Music* 2, no. 1 (1978): 3–17.

27. See, for example, his essay "Hands On, Lights Off: The 'Moonlight' Sonata and the Birth of Sex at the Piano," *Musical Meaning: Toward a Critical History* (Berkeley: University of California Press, 2002), 29–50.

28. Though the informational cascade effect was developed as an economic theory, researchers have applied the theory to other fields of research: "Most doctors cannot stay fully informed about relevant medical research advances in all areas. The theory of information cascades predicts fads, idiosyncrasy, and imitation in medical treatments." See Sushil Bikhchandani, David Hirshleifer, and Ivo Welch, "Learning from the Behavior of Others: Conformity, Fads, and Informational Cascades," *Journal of Economic Perspectives* 12, no. 3 (1998): 167.

29. Sushil Bikhchandani, David Hirshleifer, and Ivo Welch, "A Theory of Fads, Fashion, Custom, and Cultural Change as Informational Cascades," *Journal of Political Economy* 100, no. 5 (1992): 992–93.

30. Bikhchandani, Hirshleifer, and Welch, "Learning from the Behavior of Others," 155.

31. Bikhchandani, Hirshleifer, and Welch, "Learning from the Behavior of Others," 157.

32. The dictionary article was published separately as Joseph Kerman and Alan Tyson, *The New Grove Beethoven* (New York: Norton, 1980, 1983), 55.

33. The Wikipedia article on "Immortal Beloved," which badly needs editing for both historical accuracy and objectivity as defined by Wikipedia, does contain a review of the contesting theories.

34. Barry Cooper, "Book Review: Beethoven's Immortal Beloved and Countess Erdödy: A Case of Mistaken Identity?," *Beethoven Journal* 11, no. 2 (1996): 18–24.

35. Cooper, 18.

36. Cooper, 24.

37. Quoting from the transcription in Goldschmidt, *Um die Unsterbliche Geliebte: Eine Bestandsaufnahme*, 206. In his edition of the letters, Brandenburg did not transcribe "so mit Schmerzen," which was crossed out; see his letter no. 485.

38. Emily Anderson translated the close as "ever yours[,] ever mine[,] ever ours[.]" See her letter no. 373. Virginia Beahrs translated the close as "forever yours[,] forever

mine[,] forever us[.]" See her "'My Angel, My All, My Self': A Literal Translation of Beethoven's Letter to the Immortal Beloved," *Beethoven Newsletter* 5, no. 2 (1990): 36, 39. The sense of the close seems to be that Beethoven was ever the Immortal Beloved's, she was eternally his, and that their relationship was also eternal. Lund theorized that the "unß" referred to Antonie's child born in 1813.

39. In the letter Beethoven spells the word "seelig" instead of "selig"; because he was a terrible speller, one might not want to make too much of the misspelling, but his error combines the concept of the soul (Seele) and blissfulness (selig) into a new word.

40. Considering the topic of Beethoven retaining objects from Bettina, I should mention the Beethoven letter in the Center's collection that contains an impression that Sieghard Brandenburg identified to Ira Brilliant as one of her seals when he inspected the letter in Arizona. Since the date of the letter is 1817, this means that seven years after having met her, Beethoven either retained her seal or stationery that had belonged to her or that she had sent him. On the topic of Bettina sending blank pages to her correspondents such as Goethe, see Marjorie Goozé, "A Language of Her Own: Bettina Brentano von Arnim's Translation and Her English Translation Project," in *Bettina Brentano von Arnim: Gender and Politics*, ed. Elke Fredericksen and Katherine Goodman (Detroit: Wayne State University, 1995), 288. See Walden's discussion of the Beethoven Center letter for further details.

41. The myths of the chimera were described in Virgil's *Aeneid*, Homer's *Iliad*, Hesiod's *Theogony*, and Ovid's *Metamophoses*. Owen Jander has argued that Beethoven knew the last source in a famous 1791 Viennese edition in which the chimera is mentioned in book 6; see his *Beethoven's "Orpheus" Concerto* (Hillsdale, N.Y.: Pendragon, 2009).

42. See Elke Fredericksen and Katherine Goodman, "'Locating' Bettina Brentano von Arnim, A Nineteenth Century German Woman Writer," *Bettina Brentano von Arnim*, 24–25.

43. Fredericksen and Goodman, 14–17.

44. Ann Willison, "Bettina Brentano von Arnim: The Unknown Musician," *Bettina Brentano von Arnim*, 304–45.

45. Willison, 312. Willison provides the original German texts in her article after the translations.

46. Willison, 313.

47. Willison, 313–14.

48. Willison, 314.

49. Willison, 317.

50. Willison, 318.

51. Willison, 318–19.

52. Willison, 320.

53. I am indebted in this regard to mezzo-soprano Malin Fritz, tenor Christopher Bengochea, and pianist Patricia Stroh, who performed four songs from the set in a lecture recital at the Beethoven Center on May 1, 2008.

54. I would like to thank Corey Keating, assistant editor of *The Beethoven Journal*, for the creation of the music examples. The score of the song is reproduced from the first edition without editing. Readers who would like to obtain a copy of this score

may download it from *The Beethoven Gateway*, which is accessible at no charge through the website of the Beethoven Center (www.sjsu.edu/beethoven/).

55. See J. Edward Mornin, "National Subjects in the Works of Achim von Arnim," *German Life and Letters* 24, no. 4 (1971): 321–3. Mornin concludes, "The collection was intended to bring about a national rebirth such as is symbolized at the end of the work: the winter's ice on the river is broken up, and from an ice-floe which comes drifting downstream people rescue a child in a cradle emblematical of new life."

56. I would like to thank Adriana Rätsch-Rivera for preparing a translation of several of the poems in the set that was distributed at the lecture recital mentioned above. I have made minor alterations of her translations to make them more literal. The remaining three strophes are: "(2) A fruit tree, heavy with fruit, hangs down its branches to the earth: a fresh wind comes from the east, it cannot be shaken. It throws asunder fruits and weak blossoms, and my dreams, which glowed so heavenly at night. (3) I love someone, but tell not who, because silent vows and virtue command me so: my completely hidden light of love must surely not reveal its flame. It pushes its pure and lucid rays to heaven; the sun is now a reflection of my pain. (4) Oh Concordia, remain in your peaceful state, never will I disturb your harmony, my only well-being and woe is thee, to you I will ever pledge my peace. O sweet last moment, there I will be able to speak, there will the stream of love break through my eyes and lips."

57. Paul Ellison has recently published a study derived from his 2010 dissertation in which he analyzes the relationship of the meanings of the Gellert set of songs to key relationships. In the dissertation, he proves, in my estimation, that Beethoven was keenly aware of the importance of key symbolism and used each key in either one or more "practices" common to the key. Ellison's theories are demonstrated in his article "Affective Organization in Beethoven's Gellery Lieder, Opus 48: Affirming Joanna Cobb Biermann's Theory on Beethoven's Intended Order of the Songs," *Beethoven Journal* 25, no. 1 (2010): 18–31. In his dissertation, Ellison argues that Beethoven used the key of E-flat Major in three different practices. The use of E-flat in this song falls into Ellison's second practice for the key.

58. See Rita Steblin, *A History of Key Characteristics in the Eighteenth and Early Nineteenth Centuries* (Rochester, N.Y.: University of Rochester Press, 1996), 245, 266, 296.

59. Willison, 323.

60. Perhaps because of the significant number of studies published on non-Antonie candidates in German, there appears to be much less acceptance of Aoki's and Solomon's theories there.

Background

$\mathcal{T}$his book is the result of almost two decades of investigation and research about the identity of Ludwig van Beethoven's so-called Immortal Beloved. Solving the mystery will open up a whole new source for analysis of Beethoven's middle years and his musical output during those years and afterward. French author and Nobel Prize winner Romain Rolland attributed Beethoven's seventh, eighth, and even sketches of his ninth symphonies to the happiness resulting from his contact with the Immortal Beloved. Beethoven's seventh was his most rhythmic, his eighth was his most joyous, and his ninth, although put on hold after his romantic disappointment of 1812 but finally completed many years later, was his most monumental. It is generally acknowledged that the sudden decrease in his musical output after 1812 was related to that romantic disappointment, and analysts have struggled to discover the cause of it for more than a century.

Bettina Brentano matched perfectly Beethoven's needs and aspirations when she first met him in 1810. Beethoven was an admirer of the great German playwright, poet, novelist, and scientist Johann Wolfgang von Goethe. Bettina was a close friend of Goethe and admired him as much as if not more than Beethoven. She believed in spirituality, loved and appreciated music, and wrote music of her own. She was a Romantic idealist who constantly searched for truth. Perhaps as a result of naive optimism, she also hoped and worked through her social contacts for a solution to the political turmoil of those Napoleonic times.

Her ideals and idols were based on her own needs for music, interaction with genius, and literary creation. Goethe responded to two of them. Beethoven responded to two as well, albeit a different two. When Bettina had a minor domestic quarrel with Goethe's wife that resulted in her ostracism from Goethe in

1811, Beethoven was there to fill the gap, and the sorts of letters she previously sent to Goethe were now sent to Beethoven instead.

When she first met Beethoven, she was beautiful, unattached, and filled with a youthful energy that matched Beethoven's own. As a result of her meeting him, she considered engaging in a career in music and politics, thus foreswearing the traditional life of a wife, almost the only choice then open to privileged and educated women. Beethoven, then in his late 30s, had at that stage of his life finally achieved success and relative financial stability. When Bettina met him, he was searching for a woman with whom he could share his life, hopefully with musical talent that could possibly help him in coping with his growing deafness.

After much internal turmoil, Bettina decided instead to enter into a marriage with a handsome acquaintance only a few years older than she, Achim von Arnim, who needed a child to inherit control of an estate that would give him financial security for life. Confessing afterward that she did not marry him for love, Bettina married him nevertheless in 1811 but almost died in providing the child he needed. After her near death experience at the childbirth, she briefly concluded in 1812 that marriage was a mistake and that a life in music was what she needed and really wanted.

For artistic, emotional, and spiritual comfort, she had during her pregnancy substituted Beethoven for Goethe as her correspondent, telling Beethoven, as she had told Goethe in earlier letters, how much she loved him and how she dreamed at night of lying in his arms. Unlike Goethe, poor lovesick Beethoven, longing for sexual and emotional female companionship, hoped that her love was of a different kind than she possibly meant, and in a brief moment of physical and emotional exhaustion in 1812, he hesitatingly wrote to her of his own love and dreams: "I talk to myself and to you—[written pause] arrange that I can live with you, what a life!!!" But he never mailed his letter because Bettina arrived just after he wrote it in the summer spa town where he was trying to find a cure for his illnesses. There she told him of her decision that she could not leave her child and would remain in the role of a loyal German wife. The shock of hearing that decision devastated Beethoven. He accepted it with dignity but almost never recovered.

The story has a pathos that even Goethe could not conjure up in his novels and plays. It was at the same time a boon and a tragedy for music, and ranks with one of the greatest and most poignant love stories of all time.

Right at the outset, I would like to make clear to the reader that I am a lawyer by training. The methodology I use in this book is to present the case that Bettina is Beethoven's Immortal Beloved in the best light I can, as would a lawyer attempting to prove that case in court. The case's theory is based on two crucial letters completely overlooked in previous scholarly analyses. The first is the single surviving 1811 letter from Beethoven to Bettina written just 18 months before he wrote his letter to the Immortal Beloved. In that 1811 letter, Beethoven acknowledged having already received two letters from Bettina and begged her to write to him soon and often. Second is the love and desire for physical intimacy Bettina expressed for Goethe in at least one surviving letter to him, from which I argue that Bettina wrote similar missing letters to Beethoven.

To make my case, I set out in chapter 2 what I intend to prove, much as does a plaintiff's lawyer or prosecutor at the beginning of a trial. The supporting evidence is presented with full citations in the chapters that follow. I also critically analyze the evidence and arguments proffered on behalf of Josephine Brunsvik and Antonie Brentano, the other women currently contended to be Beethoven's Immortal Beloved, and show how they could not be. It is for the reader to judge whether I have established my case.

Chapters 3 through 11 explore in greater detail events touched on in chapter 2 and contain reference citations constituting the evidence I rely on in support of my theory. Many of the sources are in English and may be found in most reference libraries in North America. Other sources are in German and include many out-of-print or obscure books found only in libraries and archives in Europe.

Chapter 13 offers a short synopsis of the salient points of the narrative and my general conclusions as well as a summary of the most important supporting evidence. Interested readers will find additional source citations in the Summer 1999 and Winter 2002 issues of the *Beethoven Journal*, which contain two papers written by me that form the nucleus of this book.

As will be noted in chapter 3, Bettina published in 1835 after Goethe's death and when she was 50 a partly fictional book of correspondence exchanged between her and Goethe in the early years of her life, entitled *Goethe's Correspondence with a Child*. It is referred to in this book as the "*Goethe Correspondence* book" and is mentioned frequently. The only English translation of the *Goethe Correspondence* book published in North America is Bettina von Arnim, *Goethe's Correspondence with a Child* (Boston: Ticknor and Fields, 1859), but it is out of print and very rare. However an e-text of it is available online at www.hedweb .com/bgcharlton/bettina-goethe.html. A single volume in German including the book itself and the original letters exchanged between them that have been found up to now is available in volume 2 of *Bettine von Arnim Werke und Briefe*, 4 vols. (Frankfurt: Deutscher Klassiker Verlag, 1992).

The reader should be aware at the outset that Bettina intended the *Goethe Correspondence* book to be an epistolary book similar in form to an epistolary novel, a form used and popularized by Goethe for one of his own novels. She used her own letters to Goethe as the basis for her book but modified some of the original letters and may have created others. The liberties she took in doing that caused her critics to contend that she created or took similar liberties with all three letters to her from Beethoven that she published. When one of those three was found in the possession of a third party late in the 19th century exactly as she had published it, her critics contended that she concocted *in full* the remaining two because they were not found among her papers after her death. One of the purposes of this book is to establish that she did not concoct those other two. In making my argument, I distinguish between the letters she exchanged with Goethe and with Beethoven that survive today and are found in collections, archives, or libraries, with those that are not. The latter are referred to in this book as the "missing" letters. Included in the description of missing letters are those that were seen and verified by reliable witnesses at some time in the past. The many critics of Bettina contend that most, if not all, of the letters I describe as missing never existed at all and that she concocted them, but one of the purposes of this book is to show that most, if not all, of the missing letters did in fact exist but have been lost or destroyed.

FREQUENTLY USED PHRASES

Beethoven Description Letter: The letter written by Bettina describing her time with Beethoven in Vienna dated May 28, 1810, that is today missing but which was reproduced, probably in an edited form, in her *Goethe Correspondence* book. See chapters 4 and 7.

Teplitz Letter: The letter from Beethoven to Bettina written in Teplitz in July 1812 and handed to her as he hurriedly left town, just two and a half weeks after he wrote his letter to the Immortal Beloved. In the Teplitz Letter, he said a painful good-bye to Bettina and ended with the words "God how I love you!" The letter does not survive, but its authenticity is corroborated by the facts detailed in chapter 5.

1810 Letter Gap: The gap in the surviving letters from Bettina to Goethe starting with her partly surviving letter to him of July 28, 1810, just where she begins to describe what happened between her and Beethoven, up to her surviving letter to him of October 18, 1810. The missing letters were referred to in Goethe's surviving letters to her of August 17 and October 25, 1810. See chapter 4.

Beethoven's Letter to the Immortal Beloved

HISTORY OF BEETHOVEN'S LETTER
TO THE IMMORTAL BELOVED

*A*lthough the great German composer and pianist Ludwig van Beethoven poured out his emotions countless times in his music, he did so in a significant way only twice through the medium of written words. The first time was in 1802, in the form of a will now known as the Heiligenstadt Testament. In it, he told of struggling to come to grips with the terrible realization that he, a musician who lived in a world of hearing and creating sound, was inexorably growing deaf. The second time was in 1812, when at the age of 41 and still a bachelor, he wrote in pencil a passionate yet touching 10-page love letter to an unidentified woman. The letter was undated and presumably never sent, because it was found after his death 15 years later, hidden away in a locked and secret drawer. He did not name the woman in the letter, which began with the words "My angel, my all, my self" and ended with the words "your beloved L, forever yours, forever mine, forever us." She has come to be known historically as his "Immortal Beloved," because he referred to her that way within the text of the letter. An English translation of the complete letter is set out in appendix A, and its first and last pages are shown in illustrations 5a and 5b.

The mystery of who his love was remains unsolved to this day. Beethoven never married, but in 1816, Fanny Giannastasio del Rio, a young admirer, overheard him tell her father that "five years ago, he had made the acquaintance of a person, a union with whom he would have considered the greatest happiness of his life. It was not to be thought of, almost an impossibility, a chimera—'nevertheless it is now as on the first day' he could not get it out of his mind."[1] Whomever Beethoven was referring to, she is generally thought today to be the Immortal Beloved. Over the last century and a half, at least 10 names have been put forward as guesses as to who the woman was. The riddle was not made easier by the fact that the letter bore no year nor place of writing, saying however in one place, "Monday evening on July 6."

Clues within the letter allowed researchers to arrive at a consensus by the 1920s that the letter was in all likelihood written in 1812 when Beethoven was in Teplitz, a Bohemian spa town, and was intended to be sent to a woman in the nearby Bohemian spa town of Karlsbad.[2] This consensus and the resulting research has led The Ira F. Brilliant Center for Beethoven Studies in San José, California, to narrow the list of leading candidates today to three: Antonie Brentano, Josephine Brunsvik, and Bettina Brentano. Antonie was the only one of the three who actually was in Karlsbad when Beethoven wrote his letter, although Bettina had apparently intended to go there when Beethoven wrote his letter, but her husband changed their destination and they came to Teplitz instead, where Beethoven was. The problem with Antonie and Bettina as candidates, however, was that they both appeared to be happily married. Antonie was pregnant with her fifth child when the letter was written, and Bettina had given birth to her first child only eight weeks before. Josephine Brunsvik was the only one of the three whose marriage was disintegrating when the letter was written, but she was nowhere near Karlsbad that summer and appears not to have had any plans to go there.

THE CASE AGAINST ANTONIE

Antonie Brentano was first proposed as a candidate in the 1970s by Maynard Solomon, an eminent American musicologist. Of the three front-runners noted above, she was the only woman who *was* in Karlsbad when Beethoven wrote his letter, and Beethoven knew her well. The problem with Antonie being the intended recipient, however, is that the letter was in Beethoven's possession when he died, so it is unlikely that he posted it. Her presence in Karlsbad therefore works against her in favor of someone who intended to go there but may have somehow got word to Beethoven that her plans had changed. Solomon suggested that perhaps Beethoven did post the letter but that Antonie gave it back. That scenario appears unlikely because a return of the letter, effectively meaning rejection, would make it improbable that Beethoven would keep hidden away until his death such a painful reminder of the rejection. Solomon seems to have realized this, so he alternatively suggested that the kept letter was only a first draft, and that Beethoven recopied and posted it. This is even more improbable given the length of the found letter and the fact it was signed with Beethoven's initial. Of course if a copy was posted and received by Antonie, it should be noted that it has never been found in her papers.[3]

The principal reason Antonie is ruled out as the Immortal Beloved, however, stems from Beethoven's confession in 1816 referred to above that he had met the love of his life five years before. Alexander Wheelock Thayer, the great 19th-century biographer of Beethoven whose masterful work as edited and reedited still remains the foundation of research about Beethoven's life, carried out research and made inquiries that established that Beethoven, who was a frequent guest at the house of Antonie's father, had known Antonie even before her marriage in 1798. Proponents of the theory that Antonie was the Immortal Beloved dispute this, but for the reasons set out in chapter 12, their contention is mistaken. Accordingly, if Antonie knew Beethoven before 1798, she could not be the woman to whom Beethoven was referring in 1816. A powerful further argument against Antonie as the Immortal Beloved is reflected in the opinion of Richard Specht, a distinguished Viennese music critic and biographer, who wrote in 1933 that Antonie was married, and "marriage meant for Beethoven a divine sacrament against which it would be a sacrilege to offend." According to Specht, Beethoven "would have torn out his tongue rather than suffer it to utter words in the Immortal Beloved letter of such glowing passion and regret to another's wife."[4] Beethoven was a close friend of both Antonie and her husband and was like an uncle to their children. That Beethoven mused in his letter to the Immortal Beloved about living together virtually rules out Antonie, already the mother of four children, as being the intended recipient of the letter.

THE CASE AGAINST JOSEPHINE

Beethoven first met Josephine, the daughter of a Hungarian countess, when the countess brought her and her sister to Vienna in 1799 to take music lessons from Beethoven. Josephine was 20 at the time. That same year, her mother arranged a marriage for Josephine with a man 30 years her senior. The marriage was an unhappy one, and the husband died in 1804 after Josephine had three children by him and was pregnant with her fourth. There is no question that Beethoven fell deeply in love with Josephine sometime between 1804 and 1807, and there even exists an unsigned copy made by her of a letter from him written in 1804 or 1805 that resembles some of the language and ideas contained in the letter to the Immortal Beloved.[5] However, the copy uses the formal German "Sie" not the intimate "du" that Beethoven used in the letter to the Immortal Beloved. Use of "du," equivalent to the old "thou" in English, indicates in German a degree of intimacy between a man and a woman not lightly bestowed, especially by a woman. Also all *surviving* signed letters from Beethoven to her use the formal "Sie." From unanswered or disregarded letters from Beethoven to Josephine in 1807, it appears that she rejected him in that year,[6] and three years later she married again. The second marriage did not turn out well and was already in trouble in 1812 when Beethoven wrote the letter to the Immortal Beloved. Josephine and her second husband separated in 1813 or perhaps in the summer before, when the letter to the Immortal Beloved was written. Therefore, only she of the three leading candidates appears to have been separated or had a disintegrating marriage when Beethoven wrote his letter to the Immortal Beloved, and it is mainly for that reason that Josephine's candidacy remains alive.

The proponents of her candidacy contend that she and Beethoven continued their relationship after 1807 until her second marriage in 1810, then revived it when her marriage to her second husband began to disintegrate. There appears to be no evidence of that by correspondence or otherwise, so it must remain purely speculative.

Another problem with Josephine's candidacy is that there is no evidence that she was in, near, or even planned to go to Karlsbad when Beethoven wrote his letter. To the contrary, all evidence indicates that she remained in Vienna throughout the summer of 1812. She had gone to Karlsbad the previous summer, and her visit was routinely reported in the police travel registrations required in those days, but there is no record of her traveling there in the summer of 1812.

The strongest argument against her candidacy is that Beethoven had known her since 1799, so she could not be the woman Beethoven said in 1816 he had met five years earlier and whom he could not get out of his mind.

THE CASE AGAINST BETTINA

Beethoven first met Bettina in 1810, so she falls approximately within the five-year period mentioned by Beethoven in 1816 as when he had first met the "love of his life." Her husband hoped to take her for a rest cure in Karlsbad in the summer of 1812 around the time Beethoven wrote the letter to the Immortal Beloved, but according to the husband he was talked out of it by Bettina's sister and came to Teplitz instead, where Bettina met Beethoven again. Further, Beethoven wrote to her in 1811, about 18 months before he wrote his letter to the Immortal Beloved, a surviving letter in which he acknowledged her marriage with sadness, begged her to write to him, and used in one part the intimate German "du," which, so far as is known, he never used in any letter to any woman with whom he was romantically involved except in his letter to the Immortal Beloved.

What has caused Bettina's candidacy to be rejected in the past is that she was living in Berlin when Beethoven, who lived in Vienna, wrote the Immortal Beloved letter. Bettina appears at that time to have been happily married, had given birth to her first child only two months before Beethoven wrote his letter, and subsequently had six more children by her husband while she continued to live in Berlin. Also, because she was living in Berlin throughout 1811 and 1812, she could not have been having a physical affair with Beethoven. Most researchers assumed that Beethoven and the Immortal Beloved were having a physical affair because Beethoven tentatively expressed hope in the letter that the two might live together. Max Unger, a leading German researcher on the question of the Immortal Beloved, concluded in 1910, after careful consideration of Bettina's relationship with Beethoven, that the main reason she could not be the Immortal Beloved was that she loved her husband, whereas the letter to the Immortal Beloved suggests a recognition by Beethoven that the woman loved him. That she could not have been the Immortal Beloved was essentially the same conclusion reached by Richard Specht quoted above, but for a different reason, namely, Beethoven's idealization of the institution of marriage.

As will be shown in the evidentiary chapters of this book, Bettina in her later years published a letter from Beethoven written by him in Teplitz in 1812, only several weeks after he wrote his letter to the Immortal Beloved. If that letter to Bettina was genuine, it would prove conclusively that Bettina was the Immortal Beloved, but the original has not survived, and the authenticity is strongly doubted today. That is because when Bettina was almost 50, she published a book containing correspondence she claimed to have exchanged with Goethe (the *Goethe Correspondence* book), but when the original letters were made public in 1929, it was apparent that she had made a number of changes when she reproduced the letters in her book. As a result, her reliability and truthfulness are today under a cloud. The question of her reliability and truthfulness will be considered more fully in subsequent chapters of this book.

NOTES

1. Thayer Forbes, 646.
2. Thayer Forbes, 534, quoting Unger in footnote 15.
3. See Solomon, *Beethoven*, 243–4.
4. Richard Specht, *Beethoven as He Lived*, trans. Alfred Kalisch (London: Macmillan, 1933), 177–80.
5. Thayer Forbes, 377–9.
6. Thayer Forbes, 425.

The Case for Bettina

OPENING SUBMISSION

This chapter sets out in outline form my case that Bettina Brentano was Beethoven's Immortal Beloved. Supporting evidence with appropriate citations follows in succeeding chapters. The facts on which the case is based are set out here. Unless otherwise specifically noted, those facts are generally accepted and not disputed.

Bettina Brentano was born in Frankfurt-am-Main, Germany, in 1785. Her father, a widower with three children by a previous marriage, was a Catholic from northern Italy who moved to Frankfurt, remarried, and established there a prosperous import and banking business. Bettina's mother, a German and a Protestant, was 20 years younger than her husband. She gave birth to seven children by him, but during the marriage, she had a romantic relationship with the famous poet, novelist, playwright, and scientist Johann Wolfgang von Goethe, who was also from Frankfurt. Bettina's mother died when Bettina was eight. Her father sent her and her sisters to an Ursuline convent where she spent three years until the convent district was occupied by French armies, after which she moved to the home of her grandmother near Frankfurt. Her grandmother was a prominent writer, so the house was visited by eminent literary visitors while Bettina lived there. Bettina's older brother Clemens became a prominent German poet and lyric writer and was close to and supportive of her. In her later teens, she moved to the house of her older sister Gunda, who had married Friedrich Savigny, a professor of law. She also met, through the introduction of Clemens, Achim von Arnim, a literary collaborator with Clemens. Arnim was to become not only one of the great Romantic writers of German literature in the early 19th century but also Bettina's husband. Her literary connections included as well the Grimm brothers, who became icons of German folk literature. She spoke Italian, French, and German, learned Spanish, and had a working knowledge of English.

Clemens urged her to read the literature of Goethe. In doing so, she became particularly influenced by his novel *Wilhelm Meister*, in which a lively girl from Italy named Mignon, traveling in Germany with a troupe of players, sings a poem of longing for her native Italy ("Kennst du das Land?"), which was later set to music by Beethoven and is commonly known now as "Mignon's Song." Being descended from an Italian father, Bettina identified with Mignon and even dressed and tried to dance and act as Mignon was described in Goethe's novel. Equally important in her growing adulation of Goethe was the fact that Bettina got hold of and read the letters that the youthful Goethe had sent to her grandmother about his romance with Bettina's mother. Bettina became obsessed with Goethe and his literary output. In 1807 she traveled (dressed as a man because of the dangers posed by the occupying French army) to Weimar, where Goethe then lived, and introduced herself. He was 35 years older than she. As a result of their meeting, she began a lengthy correspondence with him that will be more fully described in the evidentiary chapters of this book. In January 1810, while still a student, she wrote a remarkable, surviving letter to him, the significance of which will be discussed at greater length later in this chapter. She was 24 at the time and unmarried; he was then 60 and married.

Although her social contacts gave her a strong background in literature, it was music that was her field of artistic choice. She studied voice and piano while a student in Munich, played the guitar, and sang in choirs in Berlin after she moved there in late 1810. In her later life, she composed songs that are still performed and recorded. She wrote that music is the most joyous wonder of human nature. In 1810, when she was 25, she began a long journey at the beginning of May accompanied by her sister Gunda, Savigny, and a few young fellow students, starting from a town near Munich where she had been studying, passing through Salzburg, then to Vienna, then to her family's estate in Bohemia, then to the Bohemian spa town of Teplitz, and finally around the middle of August to Berlin, where she stayed at the new home of Gunda and Savigny. That journey was pivotal in her life. In the early part of the trip, she formed a close romantic relationship with one of the students with whom she was traveling.

She arrived in Vienna around May 8, where she, Gunda, and Savigny stayed at the house of Bettina's half-brother Franz and his wife, Antonie, for the better part of a whole month. Toward the end of May during their stay, Bettina looked up the famous Beethoven, who already knew Antonie, Franz, and Antonie's father. (Proponents of the theory that Antonie was the

Immortal Beloved contend that Franz and Antonie did *not* know Beethoven
when Bettina met Beethoven, but as shown in chapter 12, their contention is
erroneous.) Here is a part of what Bettina wrote in her *Goethe Correspondence*
book about her meeting with Beethoven:

> I had been told that he was unsociable and would converse with nobody.
> They were afraid to take me to him; I had to hunt him up alone. . . .
> He was very friendly and asked if I would hear a song that he had just
> composed; then he sang, shrill and piercing, so that the plaintiveness re-
> acted upon the hearer [Mignon's Song]. "It's beautiful, is it not," said he,
> inspired, "most beautiful! I will sing it again." . . . He accompanied me
> home and it was upon the way that he said many beautiful things upon art,
> speaking so loudly and stopping in the street that it took courage to listen
> to him. . . . They were much astonished to see him enter a large dinner
> party at home with me. After dinner, without being asked, he sat down at
> the instrument and played long and marvelously. . . . Since then he comes
> to see me every day, or I go to him. For this I neglect social meetings, gal-
> leries, the theater and even the tower of St. Stephen's. Beethoven says "Ah!
> What do you want to see there? I will call for you towards evening; we will
> walk through the alleys of Schönbrunn." Yesterday I went with him to a
> glorious garden in full bloom, all the hot-beds open—the perfume was be-
> wildering. . . . He took me to a grand rehearsal, with full orchestra—there
> I sat in the wide, unlighted space, in a box quite alone.

Bettina left Vienna to travel to Prague around June 3, then went on to
a nearby estate that the Brentano family owned, where she stayed for almost
a month. While she was there, Arnim traveled down from Berlin and proposed marriage, fully expecting that she would accept. He needed to marry
and have at least one legitimate child in order to gain control of his wealthy
grandmother's estate. But the time Bettina had spent with Beethoven only a
few weeks before had left such a deep impression on her that she told Arnim
she was considering forgoing marriage to devote her life to music and political causes. Arnim returned to Berlin in a state of shock, judging from his next
letter to her.

Bettina traveled in August from the Brentano estate in Bohemia to the
nearby spa town of Teplitz, where Goethe was spending his summer vacation
without his wife. Bettina surprised him with her visit, and papers discovered
after her death suggest he may have made sexual approaches that changed the
nature of their relationship from one of worshipful admiration of him by a
"child" to a more mature and ambivalent relationship of an aging man with an
attractive and dynamic young woman. It may be significant that Bettina reached
the age of 25 that year, the age of legal majority for women at the time.

After leaving Goethe and Teplitz, she traveled on to Berlin in mid-August, staying with Gunda and Savigny in their new home. Waiting for her there was Beethoven's first letter to her dated August 11, 1810, with which he enclosed a copy of "Mignon's Song" and a song entitled "New Love, New Life," both set to poems by Goethe. Because this letter does not survive, its authenticity is disputed, but its genuineness will be proven in the evidentiary chapters of this book. Its text is set out in the body of chapter 7. It is corroborated by a found dedication to Bettina in Beethoven's handwriting on the title page of "New Love, New Life" bearing fold marks consistent with its being included with a letter. That title page is shown in illustration 6.

Meanwhile Arnim, who lived in Berlin, continued his entreaties that they marry. Bettina, for her part, began her correspondence with Beethoven, writing to him twice before February 1811.

In December 1810, Bettina finally agreed to marry Arnim, making him promise, however, that he would not interfere with nor be jealous of her close connection with Goethe. The marriage took place in a surprise and secret ceremony the following March. Bettina told a friend twice over the course of a long acquaintance that she did not marry Arnim for love but because he had paid her the honor of bearing his child.

In mid-February 1811, not too long before her wedding, Bettina received a second letter from Beethoven (which survives and is shown in illustration 7) in which he acknowledged already receiving two letters from her since she left Vienna in 1810 and addressed her near the end in the intimate German "du." Its text, translated into English, is contained in appendix B. Bettina also received around that time, presumably accompanied by an unpublished letter to her from Beethoven that has not survived, a sonnet he wrote for her lamenting but congratulating her on her marriage. The authenticity of this sonnet has also been disputed, but its genuineness will be proven in the evidentiary chapters of this book. A facsimile of it is shown in illustration 12, and its text in both German and English is set out in chapter 8.

Bettina wrote to Goethe soon after her marriage, telling him how happy she was. She engaged in performing and composing music, and helping Arnim in his writing. In the summer of 1811, the newly married young couple took a belated honeymoon to the Brentano family summer home on the Rhine near Frankfurt. On the way, they stopped in Weimar, where Goethe lived. After a few days there, Goethe's wife publicly quarreled with Bettina, tore off Bettina's glasses, and stomped on them. Goethe, at his wife's behest, ceased all written and personal communication with Bettina until after his wife's death some years afterward.

By autumn of that year, Bettina had become pregnant. The pregnancy was not a happy one. She wrote afterward that a pregnant woman carries death in her heart and finds it difficult not to hate the man who put her in that state. She confessed to being moody. At the childbirth in May 1812, she almost died, crying out to the midwife to save the child even if it meant her own death. Afterward she became bedridden, and her doctor prescribed a rest cure for her. Arnim accordingly resolved on a trip to the mineral bath spas in Bohemia. He wanted initially to go to Karlsbad to join his brother, who would be vacationing there, but he later wrote that Gunda, who was to accompany them, had talked him into going to Teplitz instead. On June 18, Arnim's brother checked into the mineral baths at Karlsbad. On the same day, Bettina with Arnim, their infant, and Gunda finally left Berlin, their departure delayed because of Bettina's health. Instead of going to Karlsbad as Arnim wanted, they were on their way to Teplitz. Both Goethe and Beethoven were there.

While Bettina was recuperating from the life-threatening birth of her first child and Arnim was making plans for her Bohemian rest cure, initially as noted before to be in Karlsbad, Beethoven set out from Vienna on June 29, 1812, and arrived in Teplitz at 4 a.m. on Sunday, July 5, exhausted from an arduous journey in which his coach became mired for a time in mud. The next morning, July 6, he started his letter to the Immortal Beloved in pencil and continued it in intervals over the next day and a half, mentioning that he wanted to get it posted in time for the next mail pickup for "K" (Karlsbad), which he thought would be on the following Thursday. In fact, mail deliveries were daily that summer, but for some reason he appears not to have sent the letter, probably because he received a letter from Bettina that she would not be going to Karlsbad after all. Beethoven, depressed, continued to stay in Teplitz, writing to an acquaintance on July 14, "There is not much to tell you about T [Teplitz], for there are few people here and no distinguished ones among the small number. Hence I am living—alone—alone! alone! alone!"

But his depression was lifted by the unexpected arrival in town of his hero Goethe, whom both he and Bettina virtually worshiped. Bettina had introduced the two artists to one another through correspondence, and they had exchanged letters in which they mentioned Bettina as their common point of reference. The two artists visited one another over the next three or four days, and on one occasion, Beethoven played the piano for Goethe. On another occasion, the two strolled together in the town park. According to a letter to Bettina from Beethoven that she published many years afterward but which has not survived, the two encountered a group of royalty from Saxony as well as the Austrian empress and probably the duke for whom Goethe worked strolling in the opposite direction on the park path. Goethe suggested that he and Beethoven give way, but Beethoven answered that the two of them were the kings and princes of the earth, and he marched with hat down through the oncoming group while Goethe stood to the side bowing. Beethoven teased

Goethe about this, which appears to have annoyed Goethe, who later wrote that while Beethoven was undoubtedly a great artist, he had an "untamed" personality. Beethoven wrote that "court air suits Goethe too much."

On July 23, the same day that Beethoven and Goethe walked together in the park, the Arnims arrived in Teplitz, only two and a half weeks after Beethoven wrote his letter to the Immortal Beloved. He was surprised and ecstatic. He sent a letter the same day to his publisher in nearby Leipzig asking that "Mignon's Song," which he had first played and sung to Bettina two years before when she came to his lodgings in Vienna, be sent to him in Teplitz. "Have an offprint made on the thinnest finest paper as quickly, as speedily, in the quickest way, with the greatest expedition and so quickly that one cannot express it in words, and send it to me here on the wings of thought; and be sure to have it made on the thinnest and finest paper." Over the course of the next several days, Bettina met both Goethe and Beethoven. Her husband wrote in a contemporary letter, "Goethe and Beethoven are here, but my wife is not especially happy about it, since the former will have nothing to do with her, and the latter can barely hear her; the poor devil is becoming more deaf all the time and his friendly smiles make it all the more difficult to watch."

Whatever Bettina said to Beethoven, he suddenly left town in a day or two, neglecting to even take his travel papers with him. As he departed, he handed to Bettina a letter in which he wrote that "even minds can love one another," begged her to write to him in Vienna "soon and fully," and closed with the words "God, how I love you." The authenticity of this letter, which has not survived, has been disputed, but its genuineness will be proven in the evidentiary chapters of this book. A copy of one page from it made by Bettina in her own handwriting is shown in illustration 8. Its full text, translated into English, is set out in appendix C.

Beethoven did not return to Teplitz until early September, about the time Bettina was to return to Berlin. Whether the two met there at that time is not known. There is some evidence, however, that they continued to write one another. As noted above, in the letter Beethoven handed to Bettina as he precipitously left Teplitz in July, he begged her to write to him in Vienna "soon and fully." In 1816, as noted in chapter 1, Beethoven told the father of young Fanny Giannastasio that his relationship with the love of his life was *the same then as it was on the first day*. In 1817, Beethoven wrote a letter to Bettina's half-brother bearing a "double B" seal that closely resembled a seal then being used by Bettina on some of her writing, indicating that he and Bettina may have been corresponding with one another around that time and affixing similar seals beside their signatures. A copy of the last page of Beethoven's 1817 letter bearing the "double B" seal and the similar seal used by Bettina are shown in illustrations 9 and 10 respectively. The evidence of continuing correspondence between Beethoven and Bettina will be more fully detailed and explored in chapter 3.

In 1843, Bettina, then in her middle years, was interviewed by Anton Schindler, who had been Beethoven's secretary in Beethoven's later years and became one of his early biographers. He noted afterward that when he asked about her relationship with Beethoven, she "wrapped herself in a deep cloak of silence, pretending to hear nothing I said." What was she attempting to hide? Around the same time, she gave away to Philipp Nathusius, a young literary disciple, one of her letters from Beethoven. In the accompanying letter to Nathusius, she wrote that she felt the need to atone to Beethoven's spirit for a promise she had made to Beethoven and then broken. The original of the letter to her from Beethoven that she gave to Nathusius was found among Nathusius's papers.

In her old age, Bettina confided to a friend that Beethoven had loved her until he died, and that his love was not just platonic. This suggests she was communicating with Beethoven right up to the time of his death. Further, found among Bettina's possessions after her death was a medallion-sized plaster relief of Beethoven's face, very probably a gift to her from Beethoven. It is shown in illustration 11. Among the effects of one of Bettina's daughters was an ornamented album page containing pressed flowers and foliage from the grave of Beethoven. It is not known how the daughter or her mother obtained it.

BETTINA'S LETTER WRITING

As noted earlier, Bettina's first love in life was music. She was also a compulsive letter writer. It is difficult to count how many found letters from her there are because of her habit of continuing letters over a number of days, sometimes with and other times without full dates. A 1929 auction catalogue of her effects lists 44 from her to Goethe, 10 to the Grimm brothers, two to Goethe's wife, one to Goethe's mother (another three have also been found), and one to Moritz Carrière, a prominent philosophy professor. She wrote many lengthy letters to her husband while they lived apart, a number to a young student with whom she became romantically involved while traveling to Berlin in 1810, several to a friend with whom she may have become romantically involved after her husband died, and a large number to a male friend while she and her husband were separated. The Goethe Archive in Düsseldorf has the originals of approximately 50 she wrote to two of her younger literary disciples, Philipp Nathusius and Julius Döring (she gave one of her Beethoven letters, the only one that survives, to Nathusius). She wrote frequent letters to her children, and to her sisters and brothers and their spouses. These are only a few examples. Their length and number are astonishing. The fact that Bettina had already written to Beethoven twice before his February 1811 letter to Bettina in the few months after she left him in Vienna is in itself remarkable. She wrote those two at a time when she was traveling from Bohemia, meeting Goethe in Teplitz, being courted by Arnim in Berlin, and then making arrangements to marry him. Events in her life in that short time period were occurring at a frantic pace, and yet she found time during that period to write not only *twice* to Beethoven but *five* times to Goethe.

One aspect that should be noted before an analysis is made as to the circumstances leading up to Beethoven's letter to the Immortal Beloved is the style Bettina used in writing most of her letters to others. She would begin many of them on one day, then continue them much as one does a diary over a number of ensuing days, until she finally ended the letter with its continuations and post it. Sometimes she inserted the day and month, sometimes only the month. She frequently omitted the year. *This is exactly the style used by Beethoven in his letter to the Immortal Beloved.* His letter was continued over several days, and only the day and month were included, not the year. This was not his usual style of writing letters, which were for the most part fully dated and specific, not long and rambling like Bettina's stream-of-consciousness letters. I submit that in his letter to the Immortal Beloved, he emulated Bettina's style.

Keeping this history and methodology in mind, I now ask the reader to consider two remarkable letters that survive and today can be looked at, one from Beethoven to Bettina, and one from her to Goethe. Neither letter has been considered in previous analyses as to the identity of the Immortal Beloved. I submit that two crucial conclusions can be drawn as a result of a close examination of these letters that are important in establishing that Bettina was Beethoven's Immortal Beloved. In considering the two letters and drawing these conclusions, I ask the reader to keep in mind two basic principles of Anglo-American common law.

The first principle is the fundamental distinction between the proof required in a criminal as opposed to a civil case. In the former, the law requires the case to be proven beyond a reasonable doubt. In a civil case, the burden can be satisfied if the trier of fact (judge or jury) is satisfied that the case has been proven on the balance of probabilities.

The second principle is the law of "similar fact" evidence. If evidence is admitted proving that a person has engaged in a certain unique and unusual behavior in past instances, it can be used to assist in reaching a conclusion that the person acted in the same or a similar fashion in the case at hand. If the judge determines that the similar fact evidence may have some probative value and is not unduly prejudicial, it may be admitted and used to permit a conclusion that the person acted in a similar fashion in the case at hand, based in a civil case upon the balance of probabilities.

Consider now the two remarkable letters.

THE SURVIVING 1811 LETTER
FROM BEETHOVEN TO BETTINA

The only letter to Bettina from Beethoven that today survives is dated February 10, 1811, about 18 months before he wrote his letter to the Immortal Beloved. Its English translation is set out in appendix B, and both pages of the original are shown in illustration 7. In the letter, Beethoven recognizes that Bettina will soon be marrying Arnim or has already done so. In the very last sentence, he addresses Bettina in the intimate German "du." So far as is now known, it is the only time Beethoven used this form in any letter to a woman with whom he was romantically connected other than the Immortal Beloved. He did not use that form in any of his surviving letters to Josephine or Antonie. In this 1811 letter to Bettina, Beethoven tells her that he carried her first letter to him around with him all summer, and that it made him supremely happy. I submit that those are the words of a man in love. Beethoven also acknowledges, as noted previously, that he has already received *two* letters from Bettina, and he apologizes for not writing to her "often" up to then, an indication that he has written to her before. In the most important sentence, Beethoven begs her to write to him, despite her marriage, "soon and often."

As noted earlier, a few months after Bettina received this letter, she was cut off from correspondence with Goethe by Goethe's wife. She admired and was attracted to genius. Beethoven was a genius in her own chosen field of music. She was a compulsive, almost obsessive letter writer. That Beethoven would have been a natural substitute for Goethe in her correspondence follows inevitably. Given all these circumstances, I submit that it is inconceivable that she would not have responded to Beethoven's plea to write to him "soon and often."

I therefore invite the reader to conclude, based on the contents of this found letter and its surrounding circumstances, that Beethoven and Bettina corresponded after this 1811 letter to her. I also submit that this conclusion is free from any reasonable doubt and would therefore even meet the very high burden of proof required in a criminal case, not just the lesser burden based on the balance of probabilities required in a civil case.

Yet only one letter from Beethoven to her survives, and none from her to him. *Where are her letters to him, and more importantly, his to her?* The likely answer follows in the Argument section of this chapter.

And more importantly, what would she likely have written to Beethoven in their correspondence? To determine that, I ask the reader to carefully consider a remarkable letter Bettina wrote to Goethe in 1810.

THE SURVIVING 1810 LETTER FROM BETTINA TO GOETHE

The 1810 letter Bettina wrote to Goethe does not directly involve Beethoven, but the principle of similar fact evidence establishes its relevance as to what the unfound letters from Bettina to Beethoven after 1811 may have said. Bettina's remarkable letter to Goethe was written in January 1810, two and a half years before Beethoven wrote his letter to the Immortal Beloved, and just over one year before Beethoven wrote his 1811 letter to Bettina described above. At the time she wrote the letter to Goethe, Bettina was studying music in a small town near Munich, was still unmarried, and was approaching the majority age of 25. Goethe was then 60 and apparently happily married. The text of the first portion of the letter translated into English is set out at the beginning of chapter 6.

In her letter to Goethe, she writes of her deep love for him. "Don't burn my letters . . . so steadfastly and truly alive is the love that I express in them for you, that I can only speak of it aloud [to myself] but show them to no one." She also writes that although she may be far away from him, in her thoughts she sleeps every night in his arms, and will repay him for introducing the world of nature to her through his literature by embracing him with her "warm loving arms." She describes that she dreams of falling asleep with her hand in his lap and awaking the next morning with him, when "you would certainly kiss me, and call me a thousand affectionate names, and call me your very own."

In Beethoven's letter to the Immortal Beloved, he writes, "As much as you love me, I love you still more." I submit that Bettina's letter to Goethe demonstrates her state of mind with regard to persons of genius, especially in the field of artistic expression such as literature, poetry, and music. The psychology of her attitude toward love (physical, emotional, and platonic) will be explored more fully in chapter 6. Her letters to Goethe described in that chapter, and especially this surviving one that she wrote to him in January 1810, may reasonably lead to a conclusion that Bettina wrote similar words of love, admiration, and the possibility of physical intimacy to Beethoven. Both Beethoven and Goethe were geniuses, one in literature, the other in her intended field of music. Both were significantly older than she. Both were then far away. In Beethoven's letter to the Immortal Beloved, not only did he accept as a given the woman's love for him, he even hesitatingly suggested that they might live together. I ask the reader to conclude on the basis of this letter to Goethe that in one or more of the letters that Bettina sent to Beethoven after 1811 and before July 1812, she professed a love for Beethoven as well as the prospect of physical intimacy in much the same way she had for Goethe less than two years before. Beethoven would have been even more connected to her admiration for genius and artistic expression, because her intended outlet for artistic expression, like Beethoven's, was primarily music. This conclusion, I submit, is more probably true than not. In other words, it meets the test of proof on the balance of probabilities.

As to what Bettina wrote to Beethoven after his 1811 letter to her and before his letter to the Immortal Beloved, I will be asking the reader to come to two further conclusions, based not on the rule of similar fact evidence, but rather on the rule of the balance of probabilities arising out of the evidence I will be presenting. The first is that Bettina wrote to Beethoven of her depression during and after her pregnancy and her brush with death at the birth of her child. This conclusion is based on the sentence in his letter to the Immortal Beloved lamenting that she had apparently told him that she was suffering. The second is that Bettina also wrote in her letters to Beethoven that she considered marriage to have been a mistake, and that what she really wanted in life was a career in music. This conclusion is based on the unusual circumstances surrounding her marriage described earlier in this chapter.

SUMMARY OF THE CRUCIAL EVIDENCE

Set out below is a summary of the crucial pieces of evidence and reasonable conclusions arising therefrom on which I will base my argument.

1. The surviving dedication to Bettina in Beethoven's handwriting on the title page of his song "New Love, New Life," accompanying his first letter to her (missing) of August 1810.
2. The contents of the single surviving 1811 letter from Beethoven to Bettina establishing that she had already written to him twice and he to her at least once; his entreaty to her in it to write to him soon and often; his resigned acceptance in it of the fact that she was or would soon be married; and his addressing her in part of it in the intimate German "du."
3. The fact that one of the two letters Bettina sent to Beethoven after she left Vienna in 1810 made Beethoven so happy *he carried it around with him all summer*, as he told Bettina in the surviving 1811 letter to her referred to in item 2 above.

4. The conclusion that beyond any reasonable doubt, based on the contents and surrounding circumstances as to the surviving 1811 letter from Beethoven to Bettina described above, Beethoven and Bettina were corresponding with one another after 1811.

5. The refusal of Bettina to Arnim's initial marriage proposal, saying that she was considering devoting her life to music and political activism, and the unusual circumstances that had led Arnim to make his marriage proposal in the first place, based on economic necessity and convenience.

6. The sonnet that Beethoven wrote for Bettina and sent to her as a marriage gift.

7. The fact that Arnim and Bettina originally intended in 1812, the year in which Beethoven wrote his letter to the Immortal Beloved, to travel to Karlsbad, where Beethoven believed the Immortal Beloved to be, but they changed their destination to Teplitz, possibly at the last moment.

8. The conclusion that on the balance of probabilities based on the contents and surrounding circumstances as to the surviving 1810 letter from Bettina to Goethe, Bettina wrote similar words of love, admiration, and the prospect of physical intimacy to Beethoven in the correspondence they exchanged after 1811 and before his letter to the Immortal Beloved in 1812.

9. Bettina's acknowledged illness during and after her pregnancy and her near death at the birth, considered in conjunction with Beethoven's statement in his letter to the Immortal Beloved that the woman was "suffering"; also her illness appears to have resulted in a postponement of her rest-cure trip to Bohemia.

10. Beethoven's excited surviving letter to his publisher shortly after Bettina's arrival in Teplitz to mail to him *in Teplitz* the song he had sung to Bettina when they first met two years before.

11. Beethoven's sudden and unexpected departure from Teplitz a few days after Bettina arrived, and the poignant letter he handed to her as he left Teplitz only two and a half weeks after he wrote his letter to the Immortal Beloved. In this missing letter to Bettina, he wrote that "even minds can love one another" and ended with the words "God, how I love you!"

12. Bettina's refusal to discuss her relationship with Beethoven when interviewed by Schindler in 1843.

13. Bettina's confession in giving Nathusius in the 1840s the single letter to her from Beethoven that survives, saying that she wanted to atone to Beethoven's spirit for breaking a promise she had made to him.

14. Bettina's confession to a confidant in her late years that Beethoven had loved her until he died and that his love was not just platonic.
15. The similarity between Bettina's letter-writing style and the writing style (unusual for Beethoven) used by him in his letter to the Immortal Beloved.
16. The "double B" seal used by Beethoven in an 1817 letter to Bettina's brother that is similar to Bettina's personal "double B" seal.
17. The finding of a medallion-sized plaster relief of Beethoven among Bettina's possessions after her death, most likely a gift from him to her.
18. The finding of pressed leaves and foliage from Beethoven's grave in the effects of Bettina's daughter.

ARGUMENT

As noted in chapter 1, both Richard Specht and Max Unger believed that Bettina met the psychological, geographical, and timing requirements necessary for her to be the Immortal Beloved. But they both rejected her for slightly different reasons. Unger believed that because she loved her husband, she could not be the Immortal Beloved, since in the letter to the Immortal Beloved, Beethoven seemed convinced from something that the woman wrote or said to him that she loved him (Beethoven). Specht's reason was that Beethoven's idealization of the institution and sanctity of marriage would prevent him from writing the passionate tender words to another man's wife.

What follows is my reconstruction of the salient facts in the lives of Bettina, Goethe, and Beethoven, and my argument as to why the conclusions of Specht and Unger in ultimately rejecting Bettina as the Immortal Beloved were mistaken.

In the last half of 1811 and the first half of 1812, Bettina was beset by problems: the emotional devastation she must have suffered because of the rupture with Goethe; the melancholia probably induced by a typical Berlin winter in 1811–12; the difficulties that emanated from her pregnancy and likelihood that she became depressed; the restriction on her musical endeavors resulting from her confinement; her near-death experience during the birth of her first child in May 1812; and the unknown physical or psychological symptoms that caused her to be bedridden after the birth, possibly including postpartum depression. They all occurred in the months after she received a letter from one of the greatest musical geniuses in history who acknowledged having already received two letters from her and *begged* her to write to him "soon and often." That she would confide her troubles to an adoring musical genius and that he would have responded with words of comfort may be inferred from words in the letter to the Immortal Beloved such as "Why such deep sorrow ?" and "You are suffering, my dearest creature."

A further question arising out of the words used by Beethoven in his letter to the Immortal Beloved that has intrigued all commentators (and even led to outlandish theories) is that Beethoven acknowledged in his letter that the woman loved him. How can this be linked to Bettina? As noted previously, and as will be more fully explored in chapter 6, Bettina had in her letters to Goethe written words about her love for him, apparently ranging from platonic to intensely physical. I submit, as stated above, that in writing to Beethoven in answer to the plea in his 1811 letter to write to him "soon and often," Bettina used the same kind of language of love for Beethoven that she expressed in her January 1810 letter to Goethe. That conclusion would counter Unger's rejection of Bettina as Beethoven's Immortal Beloved because he believed that she loved her husband. She undoubtedly did love her husband, as shown in chapter 6, but in a different way, so it would not have stopped her from writing to Beethoven, as she did to Goethe, expressing also her love for him because of what his genius had brought to her in music.

Specht rejected Bettina as the Immortal Beloved because she was a married woman and Beethoven had reverence for the institution of marriage. However, Beethoven had met and fallen in love with Bettina *before* her marriage. If she had written to him in reply to his found 1811 letter explaining the reasons behind the marriage, her reservations about it, and her continuing dream of devoting her life to music and political activism, this would have salved Beethoven's conscience, since he was not inducing the breakup of a customary marriage.

I turn now to a probable reconstruction of the facts leading up to what happened after Beethoven wrote his letter to the Immortal Beloved. Beethoven expected when he arrived in Teplitz that he would hear almost immediately from Bettina that she had safely arrived in Karlsbad, as Arnim had previously planned. As noted earlier, their departure from Berlin had been delayed as a result of Bettina's illness. Knowing that Beethoven was probably already in Teplitz, she wrote to him there, telling him of the delay, so Beethoven withheld posting his Immortal Beloved letter until he had received a letter from her saying that she had arrived in Karlsbad. When she unexpectedly arrived in Teplitz instead of Karlsbad, he did not need to post his letter but kept it until he died. Upon her arrival in Teplitz, Beethoven's excitement was apparent from his letter to his publisher on the same day that she arrived. As noted previously, he asked that he be sent in Teplitz a copy of "Mignon's Song" *right away!* What did he hope for?

Also as noted previously, Bettina in her middle age gave Nathusius one of her letters from Beethoven, noting that she felt the need to atone to Beethoven's spirit for a promise she had made to Beethoven and then broken. What was that promise? I submit that Bettina had written to Beethoven in the months before she came to Teplitz not only of her love for him, but also that her marriage was a mistake, and that a life in music was what she always wanted. Now that she had borne Arnim the child he needed to gain control of his wealthy grandmother's estate, she was free to follow her own desires, and she may have promised Beethoven to join him in Vienna to pursue a life in music in collaboration with him as his muse and assistant.

But when Bettina arrived in Teplitz, she likely told Beethoven that she had changed her mind and would remain in her marriage. She was emotionally stronger than when she wrote him after the childbirth, and now could not consider leaving her child and husband for a life in music with Beethoven. Beethoven must have been shattered. He left town precipitously, forgetting to take even his travel papers with him. As he left, he handed Bettina a tender letter of resigned acceptance as noted above, telling her how much he loved her, that "even spirits can love one another," and exclaiming "God, how I love you!" The inevitable conclusion, I submit, is that Bettina was Beethoven's Immortal Beloved. In many ways, his disappointment must have been as tragic for him as the increasing deafness he had faced and finally come to terms with seven years before.

But what happened to the missing letters that we know Bettina had sent to Beethoven, and the letters from Beethoven to Bettina, all of which, except for the one she gave to Nathusius, are today missing? It is possible that the two destroyed them by mutual agreement, as did Brahms and Clara Schumann with some of their correspondence years afterward, but this is only a surmise. To Beethoven, the letters were so important that he carried one of them around with him all summer. As for Bettina, she had the originals of the three of them in 1839 when she had them published, because they were seen and verified by two reliable witnesses. I will discuss the matter at greater length in chapter 4. If she did destroy the letters for the reasons discussed in that chapter, it is obvious that she could not destroy the letter to her from Beethoven that she gave away to Nathusius, and she did not destroy but rather treasured the sonnet Beethoven had composed for and gave her.

· 3 ·

Beethoven and Bettina after 1812

BETTINA

$\mathcal{A}$fter Bettina left Teplitz in September 1812, she returned to Berlin and, over the years, had six more children with Arnim. But she began to live apart from him in 1820. Although she resumed her friendship with Goethe after his wife died in 1816, the relationship was not the same as before. He had become quite elderly, and she was busy with a growing family. She nevertheless continued to revere him until his death in 1832. In 1835, when she was almost 50, she published her *Goethe Correspondence* book to raise money to build a monument in his honor.

In 1839, in a literary and political journal, Bettina published three letters she claimed to have received from Beethoven, one in 1810, the second in 1811, and the third in 1812. The authenticity of these letters as well as the letters she supposedly received from Goethe contained in the *Goethe Correspondence* book became a subject of great controversy in Europe, as will be explained in greater detail in the evidentiary chapters of this book. In 1846, when she was 61, she also published a book entitled *Ilius Pamphilius und die Ambrosia* (the "*Ilius* book"), which contained correspondence she had exchanged some years before with two young literary acolytes, Philipp Nathusius and Julius Döring. Because the book was modeled on the form of epistolary novel popularized by Goethe in one of his books, the names of the letter writers were changed, she becoming Ambrosia and Nathusius becoming Ilius. In that book, she published the same three letters from Beethoven that she had published in the literary journal seven years before, as well as three letters she claimed to have received from Goethe's mother. In one of her letters to Nathusius, she describes giving him *one* letter from Beethoven and *one* from Goethe's mother for his autograph collection. The Beethoven letter turned up in Nathusius's estate and is the only one that survives today. In a surviving letter published in the *Ilius* book, responding to Nathusius's request for the Beethoven letter for his autograph collection, she writes:

> as for the letter of Beethoven, I am holding it with both hands, it is a relic of the greatest spirit not only of our but of all times. His was a heart that, turned towards the spirit, was finally born anew from the motherly womb of the ether into the world of the senses. There he discovered through his innate genius and through the spiritual joy of the senses the music of the language of love that can satisfy the spirit. But his heart needy as a newborn child, strained after the treasures of life, searching for playmates, and he saw me, and the sparkling diamonds of ancient longing lit up in his heart. For it was as if I had to be one of those sensual hearts which, in earlier times, intoxicated with love, filled themselves with his image or still want to do so; this is why I hold the letter so firmly.—Now that his heart reposes in the dust, [I] beg his forgiveness for not having always waited at the door when he went in or out, for not having cushioned the ground under his feet with my hands, not having listened when the spirits spoke with him and he confided to them the rhythms of the most profound surge [of his soul]. Yes, I hold this letter so firmly, mindful of the vows that the spirits pressed upon me, that I should not refuse anything to him who demands, and there I read that he pressed the seal of his love upon my brow, and that fills me wholly with melancholy; I feel the waves of his genius brimming over in my bosom because I did not atone to him for his loss according to my vow. And I am giving you this letter because you asked me for it, because—if I am to fulfil my vow—I must never refuse.[1]

What did she mean when she wrote "I did not atone to him for his loss according to my vow?" Was she referring to the loss of his hearing, or the loss of her? What was her vow? The possible answer to these questions will be explored more fully in the evidentiary chapters of this book. Until her death, Bettina remained an ardent advocate of the music of Beethoven, but so far as is known, she never saw him again. Shortly before her death, she told an acquaintance of the many years that Beethoven loved her until he died, and that his love was not platonic. She died in 1859 at the age of 74. As noted in chapter 2, found in her belongings after her death was a medallion-size plaster relief of Beethoven's head (see illustration 11). It is described by the Goethe Museum in Frankfurt, where it is located today, as quite possibly a gift to her from Beethoven. Found in the belongings of one of her daughters was an album page, ornamented with the daughter's painting, that holds dried and pressed leaves and foliage from Beethoven's grave. The album page is today located in the Goethe Museum. How the daughter got the leaves and foliage is not known.

BEETHOVEN

As noted in chapter 2, Beethoven suddenly and unexpectedly left Teplitz two or three days after Bettina arrived, neglecting to take even his travel papers with him. Teplitz was a small town, and repeated encounters with Bettina would likely have been painful for him. As he left town, he handed to her the long poignant parting letter described in chapter 2. Here is part of what it says:

> If God spares me a few more years, then I must really see you again, my dear, dear Bettina. . . . Spirits too can love one another and I shall always pay court to yours. . . . Adieu, Adieu, dearest . . . your last letter lay on my heart for a whole night and refreshed me there. God, how I love you!

Beethoven went from Teplitz to Karlsbad, where he joined his friends Franz and Antonie Brentano and one of their children, then afterward traveled to another nearby spa town, blaming his travels on orders from his doctor, trying to find a cure for his physical ailments. He then came back to Teplitz in September shortly after Bettina was scheduled to leave. It is not known whether he saw Bettina or Goethe then. Also as noted in chapter 2, he wrote a letter in August criticizing Goethe for being too solicitous toward royalty. Goethe wrote a letter also in August praising Beethoven's talent and energy but criticizing his manners and decorum.

As noted earlier in this book, the Nobel Prize winner Romain Rolland attributed the pulsing and joyous ideas evident in Beethoven's seventh and eighth symphonies, and even the inspiration for early drafts of the ninth, to Beethoven's communication with the Immortal Beloved around 1811–1812.[2] However, his musical inspiration seems to have ended near the end of 1812, and his creative output declined considerably for the remainder of the decade, as noted by Thayer.[3] I submit to the readers of this book that during the happy period when Beethoven was corresponding with Bettina in the last half of 1811 and the first half of 1812, he was working simultaneously on his seventh, eighth, and ninth symphonies, inspired by her confessions of love for him, as she had previously relayed to Goethe in her found letter to him of January 1810, described in chapter 2. Beethoven's seventh and most of his eighth were completed before he went to Teplitz in 1812,[4] but after he received the devastating news from Bettina in July, he must have stopped work on his ninth, because he did not start it again until 1817,[5] and he did not complete it until 1824, 12 years after what happened in Teplitz. What caused his creative diminishment has never been explained, although many believe it was related to something that happened between him and the Immortal Beloved.

It is clear that Beethoven was devastated by what Bettina had said to him when they met in Teplitz, where she had apparently, as she explained in her 1840 letter to Nathusius quoted above, broken her vow to Beethoven. What was that vow? The possible answer will be explored in chapter 4.

CORRESPONDENCE BETWEEN BEETHOVEN AND BETTINA AFTER 1812

In the early years of my research, I believed that the correspondence between Bettina and Beethoven ended after she broke his heart in Teplitz in 1812, when she announced her decision to stay with her husband instead of pursuing a life in music. There is some evidence, however, indicating that she and Beethoven may have been corresponding afterward. In the 1812 Teplitz Letter that he handed her as he hurriedly left Teplitz, he begged her again to write to him "soon, soon, and quite fully." In a letter she wrote to an acquaintance in 1832, she reveals details that appear to have been related to her by Beethoven *after* their final meeting in Teplitz in 1812.[6] In 1816, as explained in chapter 1, the young Fanny Giannastasio overheard Beethoven say that five years before "he had made the acquaintance of a person, a union with whom he would have considered the greatest happiness of his life." Then Fanny quotes Beethoven as saying "nevertheless it is now as on the first day."[7]

Another clue arises out of a confidence Bettina shared in her later years with the well-known Berlin actress Karoline Bauer, whom she told that Beethoven loved her *until he died*.[8] Would she know that because they were corresponding up to the time of Beethoven's death in 1827?

A more intriguing clue arises out of a symbol on a surviving 1817 letter from Beethoven to Bettina's half-brother Franz Brentano (the husband of Antonie) presently in the collection of the Beethoven Center in San José, California. The symbol is a "double B" in blue ink that appears next to Beethoven's signature at the end of the letter, so it was very probably stamped on it by him (see illustration 9).[9]

In 1809, before Bettina had married and when her maiden name was Bettina Brentano, she had been given a "double B" seal standing for her initials for use on her correspondence. Before and after she married, she used for some of her writing and music the pseudonym "Beans Beor," derived from a Latin expression meaning "when I make [others] blessed, I become blessed myself." Two songs written by her in 1810 that will be referred to in chapter

10 were written under that pseudonym.[10] For the purpose of using that pseudonym, she apparently had made and used a "double B" seal similar to the one given to her in 1809 but with "Beans Beor" inscribed around the outside of the symbol (see illustration 10). In Beethoven's 1817 letter to Franz, the two "B"'s in the symbol appearing next to Beethoven's signature are not separated as on Bettina's seals but are intertwined, and the symbol appears to have been pressed onto the paper from a seal that, in the opinion of a curator in the Goethe House in Frankfurt, was probably made of rubber. If that is so, it likely was specially and artistically manufactured. Beethoven did not use the symbol on the single surviving 1811 letter from him to Bettina, possibly because there was no room at the end of the page beside his signature (see illustration 7).

Whether Bettina used her own "double B" symbol on her letters to Beethoven is not known, because *none* of them have survived. While Beethoven's use of a "double B" seal in 1817 similar to that used by Bettina during those years may have been coincidental and have no connection to Bettina, the similarity with her personal seals is striking. It could indicate that Beethoven and Bettina were corresponding with one another around 1817, with the two of them affixing similar "double B" seals on their letters to one another. As noted above, Beethoven used it on the letter he sent to Franz in 1817. Franz was a literary giant and an acquaintance of Beethoven, and possibly in on the secret of Beethoven's love for Bettina.

NOTES

1. *Ilius*, 2:623. The author thanks Dr. Hans Eichner and his wife Dr. Kari Grimstead for their translation of this difficult passage. The original letter of Bettina to Nathusius in Bettina's handwriting containing this passage may be found in the Goethe Archive in Düsseldorf.

2. Romain Rolland, "La lettre de Beethoven à l'Immortelle Aimée," *La Revue Musicale* 11 (1927): 201.

3. Thayer Forbes, 483–4. Thayer thought Beethoven's "dry period" began around 1810, but as pointed out in Thayer Forbes, Thayer did not know that the ideas for the seventh and eighth symphonies and other important works occurred in 1811–12, and as pointed out by Forbes, the "dry period" in fact began in 1813. It is a reasonable surmise that the dry period resulted from Beethoven's devastation at learning his hoped-for union with the Immortal Beloved would not come about.

4. Thayer Forbes, 483, 543.

5. Thayer Forbes, 691.

6. Sonneck, *Impressions*, 84–88. In her 1832 letter, Bettina tells the friend, Pückler, details about how Goethe reacted emotionally to Beethoven's playing for Goethe in Teplitz in 1812, as well as the differences between the reactions of Viennese and

Berlin audiences to his playing. While it is possible that Beethoven told Bettina these details when they met in Teplitz in 1812, their time together there was very brief, and they undoubtedly had more important things to talk about. It seems more likely that Beethoven related these details in their subsequent correspondence, since she could not tell Beethoven about his playing for Goethe when they were together in Vienna in 1810. He had not then met Goethe.

7. Thayer Forbes, 646.

8. *Sie sassen und tranken am Teetisch: Anfänge und Blütezeit der Berliner Salons, 1789–1871*, ed. Rolf Strube (Munich: Piper Verlag, 1991), 191, quoting Karoline Bauer, a well-known Berlin actress.

9. Anderson, Letter No. 758; Brandenburg, Letter No. 1083, dated February 15, 1817.

10. Ann Willison Lemke, *Bettine's Song: The Musical Voice of Bettine von Arnim, née Brentano*, doctoral dissertation (Ann Arbor, Mich.: UMI Dissertation Services, 1998), 32.

• 4 •

The Mysterious Missing Letters

THE MISSING LETTERS FROM BETTINA TO GOETHE

In chapter 2, I raised the question as to what may have happened to the missing letters exchanged between Bettina and Beethoven. There are also missing letters exchanged between Bettina and Goethe, as shown below. This chapter attempts to explain what happened to them and what they might have said.

The year 1810 was one of the most significant of all the 74 years Bettina spent on earth. As noted in chapter 2, within that year she turned 25, the age of legal adulthood at the time. She met Beethoven in Vienna. A few weeks later, her future husband, Achim von Arnim, proposed marriage. In August, she visited Goethe for the second time, and it is quite possible that he and she had some kind of brief sexual encounter (see below), changing the tone of their correspondence from that of a worshipful child exchanging letters with an older, world-famous artist to the more mature give and take of a male-female relationship. Later that year, she received her first adoring letter, dated August 11, 1810, from Beethoven, who begged her to write to him. The authenticity of that missing letter will be established in chapter 5. In December, she and Arnim became engaged.

As noted in chapter 2, at the beginning of that fateful year, Bettina was studying music and languages near Munich. In May, she with her sister Gunda, Gunda's husband Friedrich Savigny, and a few student friends began an extended journey that would take her through Vienna, where she met Beethoven, then to her family estate in Bohemia, where Arnim came to meet her and propose marriage, then to Teplitz in Bohemia, where she met Goethe again, and finally in August to Berlin, where she began to live with Gunda and Savigny in their new home.

27

Through the course of that year, she wrote nine lengthy letters to Goethe that survive (even more if one considers their extensions and additions as separate letters). She described in them her adventures on her journey as well as her thoughts and philosophy about music, art, literature, and religion. Their length and detail are astonishing. They run to more than 13,000 words.

Goethe kept these and the other letters written by Bettina to him before and after 1810, and after his death Bettina obtained their return from his legal administrator. As noted in chapter 1, Bettina used the originals as the basis for a freely edited, expanded, revised, and partly fictional book in epistolary form entitled *Goethe's Correspondence with a Child* (the "*Goethe Correspondence* book") that she published in 1835 when she was 50. In considering the analysis that follows, it is important for the reader to distinguish between the letters Bettina wrote to and received from Goethe that survive, and those letters as they appeared in the *Goethe Correspondence* book. As will be noted in chapter 11, some letters appeared in the book that are today missing, and at least one letter that survives did *not* appear in the book. As well, she made some deletions, additions, and changes to the surviving letters when she included them in her book, examples of which will be analyzed in chapter 11.

Surviving today are 13 letters to Bettina from Goethe and 44 letters from her to him. Many of them are reproduced accurately and in their entirety in her book. What she did, however, was rearrange them, edit some of them, redate others, create new passages, and delete others, so as to create a flowing sequential narrative. Because she did not date many of her own original letters, or wrote continuous extensions of them as if she were keeping a diary that she saved for mailing in a single bundle, it would have been necessary and logical for her in her *Goethe Correspondence* book to reorganize many of them, especially her own lengthy writings, in order to make a coherent readable sequence. Editing and reorganizing by Bettina was also necessary because of her peripatetic wanderings during the period of her correspondence with Goethe. Goethe traveled frequently as well.

Bettina never pretended that her book was simply an edited version of her correspondence with Goethe, but rather viewed it as a "poetic epic" of her own intellectual and emotional development as stimulated by the actual letters, looked at from the perspective of her own greater maturity.[1]

The first thing that stands out in looking at the surviving correspondence between Bettina and Goethe, which is presently in the Morgan Library in New York, is the gap in the surviving letters from Bettina to Goethe during 1810 (the "1810 Letter Gap"). That gap raises intriguing questions. It begins in the middle of a surviving letter to Goethe that she started to write while in Bohemia on July 6, 1810, and added to on July 7, 10, and 28. The surviving portion of that letter consists of two four-page folios, and the text ends in midsentence on the last sheet of the second folio, just where she begins to describe Beethoven. The subsequent folio or folios of the letter are missing. The next surviving letter from Bettina to Goethe is dated October 18, 1810, and was written from Berlin.

Within the 1810 Letter Gap are the missing part of the letter begun in Bohemia on July 6 ending just where she began to describe Beethoven, other letters that she sent or handed to Goethe when she visited him in Teplitz in August, and a letter she sent to him dated August 27. All of them were referred to in Goethe's surviving letters to her of August 17 and October 25.

Bettina was meticulous in preserving letters from others and, whenever possible, recovering letters she herself wrote. So what was the reason for this gap in her surviving letters to and from Goethe? There are three possible answers: (1) Goethe destroyed them, (2) they were inadvertently lost, or (3) Bettina destroyed them.

The possibility that Goethe would have destroyed the missing letters is remote. He had no reason to do so, except for Bettina's single letter to him of August 27 if it referred to the sexual incident that may have occurred in Teplitz in mid-August, described below. Her letter to him of August 27 did exist, because it was referred to in Goethe's surviving letter to her of October 25. However, it fell within the 1810 Letter Gap and was not reproduced by Bettina in her *Goethe Correspondence* book, at least in a form bearing that date.[2]

The possibility that the letters in the 1810 Letter Gap were inadvertently lost is unlikely, given the significance of their contents, especially since others survive that are less significant. Goethe's surviving letter to Bettina of August 17 referred to the missing letters as the most interesting of all she had sent to him.

The possibility that Bettina destroyed them is not as far-fetched as might first appear. As will be seen in chapter 10, Max Unger, by then an avowed Bettina skeptic, raised just such a possibility, but for reasons that would support his suspicion of her. Alternatively, Bettina's motives in destroying them might be based on two life-altering events that happened to her within the period of the 1810 Letter Gap. The first is her meeting and the time she spent with Beethoven in Vienna in late May and early June and what happened between them. The second is the possibility of a brief sexual encounter with Goethe in Teplitz a month and a half afterward, described below.

Few clues shedding light on the mystery of the 1810 Letter Gap can be found from the way she dealt with it in the *Goethe Correspondence* book. There she included the missing portion of the surviving letter begun July 6 by describing her meeting and memories of Beethoven in great detail. She cast it, however, as a completely separate letter dated May 28, 1810 (the day she likely first met Beethoven), and not as a continuation of the long surviving travelogue letter that preceded it. She also included in the *Goethe*

Correspondence book, following the separate letter describing her time with Beethoven, the text of three other letters she ostensibly sent to Goethe during the 1810 Letter Gap. Since none of the four survive and lie within the 1810 Letter Gap, they are portrayed as pure fiction by Bettina critics, yet they *did* exist because they were referred to by Goethe in his surviving letters. They are most likely edited versions of the originals, deleting whatever Bettina may have been trying to hide from her family or the world.

In the *Goethe Correspondence* book, at the end of the fourth missing letter from Bettina to Goethe that lay within the 1810 Letter Gap and immediately preceding Goethe's surviving letter to her dated August 17, she wrote: "Here there is a gap in the correspondence." Thus there may have been more letters from her to Goethe than the four she edited or created for the book. Goethe's letter to her dated August 17 was included in the book exactly as he wrote it except that she left out the date. The surviving original includes Goethe's effusive praise for the partially missing letter or letters to him from her. In a footnote, however, she wrote "the letters and pages [referred to by Goethe] are missing."

As we consider what may have happened between Bettina and Goethe when they met that summer, some light may be shed by several sketches found in her papers after her death that describe a brief sexual encounter with Goethe when she looked him up in Teplitz in mid-August. According to the sketches, the encounter was at least in part instigated by her. This is what one of them says (the other is substantially the same):

> The twilight of evening was falling, this hot August day. . . . He was sitting at the open window, while I stood before him, my arms around his neck, my eyes piercing his to their depths, like an arrow. Perhaps he could withstand my gaze no longer, for, to break the silence, he asked me whether I felt hot, and whether I would not like to be cooler? . . . I nodded assent. He went on, "Why not open your breast to the evening breeze?" As I did not object, although I blushed, he undid my bodice, looked at me, and said "The glow of summer has reddened your cheeks." He kissed my breast and rested his head on it. "No wonder" said I "for my sun is sinking to rest upon my bosom." He gazed at me for a long time, and we were both silent. He then asked, "Has anyone ever touched your breast?" "No" I replied; "it is so strange that you should touch me in that way." Then he showered kisses on me, many, many, violent kisses. . . . I was frightened . . . he should have let me go; and yet it was so strangely beautiful. In spite of myself I smiled, yet feared that this happiness should not last. His burning lips, his stifled breath—it was like lightning. I was in a whirl of confusion; my curly hair hung in loose strands. . . . Then he said, softly: "You are like a storm; your hair falls like rain, your lips dart lightening, your eyes thunder." "And you, like Zeus, knit your brows and Olympus trembles."

"When you undress at night, in the future, and the stars shine as now upon your breasts, will you remember my kisses?" "Yes" "And will you remember that I should like to cover your bosom with as many kisses as there are stars in heaven?" . . . The memory of it tears me apart, I long to dissolve in tears like a cloudy sky.—Never repeat what I confide to you this lonely night. I have never told it to anyone before.[3]

One Bettina expert has expressed to me a belief that the sketches are pure fiction, nothing more than a romantic fantasy on Bettina's part. Another expert, the late Konstanze Baumer, expressed to me a contrary belief, namely, that the sketches were a reasonably accurate description of what happened and were *not* fiction. The latter view is supported by Goethe's surviving letter to Bettina dated August 17, 1810, mentioned above, written just *after* the sexual incident would have taken place, if it did. In it, Goethe uncharacteristically praises, as noted above, the long letters Bettina sent him that are within the 1810 Letter Gap, then ends with the following:

Please send your next letter to me in care of "X" [coded name] and "Y" [coded address in Dresden, not Weimar where Goethe lived with his wife] that follows. How ominous! Oh pain! What will it say?[4]

Why did Goethe fear what Bettina's letter of reply might say? Why did he want it to be sent to a coded addressee and address? As noted above, the reply did exist because Goethe referred to it in a surviving letter he wrote to Bettina in October, but he may have destroyed the reply because he did not want his wife to see it. Alternatively, it is possible Bettina destroyed it if it referred to the sexual incident because she did not want the contents revealed to her family or the world after her death. The draft sketches about the sexual encounter found in her papers suggest that Bettina may near her death have been mulling over the wisdom or folly of revealing to the world the truth about her ambivalent relationship with Goethe. She had taken pains in her *Goethe Correspondence* book to emphasize that the relationship was mainly between an elderly genius and a worshipful young admirer who had not yet come of legal age. She of course did not know when she would die, and the fact that the sketches survived does not mean that she intended the truth to come out.

It is possible that either Bettina or Goethe might have destroyed her letters to him within the 1810 Letter Gap *after* she saw him in Teplitz in mid-August because of the possible mention of a sexual incident. However, that reason does not apply to the letters within the 1810 Letter Gap written *before* August 10, the letters that Goethe called "the most interesting of all" that she had sent him up to then. As noted above, the surviving portion of her July letter breaks off in midsentence: "and so it's about Beethoven I now want to

speak to you . . . . now watch, the whole world rises and falls around him as
. . . " There the surviving portion of the letter ends and the puzzling 1810
Letter Gap begins.

The missing separate letter describing Beethoven that she included in the
Goethe Correspondence book, dated May 28, begins with the same words that
immediately preceded the start of the gap in the surviving portion of the July
letter. Because the separate letter describing Beethoven is within the 1810 Letter Gap, Bettina detractors call it a fabrication. The more likely explanation
is that Bettina had her original letter before her when she was preparing her
book, but left out those parts that she was trying to hide from her family or
the world, as theorized below.

THE MISSING LETTERS BETWEEN BEETHOVEN AND BETTINA

As noted in chapter 2, it is inconceivable that Bettina would not have replied
to the plea in Beethoven's single surviving letter to her dated February 10,
1811, to write to him soon and often. Assuming she did reply and that there
were many letters exchanged between them before his letter to the Immortal
Beloved, then the three that she did publish many years later would have been
only the tip of the iceberg. Yet except for the one letter from Beethoven she
gave away to Nathusius, no other letter to her from him or from her to him
survives. As with her missing letters to Goethe, is it possible that Bettina destroyed all her letters from Beethoven except the one she gave away to Nathusius and therefore could not destroy? If so, what was she attempting to hide?
Whatever it was, it is likely that the reason for destruction of her missing letters
to Goethe written within the 1810 Letter Gap prior to his meeting with her
in Teplitz in August is the same as for destruction of the missing letters from
Beethoven. It was probably linked to the promise she had made to Beethoven,
then broken, relating to his "loss" that she mentioned in her emotional surviving letter to Nathusius, quoted in chapter 3. As noted in chapter 2, more
than 30 years after she met Beethoven, she was visited by Anton Schindler,
Beethoven's former assistant and first prominent biographer, who asked her
about the letters and Beethoven. Schindler later wrote:

> About her relationship with Beethoven, I could not induce her to say a
> single word, though she knew of my book about him and knew she was
> personally mentioned in the book. Without asking directly if I might ex-
> amine the famous letters, I hinted that it was extremely important for me
> to see the originals. The esteemed lady would at such times wrap herself in
> a deep cloak of silence, pretending to hear nothing I had said.[5]

Why would Bettina destroy some of her letters to Goethe and all of her letters from Beethoven except the one she gave to Nathusius? And why did she not show Schindler her letters from Beethoven, at the very least the one that she gave to Nathusius that today survives?

What Bettina may have been trying to hide by destroying those letters must by necessity be speculative surmise. It could not have been a physical love affair with Beethoven (as many thought Beethoven's love affair with the Immortal Beloved was), because Bettina was in Berlin and he was in Vienna. One plausible surmise, hinted at in the letters between her and Goethe that she included in her *Goethe Correspondence* book, is that Beethoven had praised her musical ability and the songs she had written and suggested she might consider devoting herself to music. For example, see the last portion of her missing letter to Goethe replying to his missing letter of June 6, 1810, where she wrote: "Beethoven has seen them, and paid me many compliments about them; as that, if I had devoted myself to this art, I might have built high hopes upon it, but I only touch it in flight, for my art is laughing and sighing in a breath, and beyond this I have none."

It is therefore possible that Beethoven may have suggested that she become his apprentice in order to ultimately take up a career of her own in music. This of itself is harmless enough and would enhance, not hurt, her reputation, but if later letters between her and Beethoven showed that she seriously reconsidered Beethoven's offer *after* her marriage, it would indicate a basic dissatisfaction with the marriage that she would not want her children or family to know of. Did she promise Beethoven in those later letters that she would join him as his assistant and muse, then break that promise?[6] As noted in chapter 3, when she gave Nathusius one of her letters from Beethoven, she wrote about breaking a promise she had made to Beethoven. Her letters to Beethoven may have revealed her doubts about the wisdom of the marriage, and also may have contained negative references to her husband, from whom she later separated. She could not let these confessions be revealed publicly, lest her children learn of them. She always promoted her husband to her children as a great writer. In order to hide all evidence of the possibility of abandoning her marriage and becoming Beethoven's assistant and muse, she may have decided to destroy all mention of it, starting with her original letter to Goethe describing her meeting with Beethoven in Vienna in 1810, even before she decided to marry.

A few weeks after Beethoven might have raised this possibility, Bettina initially refused Arnim's marriage proposal, saying she wanted to devote her life to music and political and social causes. She did this in mid-June, and the surviving portion of her lengthy letter to Goethe in which she began to describe what happened between her and Beethoven was started on July 28, a few weeks after Arnim's marriage proposal. Faced with a choice between a financially comfortable conventional marriage and a financially risky life in a strange city collaborating with an eccentric musical genius, would Bettina write to Goethe asking for his advice? In August, on her way to Berlin to join her sister, she made, as noted in chapter 2, a detour to Teplitz, where Goethe was vacationing. Would she have asked him in person for advice she had previously asked for in the missing portion of her July letter to him? Afterward Goethe wrote a surviving letter to his wife that, during Bettina's visit with him, the young woman spoke endlessly about "old and new adventures," but it seemed to him that she had decided marriage to Arnim was the way she would go.[7] If she speculated about her long-term future in the missing portions of her letters to Goethe during the 1810 Letter Gap, it would explain why the last portion of her July letter, including what happened between her and Beethoven a few weeks before, is today missing. The description of Beethoven himself, however, would have in all likelihood been repeated by her albeit in an expurgated form in her *Goethe Correspondence* book.

If this surmise is correct, it would also explain why she would want to destroy all her Beethoven correspondence except the letter of February 1811 (which she could not destroy because she had given it away to Nathusius), because in that correspondence the possibility of her joining Beethoven *after* her marriage was again raised and discussed.

But what about Bettina's letters *to* Beethoven? As noted in chapter 2, in his surviving letter to her of February 1811, he acknowledged receiving two from her within the few months after she left Vienna in June 1810. They were apparently so important to him that he carried one of them around with him all summer. The most likely surmise is that out of a sense of chivalry, knowing that her reputation as a married woman with seven children could be seriously compromised if her letters to him were discovered, Beethoven destroyed them. But he kept his letter to her as his Immortal Beloved hidden away as a memento of his deep, unrequited love for her.

SUMMARY AND CONCLUSIONS

Based on the facts and probabilities discussed in this chapter and in chapter 3, I invite the reader to arrive at the following conclusions, as I have:

1. The missing letters from Bettina to Goethe during the 1810 Letter Gap, and some from him to her within that gap, were not destroyed by Goethe nor lost, but were destroyed by Bettina.
2. All of the missing letters from Beethoven to Bettina except the one she gave away to Nathusius were destroyed by Bettina.

3. All of the missing letters from Bettina to Beethoven were destroyed by Beethoven at her request.

4. A likely reason these letters were destroyed by Bettina or at her request is that they mentioned her ambivalence about her marriage to Arnim *before* she decided to marry him, as well as a brief intention to leave him to pursue a career in music *after* the birth of her first child. She would not want the world and especially her children and grandchildren to know of her doubts about the marriage. She wanted to appear loyal to and loving of Arnim in the eyes of her children.

5. Beethoven's letter to his Immortal Beloved was not destroyed by Bettina because she never received it, and it was not destroyed by Beethoven because it did not reveal the identity of its intended recipient.

6. The only reason Bettina allowed three letters she received from Beethoven to be published was that they were the only ones that did not mention her ambivalence about her marriage.

7. Bettina's letters to and from Goethe during the 1810 Letter Gap were faithfully reproduced by her in the *Goethe Correspondence* book but in an edited (censored) form, deleting any reference to a possible career in music as an alternative to marriage.

NOTES

1. Helps and Howard, *Bettina*, 171–2; Thayer Forbes, 492–3; and Heinz Härtl, ed., *Bettina von Arnim, Werke, Goethes Briefwechsel mit einem Kind*, Vol. 1 (Berlin and Weimar: Aufbau Verlag, 1986), 666–70.

2. See *Goethe Correspondence* book (German), 689.

3. Rolland, *Goethe and Beethoven*, 171–2.

4. *Goethe Correspondence* book (German), 688.

5. Schindler, *Beethoven*, 158.

6. This possibility was raised by Ann Willison Lemke in her doctoral dissertation *Bettine's Song: The Musical Voice of Bettine von Arnim, née Brentano* (Ann Arbor, Mich.: UMI Dissertation Services, 1998), 35. Bettina certainly aspired to become Goethe's muse. See Jan Swafford, "A Virtuoso Muse," *Guardian*, August 23, 2003.

7. Fritz Böttger, *Bettina von Arnim: Ihr Leben, ihre Begegnungen, ihre Zeit* (Munich: Scherz, 1990), 108; Heinz Härtl, *Bettina von Arnim 1785–1859: Eine Chronik* (Wiepersdorf, Germany: Stiftung Kulturfonds Künstlerheim Bettina von Arnim, n.d.), 17; Ingeborg Drewitz, *Bettine von Arnim* (Munich: Goldmann Verlag, 1989), 79.

• *5* •

The Teplitz Letter and the *Ilius* Manuscript

THE SIGNIFICANCE OF BEETHOVEN'S
1812 TEPLITZ LETTER TO BETTINA

*O*f the three letters to Bettina from Beethoven that she caused to be published in 1839, the first two chronologically were written by Beethoven in Vienna and mailed to Bettina in Berlin, one in 1810 and the second in 1811. The third (the "Teplitz Letter") was written by Beethoven in Teplitz in July 1812, and, as outlined in chapter 2, was handed to Bettina by him a few days after she arrived there just as he unexpectedly was leaving town.[1] The original of the Teplitz Letter is missing today, but if it were found and established as authentic, I believe it would prove that Bettina is the Immortal Beloved. In the published version, as explained in chapter 2, Beethoven writes a touching farewell, saying that even "spirits can love one another," and ending with the words "God, how I love you!" Appendix C contains an English translation of the letter in its entirety. It was written less than three weeks after the letter to the Immortal Beloved, the latter being intended to be sent to Karlsbad, where Bettina and her husband Achim von Arnim had planned to go. However, as noted in chapter 2, Bettina's sister talked him into going to Teplitz instead, where Beethoven was.[2] Beethoven never mailed his letter to his Immortal Beloved. The reason may be that she had just arrived in Teplitz.

Because the Teplitz Letter was not found in Bettina's possessions after her death, and because of the liberties that Bettina took with the letters between her and Goethe in her *Goethe Correspondence* book, most scholars today believe that it was concocted by her (see chapter 9). I have attempted to show in chapters 4 and 5 of this book that they are wrong, and that the reason it has not been found is that Bettina destroyed it, for the reasons set out in chapter 4. As mentioned in chapter 2, the second of the three Beethoven letters, written in February 1811, survives and is today accepted as authentic. The purpose of this chapter is to establish beyond all reasonable doubt that the first and third letters that Bettina caused to be published in 1839 (including the Teplitz Letter) were authentic and not concocted by her. The significance of establishing that the Teplitz Letter is authentic is that it proves, beyond any reasonable doubt, Bettina was Beethoven's Immortal Beloved.

THE AUTHENTICITY OF THE TEPLITZ LETTER

First of all, it should be noted that Bettina never claimed to be the Immortal Beloved, and she may not have even known about the Immortal Beloved letter because it was never mailed. A link between the issue of the authenticity of the Teplitz Letter and the issue of the identity of the Immortal Beloved has not been made because until relatively recently, most researchers thought that the letter to the Immortal Beloved was written some years prior to 1812, *before* Beethoven met Bettina.

The Teplitz Letter was in fact published three times by Bettina, twice in literary and political journals in 1839 and 1841 when she was in her 50s, and then again six years afterward in her *Ilius* book, which was, like her *Goethe Correspondence* book, modeled on the form of epistolary novel made popular by Goethe. She was urged to make the first two publications in literary and political journals by Moritz Carrière, a prominent Berlin professor, for political reasons, because of Beethoven's attack on royalty and on Goethe's fawning attitude toward it described in the Teplitz Letter. Goethe and his increasingly conservative political views were still controversial in Germany in Carrière's circles. Professor Carrière publicly stated afterward that he had seen the original and it corresponded to what was published.[3] Because of the growing controversy about the authenticity of the three Beethoven letters, including the Teplitz Letter, as published by Bettina in the literary and political journals, Alexander Thayer, the leading Beethoven biographer in the second half of the 19th century, obtained through the American consul in Nürnberg a certification by Julius Merz, the distinguished publisher of the literary and political journal in which the three letters were first published, that he had copied the text from the originals of the letters and then given them back to Bettina.[4]

As noted above, the third time Bettina published the Teplitz Letter was in 1846 in her *Ilius* book. That book contained, as noted in chapter 3, correspondence she exchanged around 1840 with two young literary acolytes, Philipp Nathusius and Julius Döring. She was then in her 50s and they were in their 20s. In that correspondence, the acolyte named Ilius in the book (Nathusius) writes asking Bettina for a single letter each from Beethoven and Goethe's mother for his autograph collection. In Bettina's letter of response, she describes giving Ilius the two letters he asked for, but she includes the text of all *three* Beethoven letters she had published several years before. Presumably for textual balance, she also includes the text of three letters to her from Goethe's mother. It is clear from Bettina's letter to Ilius, however, that she gave him only *one* letter from each of the two groups of three. The only changes that she made in the *Ilius* book to the Beethoven letters that she had previously published in the literary and political journals was that in the *Ilius* book, her own name was replaced, wherever Beethoven wrote it, with a generic name, so that "Dear Bettine," for example, became "Dear Friend." As noted in chapter 3, this was because she changed the actual names of living persons in the *Ilius* book to fictional or generic names as if it were an epistolary novel.

The single letter from Beethoven that she gave to Nathusius was found in his family property after his death in 1872. It was identical to what had been published in the literary and political journals, and except for the name change, it was also virtually identical to the letter as it appeared in the *Ilius* book. In addition to the single Beethoven letter found in Nathusius's estate, all three letters from Goethe's mother that Bettina published in the *Ilius* book survive, and except for the name changes and minor corrections of grammar and spelling, they too are identical to those letters as they appeared in the *Ilius* book.

In summary, of the three letters from Goethe's mother and three from Beethoven published in the *Ilius* book, four today are extant, but the other two, both from Beethoven, including the Teplitz Letter, are not. The four extant letters correspond almost exactly to the text of those letters as published in the *Ilius* book, except for the name changes and a few grammatical and spelling corrections made by Bettina in the letters from Goethe's mother.

THE *ILIUS* MANUSCRIPT

Papers in Bettina's estate that were auctioned off in 1929 included the original manuscript of the *Ilius* book that she sent to and got back from the printer, as well as small portions of the original printer's proof. The rest of the printer's proof was presumably returned to the printer with editorial corrections made by her that included the name changes and corrections of grammar and spelling. The manuscript found in her estate includes all three letters from Goethe's mother and all three from Beethoven carefully copied out in Bettina's own hand. *It is significant that the copies of these letters in the manuscript do not show the name changes and minor corrections of grammar and spelling that were subsequently made when the* Ilius *book was published.* Those name changes and grammar and spelling corrections must have been made by Bettina to the first proof she received from the printer.

A word-for-word comparison of the text of the four letters that today survive (one from Beethoven and three from Goethe's mother) with those letters as copied out by Bettina in the *Ilius* manuscript shows that the copies are identical to the four found originals. Bettina therefore had the originals before her when she copied them for the *Ilius* manuscript. That manuscript is located today in the Goethe Archive in Düsseldorf.[5] A copy of one page of the Teplitz Letter as copied out by Bettina for the *Ilius* manuscript is shown in illustration 8.

The fact that four of the six letters in the *Ilius* manuscript are identical to the extant originals leads to the irresistible conclusion that the other two in the manuscript—the two missing letters from Beethoven, including the Teplitz Letter—are also identical to the originals.[6]

Given Carrière's public verification of the authenticity of the Teplitz Letter as published, the certification of the authenticity of the Teplitz Letter for Thayer by its publisher Merz, and the fact that four of the six letters copied out in the *Ilius* manuscript survive and are identical to the surviving autographs, there can be no reasonable doubt that the Teplitz Letter as copied out by Bettina for the *Ilius* manuscript is identical to the original. That being so, it is equally certain that the Teplitz Letter is genuine and that Bettina is therefore the Immortal Beloved.

As to the other missing letter from Beethoven written in 1810 and published by Bettina in 1839 and in the *Ilius* book, its authenticity is established beyond any reasonable doubt based on the same evidence that establishes the authenticity of the Teplitz Letter, but with one additional piece of corroborating evidence. As noted in chapter 2, in the missing 1810 letter, Beethoven wrote that he was including with it a song he composed to a poem by Goethe entitled *New Love, New Life*. As noted in chapter 2, the first page of that song is today extant and has an inscription in Beethoven's handwriting on the reverse side saying "For Bettina von Brentano—set to music by Beethoven." The page of the song with the inscription is today in the Beethoven Haus in Bonn, and it bears fold marks consistent with being folded up in a sealed letter of the kind used in 1810. A copy of the page is shown in illustration 6. The remaining pages of the song, which were found in Bettina's belongings and were sold in 1929, are today in the Morgan Library in New York.

THE SURVIVING 1811 LETTER FROM BEETHOVEN

As noted earlier in this chapter, Bettina first published in 1839 in a literary and political journal the surviving 1811 letter to her from Beethoven, as well as two others dated in 1810 and 1812. She probably did this for the political reasons mentioned above as she was urged to do by Carrière. A few years afterward, as noted in chapter 3, Bettina wrote in a surviving letter to Nathusius that she was giving him *one* letter from Beethoven, presumably the extant 1811 letter, because it turned up many years afterward in the possession of the Nathusius family, and a facsimile of it was reproduced in the 1884 edition of Marx's biography of Beethoven, as more fully described in chapter 9.

From there, the trail of the whereabouts of the 1811 letter grows cold. Two world wars intervened, then the letter turned up in a 1990 Sotheby's auction in London, where it was sold for about $170,000 to anonymous Japanese buyers. In New York in 1998, I was able to interview the previous owner of the letter, Mrs. Felix Salzer, who had provided it to Sotheby's. It had been in the possession of her late husband, Dr. Felix Salzer. A few weeks after our meeting, she wrote me a letter, saying, "I have decided that one should really know how this particular Beethoven letter got into the possession of my late husband." As she explained, the letter came into his possession through Dr. Salzer's mother, who was the sister of the eminent Viennese philosopher Ludwig Wittgenstein.

> When we had to go to Vienna after the death of my husband's mother . . . we had to go through some of her belongings and found in an armoire of household laundry the Beethoven manuscript wrapped in a newspaper. As a matter of fact it was a newspaper printed in Vienna of the time of Hitler's regime. I do not know the date of those newspaper pages. . . . the package was hidden behind some sheets etc. on a shelf. . . . By coincidence we found it. . . . No doubt the mother of my husband was afraid that the letter could be discovered by a search of the Nazis and thought probably that this was a good hiding place, and indeed it was.

I attempted a number of years ago to contact the anonymous Japanese buyers of the letter through Sotheby's but received no reply.

NOTES

1. Edward Walden, "The Authenticity of the 1812 Beethoven Letter to Bettina von Arnim," *Beethoven Journal* 14, no. 2 (1999): 11.

2. Reinhold Steig and Herman Grimm, eds., *Achim von Arnim und die ihm nahe standen*, 3 vols. (Bern: Herbert Lang, 1970), 1:302–3.

3. Thayer English, 2:185.

4. Thayer English, 2:185.

5. The author extends grateful thanks to Prof. Dr. Volkmar Hansen (*direktor*), Fr. Heike Spies (*kustodin*), and the rest of their staff at the Goethe Museum, Düsseldorf, for the assistance they provided in research there. He also thanks Dr. Norbert Trobitz for his invaluable assistance in leafing through and helping to decipher the many pages of the lengthy *Ilius* manuscript.

6. As will be described in greater detail in chapter 11, Dr. Renate Moering of Frankfurt/Main wrote a paper entitled "Bettine von Arnims Literarische Umsetzung Ihres Beethoven-Erlebnisses," published by the Beethoven Haus in Bonn in *Der 'männliche' und der 'weibliche' Beethoven* (2004), 251–77. There she claims that the following two facts prove Bettina concocted the other two Beethoven letters: (1) the one Beethoven letter to Bettina that has been found was written on a different kind of paper in the *Ilius* manuscript than the other two Beethoven letters in that manuscript, and (2) the other two Beethoven letters in the manuscript contained many cross-outs. The short answer to these contentions is as follows: (1) One of the letters from Goethe's mother and one of the Beethoven letters (the one she gave to Nathusius) are both copied out on the same kind of paper with an 1839 watermark and were presumably copied by Bettina before she gave them to Nathusius. The other four letters are all on a different kind of paper, and must have been copied out afterward. All three letters from Goethe's mother have been found, and the different type of paper they were written on does not establish they were concocted. (2) The copies in the *Ilius* manuscript of all three letters from Goethe's mother contain cross-outs, as does the copy of the found Beethoven letter, yet all four of these have been found. In fact, the main cross-out in the *Ilius* manuscript copy of the extant Beethoven letter duplicates Beethoven's own cross-out in the original.

· 6 ·

Bettina's Concept of Love

BETTINA'S 1810 LETTER TO GOETHE

*B*ettina wrote to Goethe in January 1810, when she was 24 and unmarried and he was 60 and apparently happily married. A portion of that extant letter reads as follows:

> *Dearest, kindly Goethe! [you are] the sunshine of my life that even in mid-winter glistens from the snow-covered roofs and reflects into my room. I keep for myself my neighbor's roof, that every morning glistens in the sun as a symbol of my memory of you [and] that every morning refreshes me.*
>
> *Without you would I have become as morose as if I had been born blind, and had no concept of light from heaven; You!! A clear moon-bathed fountain from which one can catch the stars for drinking with the hollow of the hand.—We are all entwined as if enslaved children with bowed heads, but the artist like you is a free person in Nature, and carries Nature's picture in his heart, and proffers it to us to kiss and to worship.—The time will come when I will repay you, beloved Goethe; by repayment, I mean that I will embrace you with my warm loving arms.*
>
> *That I [must] express in writing [what I want to say] is as strange as if one lip was speaking to the other, [saying] "listen, I have something to say to you"; and wanted to lead it [the other lip] into a serious conversation. Consequently nothing would come out of my letters other than the conscious-ness of my love, my innermost closeness to you. . . .*
>
> *And yet it is a fact that I am far away from you, but I assure you that every evening I sleep in your arms.*

Don't burn my letters, don't tear them up, it could otherwise do you harm—so steadfastly and truly alive is the love that I express in them for you, that I can only speak of it aloud [to myself] but show them to no one—keep it hidden, like a secret beauty; my love fits you beautifully! excitingly! heavenly!

Through the night a marvelous living thing frequently awakes and flourishes, like a Turkish coffee bean, which depends on a crescent moon, but with the first ray of sunshine withers away into its roots; I would be now with you just as in the evening; the daylight would have been cleansed away, it would be quiet in the house, I would sit at your feet, would have laid my hand on your lap, look at you, sensuously warm, as if one is alone with a friend, and hears nothing from the outside world, only the barking of dogs from faraway alleys— then would you certainly kiss me, and call me a thousand affectionate names, and call me your very own. This is only a thought that wells up through the night, and fades like the Turkish coffee bean with the early morning light.[1]

BETTINA AS BEETHOVEN'S IMMORTAL BELOVED

Near the end of his letter to the Immortal Beloved, Beethoven wrote: "Much as you love me—I love you more. . . . Your love makes me at once the happiest and the unhappiest of men." About these words, the eminent 19th-century biographer of Beethoven, Alexander Thayer, wrote: "the tone of the last part of the letter particularly is that of one who is making up his mind and is attempting to convince one fully in love with him of the necessity of [a] decision." I ask the reader to conclude, as I contend in chapter 2, that Bettina wrote letters to Beethoven similar to the one to Goethe after she received Beethoven's surviving 1811 letter to her, leading him to reply as he did in his letter to the Immortal Beloved.

As was noted in chapter 1, Max Unger, one of the leading experts on the question of the Immortal Beloved in the first half of the 20th century, wrote in a 1910 paper that Bettina met all the geographical, time, and psychological requirements that would prove she was the Immortal Beloved. He ultimately concluded, however, that because Bettina apparently loved her husband, she could not be the woman. He turned then to others, and finally threw up his hands in despair.[2] Unger overlooked, however, diary notations made by Bettina's longtime acquaintance Karl Varnhagen von Ense, who lived in Berlin at the same time as Bettina in her later years, saying that she repeated to him twice over the course of 25 years that she did not marry Achim von Arnim for love but because he had paid her the honor of asking her to be the mother of his child.[3]

If Bettina did not marry Arnim for love, did she nevertheless love him? More importantly, did she love Beethoven or at least tell him she loved him? If she did not, she cannot be the Immortal Beloved.

Bettina's confession to Varnhagen reflects her ambivalence toward love and also to marriage. As noted in chapter 2, when Arnim first asked her to marry him, she told him she was considering foregoing marriage and devoting herself to "music and the causes of the time."[4] She expressed to Varnhagen's wife, Rahel, a disdain for the very institution of marriage, recorded by Rahel in her 1810 diary. Bettina's father had married twice and fathered 10 living children as well as eight that did not survive. Her mother was unhappy in her marriage and had an affair while married with the youthful Goethe. Bettina must have wondered, in those male-dominant times, if she had been put on earth only to create and be a mother to children. She loved literature, society, and above all *music*.

In a letter to Arnim before she married him, she wrote:

> Do you know why you like being with me better than with other girls? Is it because I can't love you in the same way others do, and because you don't understand that, and because you are not meant to love me like other people, but like myself. I love music, it is more to me than life, it can keep me occupied; I love nature too, the summer out of doors, when only God's hand has been active, not man's, and I love Goethe.[5]

Bettina, who like Beethoven appears to have been very self-centered, was puzzled by what love was. As she wrote to Arnim before her marriage:

> You ask me . . . what is true love: I don't clearly know the answer. We are happier when we love because we feel a life in ourselves, and more unhappy because the effort disturbs us. It always seems to me that our longings, hopes and desires for happiness are like a river torrent beating up against a dam. It is the heavenly quality of love which makes the heart struggle; that it is deviated from the dam from its course is owing to the earthliness and weakness of mankind. True love would flow so strongly that it would surmount the dam and calmly resume its majestic course, with clearly defined banks so that it is no longer the plaything of fate. I often do not know, in my great desire for love, which way to turn; I feel that I no longer have a dam to surmount, but that my shallow course runs through a wilderness, and no pleasant banks are reflected on the surface of the stream. . . . I think if one really is in love one loves the whole world, and the world becomes a mirror for the images of the loved one, like a stream reflects its banks.

It therefore becomes appropriate to consider how and if she loved the three most important men in her life: Arnim, Goethe, and Beethoven. Portraits of the handsome Arnim and the aging Goethe are shown in illustrations 4 and 3, respectively.

BETTINA'S LOVE FOR ARNIM

Despite what Bettina told Varnhagen, there nevertheless seems to be some justification for Unger's statement that she loved her husband. Consider, for example, the following extracts from her letters to Arnim.

> I am still very fond of you, I might say I get fonder every day, but I have lost my troubled longing to see you. I think this is because I have the nature of a swallow. It is spring and I should like to travel as far as the sun lights my path, not bothering about the friends I leave behind. Can you care for girls who are like swallows?

These words were written before her marriage. Six years into her marriage, she wrote:

> There was a time when the endings of your letters were like arms clasping me to your heart, this time you merely write "farewell." Farewell then Arnim, but I am annoyed with you, you are not a bit affectionate, you hug me about once in a blue moon, and you don't kiss me as I should like to be kissed.

Twelve years into her marriage, she wrote:

> You are a poet and if you were not my husband I should want to make love to you, and every poem or story you wrote would draw me closer to you: as true as I live I would not [if I were in your place] bother about your shriveled old wife, all she need get is her daily bread and a few words and marital kisses.

These quotes suggest that the love Bettina and Arnim shared was intensely physical.

BETTINA'S LOVE FOR GOETHE

As noted in previous chapters, Bettina's relationship with Goethe was complex. He had courted her married mother, and Bettina had read his letters to her grandmother rhapsodizing about her mother. Bettina also became immersed in Goethe's poetry, novels, and plays before she met him. As soon as the opportunity arose, she traveled dressed as a man, as noted in chapter 2, to faraway Weimar in 1807 to meet him. He was then already in his late 50s, but she had not achieved the age of majority, which was then 25. When she visited him again in Teplitz in 1810, they may have had a brief sexual encounter of some kind (see chapter 4). The letters they exchanged afterward show that she continued to idolize and revere him. Because of the love affair her mother had with the youthful Goethe, Bettina even fantasized that she might be his daughter.

Her letters to Goethe spoke frequently of her love for him. She wrote lines such as "It would pain me if I could not joyfully follow you, if my love could not find that path which is always near to you, even as my heart is and was to yours," and "who loves you like me sings of you in my deepest heart," and "how is it that I flourish and blossom in this wilderness? From where comes to me the dew, the sap, the warmth? . . . it is because . . . of my love for you." Goethe wrote to her in the same vein, "Love me until we see one another again," he said in his extant letter to her of October 25, 1810.[6]

One of the most extraordinary letters that Bettina wrote to Goethe was dated January 8, 1810. A portion of it is set out at the beginning of this chapter. It is so intimate that she excluded it from her *Goethe Correspondence* book. It is not entirely clear whether the love for Goethe she spoke of in her letters was love of the spirit, love of the intellect, love of the heart, physical love, or some combination of all. If the love she meant was physical, it may have led to the possible sexual encounter with Goethe when she paid him a surprise visit in Teplitz in August 1810 (see chapter 4).

Before Bettina married Arnim, she made him promise, as noted in chapter 2, that she could maintain her relationship with Goethe despite the marriage and that he would never be jealous of Goethe. At that stage in her life, she appears not to have made any distinction between the different kinds of love.

Her apparent love for Goethe continued even after he ostracized her at the behest of his wife in 1811. After Goethe's death, Bettina published her *Goethe Correspondence* book to raise money to create a sculpted monument in his likeness.

BETTINA'S LOVE FOR BEETHOVEN

There are several clues as to Bettina's initial impressions and memories of Beethoven. Two may be gleaned from what she wrote shortly after she had met him in Vienna in 1810. To a friend, she wrote in a surviving letter that she had become "excessively [*unendlich*] fond of this man."[7] To Goethe she wrote in a missing letter:

> Each day brought new joy, and each delight was a source of interesting communications. Above all this, Beethoven was prominent; the great super-spiritual one, who introduced us into an invisible world, and our impulse to the powers of life, so that one felt the confined "self" widened to a universe of spirits. Pity that he is not here in this solitude.[8]

These words from her *Goethe Correspondence* book show that Bettina at that early stage of her life (she was just 25) linked the concept of idealized spiritual love with Beethoven. Yet in what she wrote in a surviving letter to her friend Prince Hermann Pückler-Muskau 22 years later, there are hints of recollections of a physical connection between her and Beethoven.[9] In that letter, she mentioned that Beethoven let her stroke his hair while he was making musical notations to the score of one of the songs he sang to her, and that he kissed her hand when they were about to leave his apartment. She also said that when he played and sang to her at their first meeting, his voice became harsh because of *the urge of passion*. Bettina's memory of their first meeting clearly shows that she was aware of the distinction between spiritual love and physical love.

In any case, Beethoven was on her mind after she left Vienna in 1810. As noted in chapter 2, in Beethoven's 1811 letter to her that is today extant, he mentions that she had already sent him two letters. It is apparent that she did not come easily to her decision to marry. After the marriage, her pregnancy became a physical and psychological burden, and she almost died at the birth of her first child.[10] She idolized genius and could no longer express her innermost thoughts and emotions in letters to Goethe because of his ostracism of her in 1811. Her greatest artistic love was music. It would have been natural for her to rethink her initial decision to marry. That she would have substituted Beethoven for Goethe as a sounding board to express her emotional turmoil is, I submit, quite likely. After the near-fatal childbirth, she may well have asked herself whether she should remain in a traditional marriage and continue to bear her husband children, as her mother did before she died, or forgo the pleasures and agonies of that kind of life for a life in the field of music with an eccentric musical genius.

Assuming she wrote to Beethoven often between 1811 and 1812 using the same kind of language about loving him as she did with Goethe, it would, as I argued in chapter 2, have stimulated Beethoven to believe her love for him could possibly become physical as well as spiritual. The ambivalent thoughts, hopes, and expressions expressed in his letter to the Immortal Beloved looked at in this light suddenly become clear. On the one hand, his love seems spiritual in nature. As he wrote in his letter to the Immortal Beloved, "Is not our love truly a celestial mansion, yet as solid as the fortress of Heaven? . . . Yes, I am resolved to wander far away until I can fly to your arms and say that I have found my true home with you, and can send my soul, surrounded by you, into the realm of spirits." On the other hand, he wrote the following, hesitatingly, almost as if it were only a hope and wish: "I talk to myself and to you—arrange that I can live with you, what a life!!!!"[11]

In the late years of her life, Bettina appears to have had no doubt about the kind of love for her Beethoven had in mind. She told Varnhagen that Beethoven "was in love with her, not just platonically" ("nicht bloss platonisch in sie verliebt gewesen").[12]

It is too speculative to attempt to fathom the kind of love Bettina would have had in mind when she wrote to Beethoven about loving him at this difficult time in her life. Which kind or kinds of love would best fulfill what her mind, her heart, her emotions, and her body wanted and needed then? However, as submitted in chapter 2, she apparently decided that she would stay as a wife with her husband and child, and that she likely told this to Beethoven as soon as they met in Teplitz. In Beethoven's Teplitz Letter to Bettina, written only two and a half weeks after his letter to the Immortal Beloved and presumably after Bettina told him that she would stay with Arnim, he wrote: "A musician is like a poet, and by a pair of eyes he can feel himself suddenly transported into a lovelier world where mighty spirits join with him to give him daunting challenges. . . . Even minds can love one another, and I shall always court yours." (This letter, translated into English, is reproduced in appendix C.)

This was the bravest face Beethoven could put on Bettina's decision. He left Teplitz suddenly the next day, forgetting to take even his travel papers with him. His heart was broken.

NOTES

1. *Goethe Correspondence* book (German), 671–3.
2. Unger, "Auf Spüren," 52–74.
3. Wilhelm Schellberg and Friedrich Fuchs, eds., *Die Andacht zum Menschenbild* (Bern: Herbert Lang, 1970), 164.
4. Rolland, *Goethe and Beethoven*, 17.
5. All the quotes in this chapter from Bettina's letters to Arnim may be found in Helps and Howard, *Bettina*, 57–73.
6. The quotes from Bettina's letters to Goethe in this paragraph, all taken from the *Goethe Correspondence* book, are illustrative only. The quote from an extant letter of Goethe to Bettina is found in the *Goethe Correspondence* book (German), 2:689.
7. Sonneck, *Impressions*, 77.

8. *Goethe Correspondence* book, 294.

9. Sonneck, *Impressions*, 84.

10. Wolfgang Bunzel and Ulrike Landfester, eds., *Bettine von Arnims Briefwechsel mit ihren Söhnen* (Göttigen: Wallstein, 1999), 1:85.

11. This is from Virginia Beahrs's translation (see appendix A). In footnote 15 to her translation, Beahrs says that the sentence "suggests further wishful thinking on Beethoven's part in telling the Beloved and himself, still in imagination, to find a way to live together."

12. Alfred Kalischer, *Beethoven und Berlin* (Berlin: Schuster and Loeffler, 1908), 92.

1. Bettina Brentano in her youth. *Courtesy Freundeskreis Schloss Wiepersdorf, Museum Schloss Wiepersdorf*

2. Ludwig van Beethoven, oil painting by Isidor Neugass, 1806. *Beethoven Haus, Bonn, Germany*

3. Portrait of Goethe by Franz Kügelgen, 1810/1811. *Photographer © Ursula Edeimann—ARTOTHEK*

4. Portrait of Achim von Arnim, Bettina's husband, by Peter Ströhling, 1804. *Photographer © Ursula Edelmann—ARTOTHEK*

5a. Page 1 of Beethoven's Letter to the Immortal Beloved. *Bildarchiv Preussischer Kulturbesitz / Art Resource, New York*

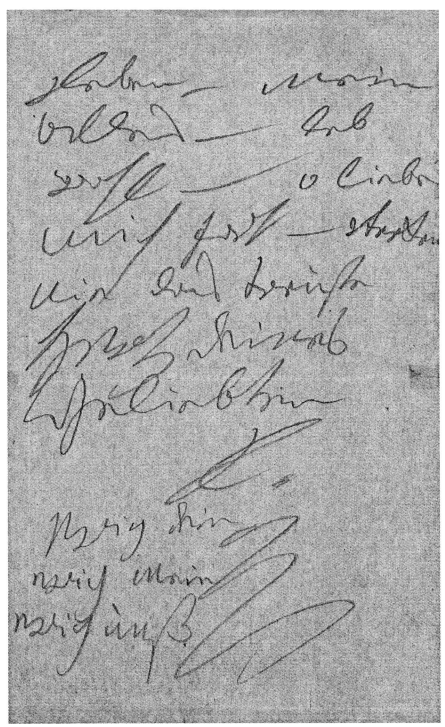

5b. Page 10 of Beethoven's Letter to the Immortal Beloved. *Bildarchiv Preussischer Kulturbesitz / Art Resource, New York*

6. First page of copyist's score of Beethoven's song "Neue Liebe, Neues Leben" ("New Love, New Life"). Along the right-hand side of the page, in Beethoven's handwriting: "For Bettine von Brentano." At the bottom of the right-hand side of the page, in Beethoven's handwriting: "Set to Music by Beethoven." *Beethoven Haus, Bonn, Collection H. C. Bodmer*

7a. Illustration of first page of Beethoven's surviving 1811 letter to Bettina, as shown in Sotheby's 1990 Auction Catalogue for the Salzer Collection. *Courtesy Sotheby's London*

7b. Illustration of second page of Beethoven's surviving 1811 letter to Bettina, as shown in Sotheby's 1990 Auction Catalogue for the Salzer Collection. *Courtesy Sotheby's London*

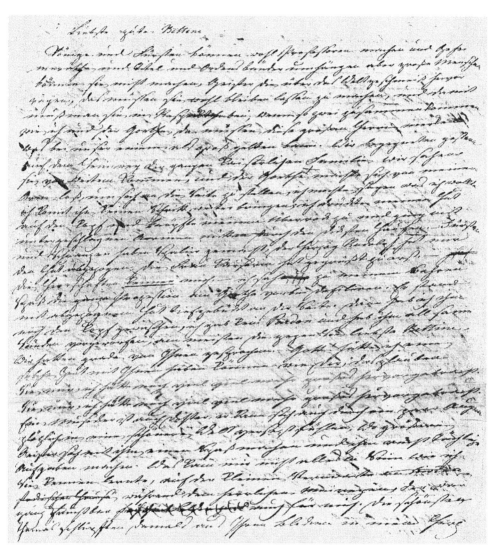

8. First page of Beethoven's 1812 Teplitz Letter to Bettina, as handwritten by Bettina for her *Ilius* manuscript. *Courtesy Goethe Museum, Anton und Katharina Kippenberg Stiftung, Düsseldorf*

9. Last page of surviving 1817 letter from Beethoven to Bettina's half brother, showing "double B" seal stamped next to Beethoven's signature. *From the collection of the Ira F. Brilliant Center for Beethoven Studies, San José State University*

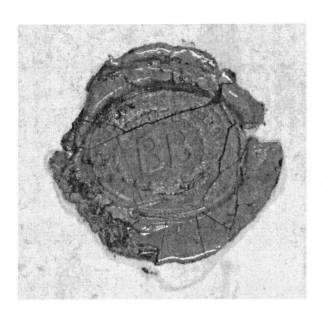

10. Illustration of "double B" seal affixed by Bettina to an 1815 letter from her. *Freies Deutches Hochstift / Frankfurter Goethe Museum*

11. Illustration of plaster relief medallion of Beethoven found among Bettina's possessions after her death. The Frankfurter Goethe Museum speculates that it was a gift to Bettina from Beethoven. *Freies Deutches Hochstift / Frankfurter Goethe Museum*

12. Illustration of facsimile of Beethoven's 1811 sonnet written for Bettina, as contained in Waldmüller's 1861 publication.

· 7 ·

The Beethoven–Bettina Romance

BETTINA'S DESCRIPTIONS OF HER
TIME IN VIENNA WITH BEETHOVEN

$\mathcal{A}$s described in chapter 2, Bettina made a long journey in 1810 with her sister Gunda and Gunda's husband, Friedrich Savigny, during which she traveled from a town near Munich eventually on to Berlin, where Savigny would take up a new post as a professor. On their way, they spent three and a half weeks in Vienna, where they stayed with Bettina's half brother Franz Brentano and his wife Antonie. While there Bettina, who had recently turned 25, looked up the famous 39-year-old musician Beethoven and, as shown later in this chapter, spent about a week exchanging visits with him. (How often she and Beethoven spent time together is disputed by Bettina skeptics but will be verified later in this chapter.) Bettina then traveled on to stay for almost a month at her family's estate in Bohemia.

She described all her adventures on the trip in astonishingly long and detailed letters to Goethe, all of which survive except those falling within the 1810 Letter Gap described in chapter 4. As noted in that chapter, her lengthy surviving letter to Goethe up to the midpoint of her stay in Vienna breaks off literally in midsentence, just where she begins to describe meeting Beethoven, but it was completed or filled in by her as a separate but today missing letter in her *Goethe Correspondence* book published many years afterward (the "Beethoven Description letter").[1] Portions of the Beethoven Description letter telling what she and Beethoven did together are set out verbatim in chapter 2 and below.

Because the Beethoven Description letter was not found in Bettina's possessions after her death and is today missing, it has been attacked by some commentators as being a complete fabrication, or at the very least partly fictional. Their judgment is based on the untrue generalization sometimes made that most of the letters in the *Goethe Correspondence* book were falsified by Bettina. As demonstrated in chapter 11, that generalization is wrong, but it shows how perceptions about Bettina were influenced by the biased views of a generation of scholars who in the early years of the 20th century prevailed over a competing camp that supported the truthfulness of Bettina, as described in chapters 9 and 10. The anti-Bettina camp, which prevailed and today thrives, believes that Bettina had very little contact with Beethoven, and that she exaggerated or falsified much of it to make herself appear more important to the world than she really was. One of the purposes of this chapter is to demonstrate that this camp is wrong, and to show what really happened between Bettina and Beethoven during and after her stay in Vienna in 1810.

As described in chapter 4, the surviving letter from Bettina to Goethe that breaks off just where her description of Beethoven begins was the last of three extensions of a found letter begun at her family estate in Bohemia on July 6, 1810, written when she finally had time to rest from traveling and had settled down for a short while. In the surviving first part of that letter and its extensions, she described her trip from the very beginning starting near Munich. The surviving part of that extended letter just where she begins to describe Beethoven is dated July 28, 1810, and contains a description of her travels into Vienna and what she did there before meeting Beethoven. In the *Goethe Correspondence* book, she continues the Beethoven Description letter exactly where the surviving original breaks off, using exactly the same transition words as in the surviving portion of her letter where it breaks off, and ascribing to it a date of May 28, 1810, which as will be shown below is likely the date she first met Beethoven. As argued in chapter 4, there is no reason to believe that the Beethoven Description letter was a total or partial fabrication. It was after all *her* letter and we know that it *did* exist. One could only state with certainty that it was a fabrication if the original survived and differed materially from the *Goethe Correspondence* book version, or if there was no reasonable proof that it existed. The letter should therefore be relied on as an authentic description of what happened between her and Beethoven unless proven otherwise, not the opposite.

In the Beethoven Description letter, she wrote the following:

(a) "they" were afraid to take her to him; she had to hunt him up on her own.

(b) she brought Beethoven back to a midday dinner party being held that day at the house of her half brother Franz and his wife Antonie.

(c) Beethoven took her to a rehearsal of a full orchestral concert.

(d) Beethoven came to see her every day until she left Vienna, or she went to him, causing her to miss social meetings, galleries, the theater, and even St. Stephen's cathedral.

(e) she and Beethoven took an evening stroll together through the Schönbrunn gardens on the outskirts of Vienna, located far from where she was staying.

Bettina repeated some or all of these details in three separate surviving letters to *other* friends. Two were contemporaneous; the third was written 22 years later.[2]

As described above and in chapters 9 and 10, Beethoven specialists became divided during the last half of the 19th century into two camps. One camp largely disbelieved Bettina and everything she wrote about Beethoven, possibly because of her politics, possibly because of her gender. The other camp, which included the American biographer Alexander Thayer, who to this day remains the preeminent and most quoted Beethoven specialist, believed in Bettina's reliability and truthfulness. In the first edition of his biography of Beethoven published in German in the 1870s, he analyzed in defense of Bettina two of the accounts written by her describing her time with Beethoven that had then published (one being the missing Beethoven Description letter, the other the surviving letter to her friend Prince Hermann Pückler-Muskau written in 1832). Wrote Thayer, "the two accounts differ, but they do not contradict, they only supplement each other. The present writer had the honor of an interview with Mme von Arnim in 1849–50, and heard the story from her lips; in 1854–6, it was his good fortune to meet her often in two charming family circles—her own and that of the brothers Grimm. Thus at an interval of five years he had the opportunity of comparing her statements, of questioning her freely and convincing himself, up to this point, of her simple honesty and truth."[3]

Now that two more surviving letters from Bettina describing her time with Beethoven have been published, modern critics skeptical about Bettina try to point out inconsistencies between the four of them in order to establish that Bettina falsified or exaggerated what happened between her and Beethoven. For example, one modern researcher contends that Bettina spent only a few hours with Beethoven while she was in Vienna.[4] Another contends that she was in contact with him for only three days in total: the day she met him and the last two days she was in Vienna. This conclusion was based on the fact that in one of the two surviving contemporaneous letters, she wrote that Beethoven stayed in her company until 10 p.m. on the day she met him, and then she added that he "even" ("noch") came to see her on the last two evenings before her departure from Vienna. But her addition to that sentence is only to *emphasize* that she had become so close to the famous Beethoven that he *even* called on her the last two days she was in Vienna. It does not purport to say how many days and times they met between the first day she met him and those last two days before she left Vienna.

Another researcher extended the reasoning of the second to claim that Bettina exaggerated the days she spent with Beethoven from three days to two weeks.[5] The basis for this contention was that at the end of the Beethoven Description letter, Bettina added a postscript informing Goethe that she hoped for a letter from him at her address in Vienna where she would be staying *another* two weeks. Bettina's reason for this was not exaggeration, but simply an editing mistake. The missing Beethoven portion of the surviving letter was started on July 28, about two weeks before she left her family estate in Bohemia. When she edited the missing portion of her letter many years afterward for her *Goethe Correspondence* book, indicating it was written by her on May 28 when she was still in Vienna, she had to adapt the postscript in the original letter to correspond to the place where she was on the date she had ascribed to it: Vienna, not Bohemia where she then was. In any case, the reasoning that Bettina deliberately tried to extend the time spent with Beethoven into a fictional two weeks is flawed, because the Beethoven Description letter *finished* the description of what happened between them. She did not pretend that she continued to see Beethoven for two weeks afterward.

How many days did she and Beethoven see one another before she left Vienna? This question may be answered with reasonable certainty by considering the following:

1. Bettina arrived in Vienna around May 8;[6] she left there on June 3,[7] and traveled to Prague, writing a surviving letter from there on June 8.[8]
2. In a surviving letter she wrote in 1852, she recalled that she met Beethoven in May 1810, and that he visited her often in her small room in the Brentano household that was perfumed by a large bouquet of May flowers.[9]
3. Beethoven in his 1812 Teplitz Letter to Bettina (see chapter 5) wrote about the "ideas that occurred to me after we were together at the small observatory during that delicious May shower."
4. The last surviving extension of Bettina's long letter to Goethe begun July 6 at her family estate in Bohemia was dated July 28; as noted above, its abrupt break-off marks the beginning of the 1810 Letter Gap described in chapter 4. The Beethoven Description letter was dated May 28 by her, when she was still in Vienna; it probably coincided with the date she first met him.

5. Thayer was convinced that the full orchestral concert that she says Beethoven took her to was one of the concerts given at the Augarten, where Beethoven conducted his own symphonies.[10]
6. Bettina mentions in the Beethoven Description letter that in addition to him coming often to where she was staying, she also went to call on Beethoven (how many times she did not say).
7. Bettina mentioned in the Beethoven Description letter and Beethoven mentioned in the Teplitz Letter that they had gone together to look at the Schönbrunn gardens, which in those days would have taken the better part of a day from where Bettina was staying.

These circumstances suggest that Bettina looked up Beethoven around May 28 or 29, that he accompanied her to the party given by Franz and Antonie Brentano that day, that she and Beethoven took the Schönbrunn stroll and he took her to a music rehearsal during the following two or three days, and that he came to call on her on June 1 and June 2, the last two nights she spent in Vienna before she set out for Prague.

Assuming this is so, the attacks on the Beethoven Description letter describing the time she spent with Beethoven in Vienna as being exaggerated are unjustified and erroneous.

BETTINA'S FIRST MEETING WITH BEETHOVEN

Another question that arises out of the circumstances surrounding Bettina meeting Beethoven in Vienna in 1810 is who, if anyone, accompanied her when she looked him up for the first time. The American musicologist Maynard Solomon, in his efforts to establish that Antonie was the Immortal Beloved as described in chapter 12, claimed that Antonie accompanied Bettina on Bettina's initial visit to Beethoven. In doing so, Solomon relied on an 1867 publication by the 19th-century Beethoven biographer Ludwig Nohl, who wrote that Antonie recounted that information to him personally. That Bettina might not have been alone when she looked up Beethoven is indicated by the words of her contemporaneous surviving letter to her young student friend Alois Bihler in which she stated that "we" waited for a good half hour for Beethoven to appear because he was shaving at the time.[11] As will be noted below, Bettina sometimes referred to herself in the first person plural (the so-called royal we), not the first person singular, so she may well have been alone when she looked up Beethoven. A second possibility was that "we" referred to Beethoven's man-servant, who chatted with Bettina while Beethoven shaved.[12] A third possibility is that Bettina was accompanied by her sister Gunda, with whom Bettina was traveling through Europe at the time. This view was expressed by Nohl in a publication made nine years after the 1867 publication on which Solomon relied (also see chapter 12 for additional details).[13]

VIENNESE MEMORIES

The time Beethoven and Bettina spent with one another in Vienna made a profound impression on each of them. In her Beethoven Description letter, Bettina wrote, as noted in chapter 2, "since then [the time she first met Beethoven] he comes to me every day or I go to him. For this I neglect social meetings, galleries, the theater, and even the tower of St. Stephen's. Beethoven says 'Ah! What do you want to see there? I will call for you towards evening; we will walk through the alleys of Schönbrunn.' . . . I went with him to a glorious garden in full bloom, all the hot beds open—the perfume was bewildering."[14] In her surviving contemporary letter to Bihler dated about four weeks after she left Vienna, Bettina wrote, "I have become excessively [*unendlich*] fond of this man. In all that relates to his art he is so dominating and truthful that no artist can pretend to approach him."[15] In her surviving letter to Pückler-Muskau written some 20 years later, she described taking Beethoven home from his lodgings to the midday dinner party being held by her half brother Franz Brentano and his wife Antonie:

> Everyone was surprised to see me enter a company of more than 40 persons, sitting at the table, hand in hand with the unsociable Beethoven. He took a seat without any demur, saying little. Twice he drew his notebook from his pocket and jotted down a few figures. After dinner the whole company mounted to the roof tower of the house to enjoy the view of the surroundings. When all had descended again and he and I were alone, he drew out his note-book, glanced over it, wrote and crossed out and said: "My song is completed." He next leaned from the window and sang it lustily out upon the air. Then he said "Eh? It sounds, does it not? It belongs to you if you want it. I wrote it for you. You incited me to do so, for I read it in your glance."[16]

See chapter 10 for an analysis of Bettina's recollections about Beethoven's Goethe songs and their connection with her.

Thayer, who as noted above interviewed Bettina several times and believed in her credibility, wrote from the notes he took in his conversations with her the following:

> There was a large [midday] dinner party that day at Franz Brentano's in the Birkenstock house and Bettina told Beethoven he must change his old

coat for a better coat, and accompany her thither. "Oh," he said jokingly, "I have several good coats," and took her to the wardrobe to see them. Changing his coat he went down with her to the street, but stopped there and said he must return for a moment. He came down again laughing with the old coat on. She remonstrated; he went up again, dressed himself properly and went with her.[17]

These incidents, in addition to showing the rapport that had already developed between Beethoven and Bettina in the few hours after they first met, may have even more significance. As more fully discussed in chapter 12, Beethoven wrote his letter to the Immortal Beloved in pencil, saying that the pencil had come from her. In Bettina's recounting set out above of Beethoven at the dinner party to which she took him, he several times made notes during the party, which obviously could not have been with pen and ink, and therefore he must have had a pencil with him. But in changing coats before going to the party, he may have left his own pencil at home and used one given or lent to him by Bettina.

During the time they spent together, it is quite probable that Beethoven mentioned the possibility of dedicating to Bettina his Mass in C. He had written it several years before on the invitation of Prince Nikolaus Esterhazy in honor of the prince's wife. The Mass was first performed in the prince's town of Eisenstadt, where Beethoven was assigned servant's quarters in the prince's castle, not the private room he would have occupied had he been considered a social equal. To make matters worse, the Mass's reception by the prince was not enthusiastic, and Beethoven may even have gotten the impression that the prince and his entourage were mocking him. The result was that Esterhazy received neither the manuscript of the Mass nor a dedication of it. That Beethoven may have discussed with Bettina the possibility of his dedicating the still undedicated Mass to her is suggested by his letter to his publisher in the autumn of the following year, after he had learned of Bettina's marriage. In the letter, he wrote, "as to the Mass, the dedication might be altered. The lady is now married, so the name would have to be changed accordingly. Hence the dedication can be omitted for the moment. Just let me know when you are publishing it; and then no doubt I shall find a saint for this work."[18]

That Beethoven may have described to Bettina how poorly the Esterhazy family treated him several years before and why he did not dedicate the Mass to them is indicated in his letter to the Immortal Beloved. There, after describing how his coach broke down on the way into Teplitz, he mentioned that the same thing had happened to Esterhazy's son, even though he took a different route and had more horses drawing his coach. Beethoven wrote in his letter that the son's similar misfortune gave him some pleasure. These words suggest that Bettina as the intended recipient of Beethoven's Immortal Beloved letter would have known who Esterhazy was from Beethoven's own lips when they discussed the possibility of him dedicating to her his Mass.

Several weeks after Bettina left Vienna and Beethoven, she wrote in one of her missing letters to Goethe reproduced in the *Goethe Correspondence* book that while she was recuperating in her family's estate in Bohemia from the arduous weeks of travel, "each day brought new joy, and each delight was a source of interesting communications. Above all this Beethoven was prominent: the great super-spiritual, who introduced us into an invisible world, and our impulse to the powers of life, so that one felt the confined 'self' widened to an universe of spirits. Pity that he is not here in this solitude."[19] It should be noted that Bettina used the first-person plural here, not the first-person singular, in referring to herself.

When Bettina was writing those words in Bohemia, Beethoven was at the same time in Vienna thinking about and writing to Bettina. Knowing she was traveling and would not arrive in Berlin until the beginning of September, he nevertheless sent to her in care of her Berlin destination (the house of her brother-in-law Savigny) a letter dated August 11, 1810. The authenticity of this letter has been attacked because it does not survive, but as shown in chapter 5, its existence is independently corroborated by a number of factors. Here is what he wrote:

Dearest Bettine!

Never was there a more beautiful spring than this year; I say this, and feel it too, because it was then that I first got to know you. You have yourself seen that in society, I am like a fish on the sand, which writhes and writhes, but cannot escape until some benevolent Galatea casts it back into the powerful ocean. I was in fact quite stranded, dearest Bettine, when I was surprised by you in a moment in which depression had totally overcome me, but truly it vanished when I saw you. I was immediately aware that you came from a different world than this absurd one, where one with the best intentions cannot open one's ears. I am a wretched man and yet complain about others!! You will quite forgive me for this from the goodness of your heart that shows in your eyes and understanding that lies in your ears; at least your ears know how to flatter when they listen. My ears are sadly a dividing-wall, through which I cannot easily have friendly communication with others. Otherwise, perhaps I might have been more self-assured with you. As it was, I could understand only the accepting look in your eyes, that made an impression upon me that I shall never forget. Dear Bettine, dearest girl! Who understands art—with whom can one converse about that great goddess? How dear to me are those few days when we were chatting together, or even more, corresponding! I have kept all the little bits of paper that bear your spirited, dear, dearest answers. Thus I have to thank my bad ears that the best parts of those fleeting conversations are written down. Since you have gone, I have had melancholy hours, dark hours for which nothing can be done. After you were gone, I paced the Schönbrunner Way, but no angel met me there, no angel seized me the same way as you did, my angel. Excuse me, dearest Bettine, for this departure from the usual key, but I must have intervals like this to unburden my heart.

You have written to Goethe about me, haven't you? I wish that I could hide my head in a bag so that I would not hear and would not see what goes on in the world, because you, dearest angel, won't [likely] be with me in it. But will I not receive a letter from you? This hope nourishes me, in fact it nourishes half the world, and hope has been next to me all my life, otherwise what would have become of me? I am sending to you with this letter a copy in my own hand of Kennst du das Land *as a memento of the moment when I first met you. I am also sending to you the other song which I composed after your departure, dear, dearest heart!*

> *Heart, my heart, what must come of it,*
> *What distresses you so much*
> *What a strange new life*
> *I don't recognize you any more.*

Yes, dearest Bettine, do answer this letter. Write to me what must come of it, since my heart has become such a rebel. Write to your most faithful friend Beethoven.

There are three things about this letter that should be especially noted. First, the title page of one of the songs Beethoven said he was sending with the letter, starting with the words "Heart, my heart," from which he quoted a few lines in his letter, has been found bearing Beethoven's signed dedication to Bettina (see illustration 6), and the balance of the song from which the title page was ripped was found in Bettina's papers. Second, in the Beethoven Description letter, she mentioned that Beethoven took her to the Schönbrunner Way, which Beethoven says in this letter he afterward went back to and paced along thinking of her. Third, most remarkably, Beethoven called Bettina "angel," not once but four times in this letter. His letter to the Immortal Beloved began with the words "My angel."

It should also be noted that in this first letter from Beethoven to Bettina of August 1810, he mentioned that he had kept the replies she had written for him when they were conversing, which must have been written in pencil. Since Beethoven did not use an interlocutor to write down conversations

· 8 ·

Beethoven the Poet

THE HISTORY OF A SONNET

$\mathcal{I}$n the 1850s, the famous Hungarian violinist and composer Josef Joachim fell in love with Bettina's youngest daughter, Gisela. She ultimately rejected him and married another suitor, but Joachim remained close to Gisela and her mother. In his younger days, he had become an advocate of the "new" style of music of Franz Liszt, but Bettina steered him toward the music of Beethoven, and there exists today a famous painting of Joachim's string quartet playing for the elderly Bettina, perhaps the music of Beethoven.

In 1858, Bettina, then in her 70s, traveled to Teplitz, where she spent three months trying to restore her health. The town must have brought poignant and possibly painful memories for her of pivotal points in her life that happened almost a half century before, including her fateful meeting with Goethe there in 1810 when she had just reached the age of majority, and her meeting with Beethoven there in 1812 when she shattered him by telling him she had decided to stay with her husband. Now, almost 50 years later, she met socially in the same small spa town a poet and novelist named Edouard Duboc, whom she apparently told some details about her relations with Goethe and Beethoven. One of those details was that Beethoven had written for her a sonnet lamenting her marriage but wishing her well in it. Duboc was intrigued and asked to see a copy. Bettina had since given it to Joachim, but she borrowed it back for Duboc to see, and he had a facsimile made (a bad one, as will be discussed below). He included the facsimile in a book that he published a few years afterward under his pen name, Robert Waldmüller.[1]

It is ironic that this surfacing of an important clue to the relations of Beethoven and Bettina occurred as a result of an apparently chance meeting of

Bettina with a traveling writer in the same small spa town where some of the most important occurrences in her life took place almost a half century earlier. Bettina, who is accused by her detractors of exaggerating her importance in the lives of Goethe and Beethoven, had never publicized or published the sonnet. It surfaced by chance late in her life and is too badly written to have emanated from her.

Bettina's detractors took it as support of their views that Bettina manufactured evidence to exaggerate her influence on Beethoven. They attacked the sonnet as they had her Beethoven letters. One detractor visited Joachim to look at the original and asserted that, in his opinion, it was definitely not in Beethoven's handwriting.[2] Another debunked it as false because it was not in the copy of Duboc's book that he looked at in a library. However, it must have been sliced out of that particular copy by someone, because it *is* in the published book.[3] As will be noted in chapter 10, Max Unger in 1910 was initially certain of its authenticity, based on his look at the published facsimile,[4] but many years later he called it a figment of Bettina's romantic imagination.[5]

In 1930, Joachim's family (he had died in 1907) offered the sonnet for sale through a Leipzig book dealer. A Beethoven expert who was engaged to authenticate the poem decided that it was a very refined and skillful forgery, so the poem was given back to Joachim's family. Its whereabouts are not publicly known today.[6]

A close examination of the facsimile (see illustration 12) reveals that the handwriting seems almost identical to Beethoven's. The writing of Bettina's name is identical to the way Beethoven wrote it in his found letter to her (see illustration 7), and most of the original letters forming the words of the poem are also identical to the distinctive way Beethoven wrote them (compare the handwriting in illustrations 12 and 7). There are some discrepancies, however. The first is that the handwriting lacks the usual scrawled flourish of Beethoven's extant letters. This could be because Beethoven, not being himself a poet, obviously labored over the poem. In several lines, words are crossed out and replaced with others to improve the rhythm and rhyming technically required in a sonnet form, showing he must have taken some care with it.

A second discrepancy is that the letter "D" has a directional curl, which is the reverse of the way Beethoven formed it. This could be due to the difficulties engravers encountered because they had to engrave on the printing block a mirror image of the original handwriting.

There are certain facts that reasonably establish the sonnet was not a forgery. First, Bettina's handwriting is so neat and controlled (see illustration 8) and Beethoven's so idiosyncratic and distinctive (see illustration 7), Bettina could never have come close to reproducing his, as some critics have hinted or expressly stated. Also, if she had forged it, she would not have labored over the cross-outs and substituted words, as Beethoven obviously did. Most importantly, Bettina gave it to Joachim, a close and respected friend of hers and a famous interpreter of Beethoven's music. She did not try to publicize it or sell it.

Other critics have acknowledged the poem to be in Beethoven's handwriting, but because Schindler said that Beethoven was no poet, they suggested it was composed by a poet friend of Beethoven's.[7] This is improbable, both because of the cross-outs and substitutions, which a professional poet would have removed before giving the text to Beethoven, and because the poem obviously is not the product of a professional poet, rather that of a wounded suitor.

Assuming the sonnet to be genuine, that alone does not prove Bettina is the Immortal Beloved. It nevertheless proves that Bettina and Beethoven kept in touch after her marriage, because in his found letter to her of 1811, he is not certain whether she is or is not yet married, so the poem must have been composed and mailed to her afterward. It also proves the deep love Beethoven retained for Bettina after she married and his anguish at her marriage decision. Finally, Beethoven addresses Bettina in the "du" form in the poem, which he never used for any woman with whom he was romantically involved except for Bettina in one portion of his found letter to her, and in his letter to the Immortal Beloved.

THE SONNET

Here is the text and English translation of Beethoven's sonnet to Bettina, as written by him but without the cross-outs in the original:

"An Bettine"

In tiefer Demuth will ich gratulieren
Tief neigund von dem Haupt den Hut mir heben
Wenn die Gedanken auch in weiter Ferner schweben
Muss ich sie doch gebahnte Wege führen
Will ich auch nicht das Schicksal gross anstieren
So wird es nimmer dennoch mich erheben
Verwirkt ist längst mein schaales Erdenleben,
Der Treue Kralle werd ich stets im Busen spüren.
Doch was wein ich und binn elende
Froh bist du und froh sey dein Leben
Ich dulde bis mir Zukunft herbes sende
Doch einen Trost sollt mir zum lohne geben,
Der Götter Huld dass ich dich glücklich sehe,
Und ferne ist mein herbes tiefes wehe.

English translation of Beethoven's sonnet to Bettina (with thanks to Dr. Hans Eichner):

"To Bettina"

I will congratulate you with deep humility,
[and] bowing deeply I will raise my hat;
Even though my thoughts may hover far away,
I must lead them along smooth paths.
Although I do not wish boldly to stare at fate,
It will none the less never lift me up;
My trivial life has long ago gone to waste;
I will always feel the pain of faithfulness in my heart.
But though I am in tears and miserable,
You are glad, and may your life be glad;
I will endure until the future will bring me [even] worse suffering.
But one consolation should I be given as a reward,
By the grace of the gods, that I may see you happy
And that my bitter profound suffering will cease.

NOTES

1. Robert Waldmüller, *Wanderstudien: Italien, Griechenland, und daheim*, 2 vols. in 1, (Leipzig: Verlag von Theodor Thomas, 1861), 2:233.

2. Theodor Frimmel, *Beethoven Handbuch*, 2 vols. (Leipzig: Breitkopf and Härtel, 1926), 1:63.

3. Donald MacArdle and Ludwig Misch, eds., *New Beethoven Letters* (Norman: University of Oklahoma Press, 1957), 90.

4. Unger, "Auf Spüren," 61–62.

5. Max Unger, "The Immortal Beloved," *Musical Quarterly* 13 (1928): 259.

6. Walter Weisbecker, "Stefan Zweig entdeckte den gefälschten Brief," *Frankfurter Allgemeine Zeitung*, January 26, 1984, 27.

7. Ann Willison Lemke, "Bettine's Song," doctoral dissertation (Ann Arbor, Mich.: UMI Dissertation Services, 1998), 38. Lemke later changed her opinion and wrote a paper published in German claiming that the sonnet was entirely Beethoven's; see Lemke, "Bettines Beethoven: Wahrheit und Dichtung," in *Masstab Beethoven? Komponistinnen im Schatten des Geniekults*, ed. Bettina Brand and Martina Helmig (Munich: Richard Boorberg Verlag, 2001), 145–58.

· 9 ·

The Tarnishing of Bettina's Reputation

MAX UNGER

$\mathcal{M}$ax Unger (1883–1959) was a well-known German musicologist who during his long career studied, wrote about, conducted, and taught music throughout Europe. Although he was born and educated in Germany, he moved to Switzerland in 1930, then to fascist Italy in 1940, from where he contributed articles about music to Nazi propaganda magazines, including one about Beethoven entitled "Beethovens vaterländische Musik." He published many other papers about Beethoven, some even before he obtained his doctoral degree from the University of Leipzig in 1911, including numerous articles about the mystery of the Immortal Beloved. One of his professors in Leipzig was Hugo Riemann, who had succeeded Hermann Deiters as editor and translator of Thayer's biography of Beethoven. Both Riemann and Deiters publicly differed and distanced themselves from Thayer's admiration of and belief in the trustworthiness of Bettina.

The transformation of Unger's views about Bettina, starting from his early writings up to his old age, illustrates how Bettina came to acquire a reputation among a number of scholars as being at best a concocter of fiction about Beethoven in the guise of made-up letters from and about him, and at worst, a forger of handwritten communications from him to her. The negative views about Bettina of Riemann, Deiters, and Unger, possibly arrived at because of her political views or gender, and perhaps correct or not, came to be cited more and more frequently as her supporters died off. And if negative opinions are cited frequently enough, they can come to be considered facts, not just opinions. Unger's final views about Bettina were a significant cause of her tarnished reputation in musical and literary circles.

A CONTROVERSIAL WOMAN

During her lifetime, Bettina became a well-known and controversial figure in Germany for many reasons. In politics, she corresponded with the King of Prussia and in some circles was considered a supporter of royal authority. Others considered her a radical because of her sympathy and support for the revolutions of 1848. She incurred the displeasure of many German anti-Semites because of her support for the legal and social rights of Jews. She claimed a close relationship with Goethe and Beethoven and was married to Achim von Arnim, one of the leading lights of 19th-century German Romantic literature, whose poetry was used by Gustav Mahler for *Des Knaben Wunderhorn*. She was a close friend to the brothers Grimm, who published and popularized German folk- and fairy tales, such as those about Hansel and Gretel, Cinderella, and Snow White. She was prominent in German musical circles and was acquainted with the famous musicians Robert and Clara Schumann, Ignaz Moscheles, Josef Joachim, Franz Liszt, and Johannes Brahms. Both Brahms and Schumann dedicated music to her. As a result of controversy about her political and social beliefs, possible envy of her fame, and possibly because she was a woman, she incurred more than her share of enemies during and after her life.

As noted in chapter 3, Bettina published in an epistolary form her *Goethe Correspondence* book in 1835. In 1839, she published in a literary and political journal three letters she claimed to have received from Beethoven, one in 1810, one in 1811, and one in 1812. Since both Goethe and Beethoven were then dead and the art of printed facsimiles was not yet fully developed, controversy arose as to whether the Goethe and Beethoven letters were genuine, especially because of the intimacies and confidences both expressed toward her in those letters. Further increasing the suspicions of the doubters, both Goethe and Beethoven had addressed her in the intimate German "du" form in parts of their letters to her as published, and she used the same form in her letters to Goethe. She never published any of her own letters to Beethoven, but Beethoven, as noted in chapter 2, indicated in the single surviving letter from him to her that she had in fact written to him before her marriage.

As a result of the controversy that swirled around her, the literary and musical establishment divided into two camps in the last half of the 19th century, one camp believing that her published Goethe and Beethoven letters were genuine, the other that they were concocted. After Bettina's death, members of her family, many of whom had been embarrassed by the Goethe letters because of the intimacies contained in them, withheld the originals from public scrutiny. That resulted in even more suspicion and controversy.

Supporters of the authenticity of the Beethoven letters included the American scholar Alexander Thayer, even today the most prestigious and oft-cited of all the Beethoven biographers. As noted in chapter 12, Thayer actually met Bettina and spoke highly of her. Other supporters were Alfred Kalischer, Ludwig Nohl, and Romain Rolland (all prominent Beethoven experts), the pianist and composer Ignaz Moscheles (who knew both Beethoven and Bettina), and Moritz Carrière, a prominent German writer and philosophy professor, who stated to Nohl that he had actually seen the originals of the three Beethoven letters, urged their publication for political reasons (as described in chapter 5), and confirmed their authenticity as published.[1]

Spearheading the rival camp was Anton Schindler, the assistant of Beethoven during the composer's last years. Schindler did not come to know Beethoven until 1814, two years after the last meeting of Beethoven and Bettina in 1812. As noted in chapter 2, Schindler visited Bettina in 1843 hoping to have a look at the three Beethoven letters she had published, but she refused even to talk to him about them. Bettina's refusal to discuss with or show him Beethoven's letters confirmed Schindler's view that Bettina had concocted them.

In 1859, Adolph B. Marx, the principal rival of Thayer as Beethoven's definitive biographer during the last half of the 19th century, published the first edition of his Beethoven biography. Marx quoted and supported Schindler's opinion about the Bettina letters from Beethoven. He even gave a detailed analysis as to why the language and style of the three letters could not have emanated from Beethoven and so must have been the product of Bettina's hyper-romantic imagination. In doing so, he quoted specific words and passages from the 1811 Beethoven letter to Bettina that he claimed Beethoven would never have used, calling them "girl-like" and "un-Beethovian."[2]

In 1860, Thayer published in the *Atlantic Monthly* a stinging review of Marx's Beethoven biography (Thayer's own had not yet been published).[3] Thayer stated with respect to the three Beethoven letters Bettina had published that he believed in the authenticity of *all of them*, and he cited examples where Beethoven had used in other letters language comparable to the language in the 1811 letter that Marx had attacked as "un-Beethovian" and "girlish."

Then around 1880, to the astonishment of the anti-Bettina camp, the 1811 letter from Beethoven was found in Nathusius's estate and was exactly the same as published by Bettina. The 1811 letter was included in facsimile form in a revised 1884 edition of Marx's biography of Beethoven. Marx had since died, so the editor of the new edition, Gustav Behncke, understandably omitted Marx's analysis as to why the language of the 1811 letter could not have emanated from Beethoven. Without missing a beat, however, he inserted an elaboration of Marx's original analysis as to why the other two letters must have been concocted by Bettina.[4]

The first part of Thayer's own biography of Beethoven appeared in three volumes between 1866 and 1879, translated into German for him by

Hermann Deiters. The dispute as to the authenticity of the three letters to Bettina became apparent in that publication because, while Thayer defended their authenticity, Deiters added a separate footnote disagreeing with the arguments that appeared in Thayer's English text. Deiters subsequently published in 1882 his own paper attacking the authenticity of all three letters. When a later edition of Thayer appeared after discovery of the 1811 letter, Thayer pointed out the mistakes made by Deiters in his 1882 paper but conceded the possible validity of one of Deiters's arguments for believing parts of the third to have been concocted.[5]

THE CONTROVERSY CONTINUES

By the time Unger entered the fray in 1909, the original antagonists, including Thayer, Nohl, Merz, Kalischer, and Carrière on the one hand, and Marx, Schindler, and Deiters on the other, were all dead, but Bettina's papers remained sealed by her family, and the debate raged on. Believers like the Nobel Prize winner Romain Rolland continued to vouch for their authenticity. On the other hand, Hugo Riemann, who succeeded Deiters as translator and editor of Thayer's biography of Beethoven, preserved Thayer's arguments in favor of the authenticity of the letters in his portion of the text of the German edition, but he added a footnote asserting his own belief that they were actually written by Bettina. And in 1921, Henry Krehbiel, the editor and translator from the German of the first English edition of Thayer, hedged his bets by saying that if the other two letters later turned up, they would have been "tricked" out of Beethoven by Bettina.[6] That unscholarly opinion illustrates the mind-set against Bettina by some who had become part of the debate.

In 1909, Unger, then a young, up-and-coming Beethoven specialist who was studying for his PhD as a student of Riemann, entered the fray with the publication of a paper attempting to establish the identity of the Immortal Beloved.[7] In it, he rejected two candidates proposed by other writers, and in doing so endorsed a new theory that the letter to the Immortal Beloved must have been written in the year 1812, when Beethoven was in Teplitz, not earlier years when Monday fell on July 6. This view is today generally accepted. Unger then suggested that Bettina might be the Immortal Beloved, based on the similarity of the three Beethoven letters published by her as well as the sonnet from Beethoven that she had given to the famous musician Joachim. He set out the full text of the sonnet and went on to suggest that if the third of the three letters to Bettina ostensibly written in Teplitz that summer by Beethoven only a few weeks after his letter to the Immortal Beloved could be found (the "Teplitz Letter"), it would prove that Bettina was the mystery woman.

This paper must have caused a stir in the academic community, because in successive papers, Unger began to back off. In 1910, he wrote a paper stating that Bettina could not have been the Immortal Beloved because she had recently married and apparently loved her husband.[8] In making that argument, he overlooked, as noted in chapter 2, a statement in the diary of Karl Varnhagen von Ense, a friend of Bettina's who also knew Beethoven, that Bettina had told Varnhagen twice over the space of many years that she did not marry Arnim for love, but rather because he had paid her the honor of asking her to bear his child, a child he needed to inherit control of his grandmother's estate.[9] Unger also showed in his 1910 paper that he had been influenced by the Bettina skeptics, including Riemann, about the Beethoven letters, because Unger stated that the Teplitz Letter to Bettina was concocted by her for reasons previously asserted by Riemann and others in the anti-Thayer camp. Unger wrote, however, that he still tended to believe in the authenticity of the 1810 letter from Beethoven to Bettina, and he also stated that there could be "no doubt" that the sonnet (included in chapter 8) was authentic. He appeared obviously puzzled by the fact that Beethoven used the "du" form in parts of the single surviving letter to Bettina published by Marx, as well as by the warmth and passion of the text of that letter.

In 1911, Unger published another paper in which he formally acknowledged having withdrawn his 1909 assertion that Bettina could be the Immortal Beloved, yet he admitted that the 1812 Teplitz Letter to Bettina had the same passion and style as the letter to the Immortal Beloved. Somewhat murkily, he wrote that "even if this letter, as has been perhaps correctly surmised, was authored in all its parts by Bettina herself, it can here be drawn upon as an entirely valid documentation, as its contents, as far as feelings and mood are concerned, probably correspond, at least in its main aspect, to reality."[10]

Meanwhile Theodore Frimmel, a prominent Beethoven scholar having seniority over Unger, visited in 1909 the famous musician Josef Joachim, to whom Bettina had given Beethoven's sonnet, as described in chapter 8. He looked at it, or possibly the facsimile of it published by Duboc, and opined that it was "definitely not in Beethoven's handwriting."[11] Frimmel's opinion must have greatly unnerved Unger, who had now been attacked by his academic superiors on two of his major published assertions. Accordingly, in a paper published in English in 1927,[12] he reversed the opinion he had expressed in 1910 that the sonnet was authentic. Now he attacked it as a figment of Bettina's imagination, thereby indirectly accusing her of forgery because of the facsimile's resemblance to Beethoven's distinctive handwriting. He also categorically asserted that the 1810 and 1812 letters were concocted by Bettina, with only the 1811 letter being genuine, thus reversing his 1910 opinion about the probable authenticity of the 1810 letter.

In 1929, the Arnim family finally permitted Bettina's papers to be inspected and later auctioned off. There were no Beethoven letters among them. But there were at least 13 letters from Goethe, and many more from her to him, so now they could be compared with what she had published in her *Goethe Correspondence* book. Bettina and Goethe did indeed address one another in the "du" form in those letters, and many portions of them were reproduced verbatim in Bettina's book. Nevertheless, as Bettina herself wrote before publication,[13] her book was not intended to be simply an edited version of the actual letters, but rather, as more fully explained in chapter 4, a "poetic epic" exploring her own intellectual and artistic development as stimulated by her correspondence with Goethe. Also as noted in chapter 4, she had rewritten, reorganized, and in many cases redated the originals to achieve a literary and sequential flow.

When Bettina's papers were made public in 1929, Unger was shocked that the Goethe correspondence had been altered at all by Bettina. He apparently had assumed the book was simply an edited version of the originals. Unger also must have taken satisfaction from the fact that there were no Beethoven letters among Bettina's papers. That supported his revised contention that the 1810 and 1812 letters were concocted by Bettina. But given that the originals of the 1810 and 1812 letters had been seen and verified by respected and reputable witnesses, as detailed in chapter 5, the fact that none were found in her estate provides greater support for the theory I postulated in chapter 4 that the Beethoven letters were destroyed by Bettina. It is also possible that the Beethoven letters were destroyed by members of Bettina's family, for the same reasons as their reluctance to make public the Goethe letters. In any case, Unger published a paper in 1936 in which he launched an almost vitriolic attack on Bettina.[14] His predisposition against her and the mistakes or oversights in his paper are so apparent that they will be separately analyzed in chapter 10. But Unger's 1936 paper makes it clear that his disenchantment with Bettina was final and complete.

THE ERROR OF OSCAR FAMBACH

After publication of Unger's 1936 paper, his views became generally accepted in the field of Beethoven scholarship. In an entirely different field of scholarship, that concerning the literary, social, and scientific legacy of Goethe, the Teplitz Letter from Beethoven to Bettina published by her was attacked from a new direction by Oscar Fambach, a prominent scholar and admirer of Goethe. Fambach, who was a professor at a prestigious German university, was appalled that Goethe was portrayed in the Teplitz Letter as a fawning admirer of royalty.

In a paper published in 1971, Fambach purported to "prove" that the 1812 Teplitz Letter was a concoction by Bettina.[15] His main reason arose from a statement made by Beethoven in the letter that the "Court" would leave the town of Teplitz "tomorrow." Fambach pointed out that the Austrian empress and her court, who were walking in the park with members of the royal family of Saxony when, according to the Teplitz Letter, they were encountered by Goethe and Beethoven, did not leave town "tomorrow" but rather several weeks later. Fambach claimed that the wrong date of the intended departure proved that Bettina had concocted the letter. But his analysis was based on a fundamental error. He overlooked that the "Court" referred to by Beethoven was not that of the Austrian empress but of the royal family of Saxony, which did in fact leave Teplitz "tomorrow," as Beethoven said they would.[16] Fambach had used the wrong royal group as the basis for his argument. Presumably because of witnesses who had seen and verified the authenticity of the Teplitz Letter that Fambach attacked, Fambach in his paper expressly claimed that the Teplitz Letter was a forgery (discussed more fully below).

ATTACKS AND ANSWERS

As a consequence of the ascendency of the anti-Bettina camp through the writings of scholars like Unger and Fambach, a whole new generation of Bettina scholars has arrived on the scene today trained by their academic superiors to disbelieve, or at the very least regard with suspicion, almost everything that Bettina wrote or did. The stalwarts of the pro-Bettina camp, such as Thayer, Nohl, Carrière, Moscheles, Rolland, and Kalischer, are long gone, and few specialists today defend Bettina as did those careful and reputable scholars. The new generation of scholars often cite or repeat accumulated negative views about Bettina made by their skeptical predecessors as if they are facts, not merely opinions deserving scrutiny. What follows are discussions of and answers to the most frequently cited modern attacks made against Bettina and her trustworthiness, including attacks made on the authenticity of the Teplitz Letter. The authenticity of the Teplitz Letter, however, was established by the evidence presented in chapter 5. And as conceded by Unger himself in his 1909 paper, if the original were to be found or established to be authentic, that alone would prove conclusively that Bettina was the Immortal Beloved.

Attack 1

Bettina doubters argue that the August 15 date of the Teplitz Letter that appeared in *Ilius* is manifestly wrong, since Beethoven was far away from Teplitz on that date, while Bettina was in Teplitz.[17]

Answer. Beethoven noted the place of writing and exact date of virtually all of his letters at the head of the first page of the letter, as is customary today. Yet the date and place of the writing of the Teplitz Letter as first published by Bettina in 1839 reads "Teplitz, August 1812" (no day). Those words appear at the end of the letter, on the left side of the page across from Beethoven's printed signature. This indicates that the notation did not emanate from Beethoven but was most likely a marginal note made by Bettina when she delivered the original to her Nürnberg editor for publication, remembering as best she could almost 30 years afterward the place, year, and approximate month when she received it. When she copied out the letter from the original for her *Ilius* manuscript some years later (which as shown in chapter 5 is almost certainly an exact replica of the Teplitz Letter), she plugged in "Teplitz, 15th August, 1812," underneath, not across from, her replication of Beethoven's signature. These facts confirm that the place and date of writing was not written on the face of the letter by Beethoven and that in all likelihood it was handed undated to Bettina shortly before he precipitously left Teplitz, when he forgot even to take his travel papers with him. He would not have endorsed its place of writing and date had he handed it to her. Edouard Duboc, who, as noted in chapter 8, met Bettina in Teplitz shortly before her death and learned from her about Beethoven's sonnet to her, published the Teplitz Letter in his book and confirmed that it was undated.[18] Presumably he learned this from Bettina.

Attack 2

Bettina's critics point out that the paper used to write out the single surviving letter from Beethoven to Bettina in her *Ilius* manuscript, referred to in chapter 5, is different from the paper used to write out the copies of the two letters which do not survive. As well, the copies of the two letters in the *Ilius* manuscript that do not survive contain cross-outs, which critics see as an indication that Bettina was drafting the letters herself.[19]

Answer. The three letters from Goethe's mother also in the *Ilius* manuscript are written on different sorts of paper, but all three survive. Bettina made cross-outs in copying out the three letters from Goethe's mother in her *Ilius* manuscript, yet all three survive and were not concocted by her. The cross-outs in the surviving 1811 Beethoven letter correspond exactly to Beethoven's own cross-outs in the original. The surviving 1811 letter from

Beethoven to Bettina was likely copied out by Bettina before she gave it to Nathusius (as described in chapter 3), while the other two were likely copied out some years afterward as she was collating the *Ilius* manuscript, hence the difference in the paper.

Attack 3

As noted above, Beethoven wrote in the Teplitz Letter that he had walked in the park with Goethe "yesterday" when they met coming the other way the Austrian empress in company with the royal family of Saxony, in all probability Goethe's duke and several other members of the nobility. He also wrote that the "Court" would leave town "tomorrow." Goethe's diary shows that he walked in the park with Beethoven on July 23. This means that the Teplitz Letter, if genuine, would have been written on July 24, and that the court would leave on July 25. Oscar Fambach pointed out that the Austrian empress and her court did not leave town until the middle of August, and he concluded that the Teplitz Letter must therefore have been concocted by Bettina.[20]

Answer: As noted above, Fambach chose the wrong "Court." The members of the royal family of Saxony left town for Dresden on July 25, the day after Beethoven wrote his letter, accompanied for part of the journey by the empress.

Attack 4

Bettina wrote to her friend Pückler-Muskau more than 20 years afterward that Beethoven had come running to "us" making fun of Goethe's obsequious bows to the party of nobility they met in the park. Why would Beethoven describe to Bettina the same event in the Teplitz Letter if he had already told her about it in person? This is the question raised by Deiters that troubled Thayer the most.[21]

Answer: Beethoven wrote the Teplitz Letter on July 24, the day after he walked with Goethe in the park. He left town precipitously on the next day or two. It is quite possible that he had already written the Teplitz Letter when he approached Bettina and her family group, which would have included Bettina and her husband and sister and perhaps other friends in the course of a social gathering. The town was crowded with nobles and hangers-on. He may have described the incident to a relatively large group at the same time as he slipped the already written Teplitz Letter to Bettina, having determined to leave town as soon as he could arrange a coach seat. Bettina wrote to Pückler-Muskau that Beethoven repeated the story "several" times. She may have had in mind the retelling of the story in the Teplitz Letter, which she had not yet made public at the time she wrote her letter to Pückler-Muskau.

Attack 5

Beethoven wrote in the Teplitz Letter that "Duke Rudolph" had doffed his hat to Beethoven when his group met Beethoven and Goethe in the park on July 23. Bettina's critics have taken this as a reference to Archduke Rudolph, the brother of the Austrian emperor, and point out that Archduke Rudolph was not in Teplitz on July 23.[22]

Answer: Beethoven's letter did not say "Archduke Rudolph" but rather "Duke Rudolph." There is a significant difference between an archduke and a duke, and Beethoven knew that. He always in his letters referred to Archduke Rudolph as the "Archduke." His letter probably was referring to the duke for whom Goethe worked, whose name was Karl August, but in scribbling his letter, Beethoven mistakenly wrote the wrong name. Bettina did not refer to the archduke as "Rudolph" in her own letters but by the name "Rainier," another of his names. If she had concocted the letter, she would likely have named Rudolph "Duke Rainier." The mistake was Beethoven's.

Attack 6

Critics argue that the independent witnesses Merz and Carrière, who saw and publicly attested to the autographs of the three letters from Beethoven to Bettina, did not know what Beethoven's handwriting looked like and in fact only saw copies written out by Bettina.[23]

Answer: Merz and Carrière were educated and respected literary experts. Both were familiar with Bettina's neat and distinctive handwriting. As Thayer pointed out, a number of publications had by 1839 included specimens of Beethoven's eccentrically distinctive handwriting.[24] Bettina's Nürnberg publisher Merz would have been aware of this in 1838 when he certified to Thayer many years afterward that he had in his possession the originals of the letters, and Carrière reiterated to Marx's editor more than 30 years afterward his confirmation of seeing the originals.

Attack 7

A letter to Bettina from Goethe's mother that Bettina included in her *Goethe Correspondence* book was dated after the death of Goethe's mother. From this is argued not only that the letter was concocted by Bettina, but also that many other letters from others to her that she published many years later (including ones from Beethoven and Goethe) but which do not today survive were also likely concocted by her.

Answer. As demonstrated at the beginning of chapter 11, Bettina and those with whom she was intimate and corresponding on a continuing and regular basis often did not date their correspondence, just as Beethoven did not date his letter to the Immortal Beloved nor his Teplitz Letter to Bettina. When Bettina published some of her correspondence many years afterward, she ascribed dates as she best remembered them. As more particularly described in chapter 11, the letter from Goethe's mother ostensibly dated after her death was in clear response to undated letters from Bettina describing a voyage down the Rhine she took in midsummer of that year, 1807. In attributing a date to it many years later, Bettina simply inserted the wrong month. As also shown in chapter 11, Bettina attributed a wrong date to one of the letters to her from Goethe's mother, thus causing an editor of a book of collected letters of Goethe's mother initially to claim that Bettina concocted the letter, then reversing his opinion when he was shown the autograph of the letter, blaming Bettina, however, for inserting the wrong year of its writing.

Attack 8

Bettina's doubters claim she spent only a few hours in the company of Beethoven,[25] and exaggerated the nature of her contact with him in what they claim is her fictitious letter to Goethe describing the time she spent with Beethoven in Vienna in 1810.[26]

Answer. As discussed more fully in chapter 7, Bettina most likely looked up Beethoven around May 28 or 29, and he accompanied her to a party given by Franz and Antonie Brentano that day. During the following days, she and Beethoven strolled in the Schönbrunn gardens and he took her to a music rehearsal. Beethoven came to see her every day until she left Vienna, or she went to him, causing her to miss social meetings, galleries, the theater, and even the cathedral.

Attack 9

In her *Ilius* book, Bettina reproduced three letters she claimed to have received from Beethoven, but only one today survives. According to her critics, this proves the other two were concocted by her.[27]

Answer. In the *Ilius* book, Bettina reproduced three letters she claimed to have received from Goethe's mother and three she claimed to have received from Beethoven. But the text of her covering letter to Nathusius when she sent him reproductions of the six letters makes it clear that she gave him only one original letter from each group of three. The one letter from Beethoven that she gave to Nathusius was found in his belongings after his death, and the other letter from Goethe's mother has also been found. They are both *identical* to what she reproduced in *Ilius* except that, as noted in chapter 5, she depersonalized her own name, for example changing her name in the heading from "Dear Bettine" to "Dear Friend." However, as noted in chapter 5, the letter from Beethoven copied out by Bettina as it appears in the preliminary *Ilius* manuscript today located in Düsseldorf, described in chapter 5, in which she had not yet depersonalized her name, is *identical* to the extant original. All three letters from Goethe's mother reproduced in *Ilius* have been found and are identical to what appears in the preliminary *Ilius* manuscript except for grammatical and spelling corrections.

CONCLUSION

As a result of the confluence of negative judgments about Bettina by Beethoven scholars like Unger and Goethe scholars like Fambach, Bettina's reputation as a concocter and possibly a forger of letters became entrenched in the literary establishment. The views of Thayer, Carrière, Kalischer, Nohl, Rolland, Moscheles, and others in the pro-Bettina camp have been rejected as wrong. But it is the anti-Bettina critics who have based their judgments on mistaken facts and premises, and in some cases bias, who are wrong.

NOTES

1. Ludwig Nohl, *Briefe Beethovens* (Stuttgart: Verlag Cotta'schen, 1865), 71. According to Nohl, in an 1868 English translation of this work, "I never myself had any doubts of their [the three Beethoven letters to Bettina] being genuine (with the exception of perhaps some words in the middle of the third letter), nor can any one now distrust them. . . . But for the sake of those for whom the weight of innate conviction is not sufficient proof, I may here mention that in December 1864, Professor Moritz Carrière, in Munich, . . . expressly assured me that these three letters were genuine, and that he had seen them in Berlin at Bettina v. Arnim's in 1839, and read them most attentively and with the deepest interest. From their important contents, he urged their immediate publication; and when this shortly after ensued, no change whatever struck him as having been made in the original text; on the contrary, he still perfectly remembered that the much disputed phraseology (and especially the incident with Goethe) was precisely the same as in the originals." Nohl, *Beethoven's Letters*, trans. Lady Wallace (Freeport, N.Y.: Books for Libraries, 1970), 84–85.

2. Adolph B. Marx, *Beethoven: Leben und Schaffen*, 2 vols. (Berlin: Verlag Otto Janke, 1859), 2:132.

3. Theodore Albrecht, "Thayer contra Marx," *Beethoven Journal* 14, no. 2 (1999): 57–58, referring to Marx, *Beethoven*, 2:132.

4. Marx, *Beethoven*, 4th ed., ed. Gustav Behncke (Berlin: Verlag Janke, 1884), 2:304–16.

5. Thayer German, 3:254–5, 328; Thayer English 2:227.

6. Krehbiel noted that Deiters, the original editor of Thayer German, had published in 1882 a paper claiming that all three letters to Bettina from Beethoven were concocted by Bettina. That obviously presented a problem for Riemann, who in 1907 succeeded Deiters as editor of Thayer German, because the 1811 letter had surfaced after the first volumes of Thayer German were published and just around the time Deiters's paper appeared. Krehbiel pointed out that Riemann had made a compromise suggestion to the effect that because the facts described in the 1812 Teplitz Letter appeared to be accurate, they had been put into letter form by Bettina based on what Beethoven told her. Krehbiel hedged his own bets in case the letters later turned up by suggesting that if they did, they would have been "tricked" out of Beethoven by Bettina. This shows the mind-set against Bettina by all three of the original editors of Thayer's work (see Thayer English, 2:190).

7. Max Unger, "Zum Problem von Beethoven's Unsterblicher Geliebten," *Musikalisches Wochenblatt* 26 (1909): 356.

8. Unger, "Auf Spüren," 71–74.

9. Wilhelm Schellberg and Friedrich Fuchs, eds., *Die Andacht zum Menschenbild* (Bern: Herbert Lang, 1970), 164.

10. Max Unger, "Giulietta Guicciardi: Die Unsterbliche Geliebte Beethovens?" *Neue Zeitschrift für Musik* 35/36 (1911): 504–5.

11. Theodor Frimmel, *Beethoven Handbuch* (Leipzig: Breitkopf and Härtel, 1926), 63.

12. Max Unger, "The Immortal Beloved," *Musical Quarterly* 13 (1928): 259.

13. Heinz Härtl, ed., *Bettina von Arnim Werke: Goethes Briefwechsel mit einem Kind*, 4 vols. (Berlin: Aufbau Verlag, 1986), 1:666–70.

14. Unger, "Neue Liebe, Neues Leben," 1049–75.

15. Oscar Fambach, "Eine Brieffälschung der Bettina von Arnim als Nachklang des Beethoven-Jahres," *Deutches Vierteljahresschrift* 45 (1971): 773–8.

16. Edward Walden, "The Authenticity of the 1812 Beethoven Letter to Bettina von Arnim," *Beethoven Journal* 14, no. 1 (1999): 9–15, translated, amplified, and edited by Peter Anton von Arnim, in the "Internationales Jahrbuch der Bettina von Arnim Gesellschaft," *Saint Albin Verlag* 15 (2003): 47–66.

17. Fambach, "Brieffälschung."

18. Waldmüller, *Wanderstudien*, 2:228.

19. Renate Moering, "Bettine von Arnims Literarische Umsetzung Ihres Beethoven-Erlebnisses," *Der "männliche" und der "weibliche" Beethoven* (Bonn: Beethoven Haus, 2004), 251–77.

20. Fambach, "Brieffälschung."

21. Thayer English, 2:227, but see p. 183 for a more hesitant opinion.

22. Anderson, 3:1357. It should be noted that in the 1839 publication of the letter, as well as in *Ilius* and in Bettina's handwritten copy of the letter in the *Ilius* manuscript (see chapter 5), Rudolph is identified by the title "Herzog" (duke), not "Erzherzog" (archduke).

23. Thayer English, 2:183–5, answering the arguments of both Marx and Thayer's own translator, Deiters, with whom he was at odds on the point.

24. Thayer English, 2:183–5.

25. Kopitz, "Antonie Brentano in Wien," 124.

26. Ann Willison Lemke, *Bettine's Song: The Musical Voice of Bettine von Arnim, née Brentano*, doctoral dissertation (Ann Arbor, Mich.: UMI Dissertation Services, 1998), 161–2.

27. Unger, "The Immortal Beloved," *Musical Quarterly* 13 (1928): 259.

• 10 •

Beethoven's Goethe Songs

UNGER'S ABOUT-FACE

$\mathcal{A}$s described in chapter 9, Beethoven specialists during the last half of the 19th century were divided into two camps on the question of Bettina's trustworthiness in her writings about Beethoven. One camp believed in the truthfulness and reliability of her published descriptions of him and the authenticity of the three letters from him that she published. Members of that camp included Alexander Thayer, Ludwig Nohl, Ignaz Moscheles, Alfred Kalischer, and Romain Rolland. The other camp believed she was at best a concocter of letters and at worst a liar and forger. Members of that camp included Hermann Deiters, who was Thayer's German translator, and Adolph Marx, who was Thayer's great rival as a Beethoven biographer. When Max Unger came on the scene as a young student in Leipzig in 1909 working toward his PhD, the most prominent pro-Bettina scholars except Rolland were all dead, but the anti-Bettina camp, headed now by Hugo Riemann, who succeeded Deiters as Thayer's editor and translator, was gaining strength. Riemann was one of Unger's professors at the University of Leipzig.

Unger started out in the pro-Bettina camp and even published a paper in 1909 theorizing that she could be the Immortal Beloved.[1] In August 1911, however, the year he received his PhD, he published a paper stating that he had withdrawn that theory.[2] This was possibly because of pressure from Riemann. During the next two decades, Unger gradually retreated from other pro-Bettina positions he had taken in his early publications, culminating with an anti-Bettina paper published in 1936 in the field of music. Although the French writer and scholar Romain Rolland continued to publish in Bettina's favor before his death in 1944, he seems to have been perceived as poaching on German turf. In a 1929 review by Unger of a biography of Beethoven written by Rolland, Unger appears condescending.[3] Doubts about Bettina seemed reinforced when no Beethoven letters turned up in the auction of her paper in 1929. That as well as the scholarly papers critical of Bettina resulted in the complete ascendancy of the anti-Bettina camp, as reflected in Oscar Fambach's 1971 paper in the field of Goethe literature described in chapter 9.[4] Skeptical and even derogatory views of her are today entrenched in the literary establishment.

Unger's 1936 paper was published in a musical journal and dealt with the history and background of one of Goethe's poems set to music by Beethoven entitled *New Love, New Life*, discussing in detail the history of its composition and analyzing Beethoven's musical sketches.[5] That in turn required Unger to deal with a statement attributed to Bettina that Beethoven wrote the song for her. Right from the beginning of the paper, it is evident that Unger's secondary purpose was to destroy the pro-Bettina contentions of Thayer, Nohl, Kalischer, and others in the pro-Bettina camp who were all now dead. Unger specifically stated that he wanted to correct the "foolishness" of the traditions created by those pro-Bettina writers and scholars of the previous generation.

Unger's paper is replete with mistakes, oversights, and flawed conclusions that he used to support his theory that Bettina concocted two of the three Beethoven letters she published, that the missing letters between her and Goethe that she published in her *Goethe Correspondence* book were complete fabrications, and that she created false evidence to exaggerate the role she played in Beethoven's life.

BETTINA'S CONNECTION WITH GOETHE AND BEETHOVEN

As noted in chapters 2 and 4, Bettina for many reasons had a strong artistic and emotional connection with Goethe, who was 35 years older than she. As previously described, when she was only 20, she traveled to Weimar where Goethe lived and introduced herself to him. That meeting led to a long series of letters exchanged between them, many but not all of which are extant today.

Beethoven also was a great admirer of Goethe, especially because of the political opposition to tyranny Goethe expressed in his play about the Flemish resistance hero Egmont. When Bettina met Beethoven in 1810, he was then working on setting the Egmont story to music. He was also working on or had recently finished setting to music three Goethe poems: *Mignon's Song* (Op. 75, No. 1), which Beethoven played and sang for Bettina twice when they first met; *New Love, New Life* (Op. 75, No. 2), a copy of which Beethoven sent to

Bettina in his first letter to her and which bears his handwritten inscription to her; *The Bliss of Melancholy* (Op. 83, No. 1), which Beethoven had not quite finished when he also sang it for Bettina when they first met.

The fact that both Beethoven and Bettina shared a great admiration for Goethe and that Bettina actually *knew* Goethe when she first met Beethoven obviously attracted Beethoven to her. Many years later, Bettina, then in her middle years, published four letters ostensibly written in 1810 dealing with Beethoven's settings of the Goethe poems. One of the letters is from Goethe to her, one is from Beethoven to her, and the other two are from her to Goethe. In them, her interaction with Beethoven and Goethe and her own connection to music were described in some detail. The three letters between her and Goethe were published in 1835 in her *Goethe Correspondence* book but fell within the 1810 Letter Gap described in chapter 4, and hence today are missing. As theorized in that chapter, they were likely destroyed by Bettina, but edited versions were copied or re-created by Bettina and included in her *Goethe Correspondence* book. The 1810 letter to her from Beethoven is also today missing. As described in chapter 3, it was first published by her in 1839 in a literary and political journal edited by an independent and respected editor, as more fully described in chapter 5.

A few years before Unger wrote his 1936 paper, several books were published analyzing the differences between the actual correspondence between Goethe and Bettina that had been auctioned off in 1929 and the same letters as they appeared in her *Goethe Correspondence* book. Unger called the differences "stupefying" and characterized all the missing correspondence between Goethe and Bettina during the 1810 Letter Gap that she reproduced in her *Goethe Correspondence* book as pure fabrications by the young "phantastin." In doing so, he was referring not only to letters during the 1810 Letter Gap from Goethe to Bettina, but also letters from Bettina to Goethe, even though, as noted in chapter 4, Goethe's surviving letters to her during and after the 1810 Letter Gap mentioned a number of letters to him from Bettina during the 1810 Letter Gap period. It is one thing to call a letter a fabrication if the original is found and bears no resemblance to the published version, or if there is no proof that the original ever existed. It is another thing to call the published version of a letter that has not been found a fabrication when it is proven to have actually existed. That is especially so if the writer of the published version is the acknowledged writer of the missing one. As to the missing letters from Goethe to Bettina during the 1810 Letter Gap, they are quite short, noncontroversial, and have the ring of truth (see chapter 11).

Turning specifically to the four missing letters dealing with Beethoven's Goethe songs, it becomes apparent that in claiming that they were complete fabrications, Unger overlooked or ignored strong evidence corroborating their existence and their contents. Below are summaries of what the four letters said, followed by evidence corroborating their existence and content. In considering the three missing letters between Goethe and Bettina, it should be kept in mind that, as will be described in chapter 11, Bettina often did not date her own letters, and in some cases in her *Goethe Correspondence* book, she attributed erroneous dates to them, either because after the passage of more than 20 years she could not remember the exact date when she wrote them, or because she broke up her own long undated letters into segments and attributed dates to them to provide easier reading and a sequential narrative.

Missing Letter No. 1: Bettina to Goethe May 28, 1810—the Beethoven Description letter more fully described in chapter 7. Bettina's date is wrong. The surviving portion of this letter was started in early July 1810, but the missing portion as published in her *Goethe Correspondence* book, just where she begins to describe meeting Beethoven, was broken out from the surviving portion and likely dated by her to correspond to the date she remembered as being when she first met Beethoven. Bettina says in the missing portion of this letter that when she first met Beethoven, he played and sang *Mignon's Song* for her, and seeing her pleasure, played and sang for her *The Bliss of Melancholy* that he had not completely finished and was still working on.

Corroboration of Missing Letter No. 1: A surviving letter from Bettina to her friend Hermann Pückler-Muskau written in 1832 repeats essentially what she had written to Goethe in Missing Letter No. 1, that is, that Beethoven had first sung *Mignon's Song* for her. She also wrote to Pückler that because "her eyes and cheeks were aglow" when she heard Beethoven sing it, he was stimulated to sing his almost completed *The Bliss of Melancholy* for her as well. In a cheerful surviving letter from Beethoven to his publisher dated June 6 1810, just several days after Bettina left Vienna, Beethoven wrote: "among the songs I have offered you there are several settings of poems by Goethe, including [*Mignon's Song*] which makes a great impression on listeners—you could publish these at once."[6] Beethoven's mention of the impression that the song made on listeners can reasonably be linked to Bettina, for whom he had played and sung the song only several days before.

Missing Letter No. 2: Goethe to Bettina June 6, 1810. Bettina's date is probably wrong; this missing letter was likely written in early August in response to her missing Letter No. 1. Goethe says he would like to meet Beethoven, possibly in the Bohemian spa town Karlsbad where he usually spent his summers. He also says he would like to see Beethoven's song settings of two of his poems. These were apparently mentioned and described by Bettina in portions of her Letter No. 1 that are not only missing, but even edited out of her *Goethe Correspondence* book, possibly because she did not want her children to learn that in the first year of her marriage she had seriously considered leaving her husband in favor of a career in music in collaboration with Beethoven. In a surviving contemporaneous letter to her young friend Alois Bihler (see chapter 12), Bettina mentioned that Beethoven had given her settings of songs made to Goethe poems, but she did not mention this fact in her missing Letter No. 1 to Goethe, so it must have been edited out by her.

Missing Letter No. 3: Bettina to Goethe, undated but probably written in mid–August. Bettina says in response to missing Letter No. 2 from Goethe to her that Beethoven assured her he would try to meet Goethe in Karlsbad next summer. Bettina also says she is enclosing, as requested by Goethe, Beethoven's song settings of two poems by Goethe that she does not name. Finally she says that Beethoven praised her musical abilities and told her if she applied herself to music she could have a promising future in it. As proof she said she was enclosing for Goethe two songs she herself had written.

Corroboration of Missing Letters Nos. 2 and 3: Bettina wrote to her friend Alois Bihler in a surviving 1810 letter that "during these last days I spent in Vienna, he came to see me every evening, gave me songs by Goethe which he had set, and begged me to write him at least once a month."[7] An original 1810 autograph copy of *The Bliss of Melancholy* was found in Goethe's after-effects and is now in the Goethe museum in Weimar.[8] In 1811, Beethoven and Goethe exchanged surviving letters. In Beethoven's letter to Goethe, he wrote: "Bettine Brentano has assured me that you would receive me kindly, or, I should say, as a friend."[9] In his reply, Goethe wrote: "the good Bettina Brentano surely deserves the interest that you have shown in her. She speaks of you with rapture and the liveliest affection, and counts the hours that she spent with you among the happiest of her life."[10] Goethe in fact went to Karlsbad in 1812 but afterward traveled to the nearby town of Teplitz to join his employer, where he and Beethoven finally met. In 1810 and 1812, Bettina published two songs she had written, under the pseudonym "Beans Beor" (see chapter 3).[11] When Achim von Arnim first proposed to Bettina several weeks after she had left Vienna and Beethoven, she said in response that she was considering devoting her life "to music and the causes of the time" instead of marriage.[12]

Missing Letter No. 4: Beethoven to Bettina August 11, 1810. Beethoven says that he is enclosing a copy of *New Love, New Life* and an autograph copy of *Mignon's Song*. Beethoven also asks that Bettina recommend him and his music to Goethe.

Corroboration of Missing Letter No. 4: The first page of a copy of *New Love, New Life* with Beethoven's handwritten dedication to Bettina has been found and is today in the Beethoven Haus in Bonn. The balance of the copy of that song was found in Bettina's private papers after her death and is presently in the Morgan Library in New York. As to *Mignon's Song*, because the original autograph has not been found (which is somewhat unusual for

musical publications by Beethoven, most of which have been found), Helga
Lühning of the Beethoven Haus speculates that it might have been the one
sent by Beethoven to Bettina with this Letter No. 4.[13] Also see the exchange
of the surviving letters between Beethoven and Goethe corroborating Missing Letters Nos. 2 and 3 above.

Bettina's final words on the subject of the Beethoven-Goethe songs that
we know of were recounted in the diary of her acquaintance Varnhagen von
Ense in 1856, when Bettina was in her 70s and had less than three years to live.
Bettina had been a close friend of Varnhagen's deceased wife Rahel, and Bettina and Varnhagen kept in touch socially because they both lived in Berlin.
Varnhagen noted in his diary that Bettina told him that Beethoven had wanted
to marry her and had written *New Love, New Life* for her. This fact will be
discussed in greater detail later in this chapter.

UNGER'S MOST EGREGIOUS ERROR

The most egregious erroneous attack on Bettina made by Unger in his 1936
paper may be seen in his attempted explanation of the inscription to Bettina
in Beethoven's handwriting on a copy of the front page of *New Love, New
Life*. As noted in the paragraph corroborating Missing Letter No. 4 above,
the inscription by Beethoven to Bettina on the title page of the song provides
powerful corroboration of the authenticity of Beethoven's Missing Letter No.
4 to Bettina, in which he said he was sending to her a copy of that song. Unger
speculates that Bettina, like an autograph hound, obtained the inscription in
blank from Beethoven when she met him in Vienna, then had an unknown
copyist write out the song when she arrived in Berlin and attached the inscription to the copy she had caused to be created. The facts about the inscription
to Bettina on the first page of the song as well as the balance of the other pages
of the song are these:

1. The inscription page with Beethoven's dedication to Bettina in his
   own handwriting has the first nine bars of the *New Love, New Life* song
   on the reverse side written out by Beethoven's copyist; that page is
   now in the Beethoven Haus in Bonn, and is shown in illustration 6.
2. The inscription page has fold marks consistent with it being enclosed
   in a sealed letter, presumably the missing August 1810 letter from
   Beethoven to Bettina.
3. The balance of the copy of the song from which the inscription page
   was ripped is in the Morgan Library in New York and was obtained
   by the library's benefactors from the 1929 auction of Bettina's papers.

4. The rip on the inscription page matches exactly the balance of that page that is joined to the rest of the copy of the song in New York.

5. The handwriting of the balance of the song in New York matches exactly the handwriting of the first nine bars of the song on the inscription page in Bonn, which is that of Beethoven's copyist.[14]

Unger's theory about how Bettina came into possession of the dedication is therefore totally wrong. Further, he was an expert in Beethoven manuscripts, and one wonders why he failed to recognize the handwriting of Beethoven's copyist.

The balance of this chapter deals with a few, but only a few, of the other conclusions of Unger in his 1936 paper that demonstrate an apparent lack of objectivity as well as a mind-set against Bettina in his analysis of the role she played in Beethoven's life.

BEETHOVEN'S STATEMENT ABOUT THE WRITING OF *NEW LOVE, NEW LIFE*

As noted above, Beethoven sent Bettina a copy of the song *New Love, New Life* with an inscription to her in his Missing Letter No. 4. He also said in that letter that he had composed it after she had left Vienna. Unger wrote in his 1936 paper that this was clearly wrong, a mistake that he contended corroborated his claim that Beethoven's 1810 letter to Bettina was concocted by her. Unger traced the history of the song, pointing out that an initial version of it had been written by Beethoven in 1798/1799, and that a second version had been published by him in 1809. This is true, but in February 1810, Beethoven sent to his publisher a semi-final draft of a third and final version of the song for possible publication.[15] He sent the completed version to his publisher on July 2, 1810, about a month after Bettina left Vienna, and a month before he sent his Missing Letter No. 4 to her with the inscription page described above.[16]

From Bettina's perspective, receiving a copy of the song with the first page endorsed "For Bettina von Brentano—set to music by Beethoven" would justify her believing Beethoven had written it for her, as she told Varnhagen many years later. Bettina was not a scholar who would have had the opportunity to pore over Beethoven's papers as did Unger almost a century later. And Beethoven did not lie to Bettina when he wrote to her that he had composed it after she left Vienna, because he finished the song and sent it off to his publisher in the month following her departure. As he said in his letter, "I am sending you also the other song [*New Love, New Life*] which I composed after I said goodbye to you, dear, dearest heart!" Only an unromantic academic would expect Beethoven to craft the sentence in his love letter to say "I enclose with this letter a song, which is in fact the third and final version of something I have been working on for many years and which I finally finished off and sent to my publisher after I said goodbye to you."

BEETHOVEN'S COMPOSITION OF *MIGNON'S SONG*

Unger accused Bettina of falsely claiming that Beethoven wrote *Mignon's Song* for her. She did not make any such claim to Varnhagen. In her missing Beethoven Description letter to Goethe (Missing Letter No. 1 above) and in the surviving letter that she wrote many years afterward to Pückler-Muskau, she said only that he had played and sung the song for her almost as soon as she met him and that he told her he had just composed it.[17] This would be a natural thing for Beethoven to say, given Bettina's identification with Mignon. Bettina knew enough about music to realize that one cannot create a song for someone "on the spot." She specifically wrote that Beethoven was still working on the other song, *The Bliss of Melancholy*, that he also played and sang for her after he sang *Mignon's Song*, because he took out his notebook and made notations in it for changes. With the literal mind of a scholar, Unger obviously did not understand the flirtatious ways of a 39-year-old man in the company of an adoring 25-year-old woman who identified with the subject of the song.

BEETHOVEN'S 1810 MARRIAGE PLANS

On May 2, 1810, a few weeks before Beethoven met Bettina, he wrote to a friend living near Bonn asking him to try to obtain a copy of his baptismal certificate from there, because he was not really certain how old he was (he was then in fact 39). In 1845, some years after Beethoven's death, his friend published in an academic journal that he had since learned the real purpose of the request was that Beethoven needed the certificate for a possible marriage. The question then arose among Beethoven scholars as to whom Beethoven had wanted to marry. One of Bettina's most prestigious supporters in the late years of the 19th century was Alfred Kalischer, whose publication of the letters of Beethoven continued to be the definitive version of them during much of the 20th century. In 1886, he published a paper theorizing that Bettina must have been the object of Beethoven's 1810 marriage intentions, based on the 1856 entry in Varnhagen's diary in which he mentions Bettina telling him Beethoven's love for her was not platonic and that he had wanted to marry her.[18] Kalischer reasoned that because of Bettina's closeness to Goethe, her musical sensibilities, her psychological makeup, and the timing of the request for the certificate (May 1810, the month in which Beethoven and Bettina met), Bettina's claim to Varnhagen was correct and that Beethoven indeed had planned in 1810 to marry Bettina, whom he met in late May of that year.

In 1911, Hugo Riemann, one of Unger's professors at the University of Leipzig, edited and completed a revised German edition of Thayer's biography of Beethoven, in which Riemann contended that the object of Beethoven's 1810 marriage plans was in fact Therese Malfatti, an 18-year-old Viennese woman. It appears that Beethoven did hope to marry Therese in the spring of 1810 but her parents vetoed the possible union. This was just before he met Bettina. That the object of Beethoven's marriage plans was Malfatti is generally accepted today, and it is certain that the woman was not Bettina, because the letter requesting the baptism certificate was sent several weeks before Beethoven first met Bettina.

In Unger's 1936 paper, he claimed that it was he, Unger, not his professor, Riemann, who should get credit for establishing that Malfatti was the object of Beethoven's marriage plans.[19] Then, in the context of Malfatti being the object of Beethoven's marriage plans in May 1810, Unger took the opportunity to attack both Bettina and her supporter Kalischer in reference to the claim she made to Varnhagen that Beethoven had wanted to marry her. Unger contended that Bettina had probably read the 1845 academic journal in which the reason for Beethoven's request for his baptismal certificate was revealed, then made up a false story that it was she whom Beethoven wanted to marry at that time, in order to make herself appear important in Beethoven's life.

Once again, Unger's accusation is erroneous. Bettina's claim to Varnhagen was only that Beethoven had *wanted* to marry her. She did not claim that he proposed to her or that she had refused him. Beethoven himself confided in 1816 to an acquaintance that his love for the hoped-for mate of his life had never reached a confession, that is, a proposal of marriage.[20] Bettina would have been justified in making her statement to Varnhagen on the basis alone of the words in Beethoven's found 1811 letter to her, in which Beethoven said he had learned that she was about to be married but was distressed that she had not given him the opportunity of seeing her and letting him talk to her first.

Assuming, however, that Bettina was the Immortal Beloved and that she and Beethoven exchanged many intimate letters between 1811 and 1812 leading up to his 1812 letter to the Immortal Beloved as established in chapters 2 and 4, it is clear from the latter letter that he would have wanted the woman to be his life partner, but that she could not be "his" in the circumstances. Had he written this in the exchange of letters leading up to the letter to the Immortal Beloved, this would have given Bettina even stronger justification for telling

Varnhagen what she did. That Bettina could have anticipated an academic quarrel between Unger and Kalischer as to the background of Beethoven's 1810 request for his baptismal certificate, a quarrel that occurred more than 50 years after her death, and that she claimed in anticipation of that quarrel to be the object of those plans, is patently absurd. It illustrates the perception Unger had of Bettina and her character, a perception that distorted his judgment about everything he wrote about her.

BETTINA'S DESCRIPTION OF BEETHOVEN

A further example illustrating Unger's mind-set against Bettina can be seen in his attempts to debunk Bettina's description in her missing Beethoven Description letter to Goethe (Missing Letter No. 1 above) and her surviving contemporaneous letter to Bihler that Beethoven did not know his own age and was unkempt.[21] Unger well knew from his research about Beethoven's 1810 marriage plans that in the letter Beethoven wrote asking for his baptismal certificate a few weeks before he met Bettina, he admitted not being certain of his own age. Unger speculates Beethoven knew his age when he was with Bettina in late May and early June, because he had written for his baptismal certificate on May 2, several weeks before he met Bettina. The baptismal certificate was in fact issued in Bonn on June 2 of that year and would not have been received by Beethoven until after Bettina left Vienna.[22]

As for Bettina's description of Beethoven as being unkempt, Unger did not mention that around the time Beethoven wrote for his baptismal certificate, he asked a friend to buy a mirror for him, because he was concerned about how he appeared to others.[23] Unger would or should have known about this through his research about Beethoven's marriage plans.

CONCLUSION

The above examples represent only a few of the conclusions and speculations of Unger in his 1936 paper that clearly show his anti-Bettina mind-set. What we have here is a remarkable phenomenon. Unger as a doctoral candidate in 1909–1911 published papers stating the following:

1. Bettina met all the psychological, geographical, and time requirements necessary to be realistically considered the Immortal Beloved.
2. The missing 1812 Teplitz Letter to Bettina from Beethoven appeared to be factually correct, had the ring of truth to it, and resembled in style and language the letter to the Immortal Beloved.

3. The missing 1810 letter to Bettina from Beethoven (Missing Letter No. 4 above) was quite likely genuine.

4. The sonnet from Beethoven to Bettina that had been published in facsimile form was without any doubt genuine.

As described in chapter 9, Unger in 1911, the year he received his PhD, publicly retracted the first of these contentions. Over the next several decades, he reversed himself on two of the other three, and with his 1936 paper he not only abandoned all of them but vigorously attacked those positions without mentioning that they were his in the first place. His attacks on Bettina's character were almost vitriolic. Was his reversal because he was older and wiser in 1936? Or was it because under pressure from his professors and peers he was forced as a PhD candidate to retract several of his principal contentions and thereafter to retreat from the others? Would it not be another blot on his reputation if later in his career he reversed himself once again?

NOTES

1. Max Unger, "Zum Problem von Beethovens 'Unsterblicher Geliebten,'" *Musikalisches Wochenblatt* 26 (1909): 356–8.

2. Max Unger, "Giulietta Guicciardi: Die 'Unsterbliche Geliebte' Beethovens?" *Neue Zeitschrift für Musik* 35/36 (August 1911): 505.

3. Max Unger, "Romain Rolland als Beethoven-Forscher," *Deutsche Musiker-Zeitung* 60 (May 1929): 440.

4. For an analysis of the oversights or mistakes made by Fambach in his 1971 paper, see Edward Walden, "The Authenticity of the 1812 Beethoven Letter to Bettina von Arnim," *Beethoven Journal* 14, no. 1 (1999): 9–15. For an edited version of the same paper translated into German, see "Die Briefe Beethovens an Bettina von Arnim," *Internationales Jahrbuch der Bettina von Arnim Gesellschaft* 15 (Berlin: Saint Albin Verlag, 2003): 47–66.

5. Unger, "Neue Liebe, Neues Leben," 1049–75.

6. Anderson, Letter No. 261.

7. Sonneck, *Impressions*, 78.

8. Georg Kinsky and Hans Halm, *Das Werk Beethovens* (Munich: Henle Verlag, 1955), 224. Kinsky says that the copy did not come from Bettina and speculates that it came from someone else, but cites no source for either opinion. Kinsky was firmly in the anti-Bettina camp. Unger also claims the copy came from someone other than Bettina but cites no source. The Goethe Archive in Weimar advised me by letter in 2003 that they do not know how the song came into Goethe's hands.

9. Anderson, Letter No. 303.

10. Albrecht, *Letters*, Letter No. 155.

11. William Meredith, "New Rare Beethoviana (and Brentaniana) at the Ira F. Brilliant Center for Beethoven Studies 2004–2006," *Beethoven Journal* 21, no. 1 (2006): 39.

12. Helps and Howard, *Bettina*, 71–72.

13. Helga Lühning, ed., *Ludwig van Beethoven: Drei Lieder nach Gedichten von Goethe* (Bonn: Verlag Beethoven Haus, 1999), 44–46.

14. The author thanks Dr. Michael Ladenburger of the Beethoven Haus in Bonn and J. Rigby Turner of the Morgan Library in New York for the information necessary for this summary.

15. Anderson, Letter No. 245.

16. Anderson, Letter No. 262.

17. For the letter to Pückler-Muskau, see Sonneck, *Impressions*, 84. For the complete text of the letter to Goethe, see *Goethe Correspondence* book, 283.

18. The sources for all these facts about Beethoven's marriage plans and Kalischer's surmise may be found in Unger, "Neue Liebe, Neues Leben."

19. Max Unger, "Beethoven and Therese von Malfatti," *Musical Quarterly* 11 (1925): 63–72.

20. Thayer Forbes, 646.

21. For letters to Bihler and a portion of Bettina's letter to Goethe, see Sonneck, *Impressions*, 76 and 79. For the complete text of her letter to Goethe, see *Goethe Correspondence* book, 283.

22. Donald MacArdle and Ludwig Misch, trans., *New Beethoven Letters* (Norman: University of Oklahoma Press, 1957), Letter No. 72.

23. Anderson, Letter Nos. 259 and 260.

A Modern Analysis

FACTS OR ROMANTIC MYTHS

$\mathcal{S}$ome contemporary reviewers were harsh in their comments about the published letters Bettina claimed to have received from Goethe, Goethe's mother, and Beethoven. George Henry Lewes, whose *Life of Goethe* was published in 1864, for example, noted a number of problems with Bettina's *Goethe Correspondence* book. As Bruce Charlton explains in his preface to a Web edition of Bettina's book, Lewes faulted Bettina for, among other things, claiming that she inspired poems by Goethe that were in fact addressed to others, and concocting letters by paraphrasing lines from some of Goethe's poems. Given these and other problems, Lewes concluded: "The correspondence has been so tampered with as to have become, from first to last, a romance."[1]

Later assessments could also be dismissive. Charlton points to the 1976 *Oxford Companion to German Literature* judgment that the *Goethe Correspondence* book "is a free and imaginative rehandling of a correspondence," and he remarks that "her cutting, compressing and invention and (sin of sins!) destruction of original manuscripts means that she is not popular with scholars."[2] "Other contemporary commentators have been equally skeptical about the words attributed to Beethoven by Bettina in the missing 1810 and 1812 letters from him, as well as about the quotes attributed to him by Bettina in the Beethoven Description Letter. Those commentators believe that Beethoven did not say things like that, that the words were Bettina's, not Beethoven's.[3]

But what are the facts?

LETTERS FROM GOETHE'S MOTHER

In her *Goethe Correspondence* book, Bettina included nine letters she claimed to have received from Goethe's mother, and approximately 10 letters she claimed to have sent to Goethe's mother. It is difficult to make an exact count of Bettina's letters because of her habit of including separate extensions or continuations of an original letter which sometimes bore a date and sometimes not—similar, as noted in chapter 2, to the way Beethoven wrote his letter to the Immortal Beloved.

None of the letters from Goethe's mother in the *Goethe Correspondence* book survive today, and many commentators believe they are complete fabrications, citing as proof that the last two from Goethe's mother were dated after her death on September 13, 1808. However, the explanation for the wrong dates is simple. Bettina took a Rhine journey in August and early September 1808, finally returning to her home in Frankfurt in the second week of September, where she visited Goethe's mother on September 12, then set off on September 13 on a long journey to Munich. On the same day she left for Munich, Goethe's mother died.

An examination of the contents of the two suspect letters from Goethe's mother dated in the *Goethe Correspondence* book after her death, and Bettina's two undated replies to them, shows that they were written while Bettina was on and returning from her summer Rhine journey, when Goethe's mother was still alive. The first from Goethe's mother warns Bettina not to continue her Rhine journey too long, and Bettina's letter in response includes a lengthy travelogue description of Cologne, which she visited in mid-August. The next and final letter from Goethe's mother responds to Bettina's description of her visit to Cologne. This letter and Bettina's reply to it clearly show that both were written in early September while Goethe's mother was still alive and just before Bettina returned to Frankfurt to begin her trip to Munich. When Bettina copied out the letters almost 30 years later, and assuming the originals from Goethe's mother were undated (which they sometimes were), it is apparent that Bettina, working from memory, simply inserted the wrong dates. Their months of writing should have been August and September, respectively, not September and October. This would make their dates coincide exactly with the external events described in them.

In fact, four letters to Bettina from Goethe's mother not included in the *Goethe Correspondence* book (three of which were included in her *Ilius* book, described in chapter 5) have been found, and they are entirely consistent in content and style with the missing letters reproduced in the *Goethe Correspondence* book. Two of the four were not dated by Goethe's mother. A comment by the editor of a book of collected letters of Goethe's mother in which the four are included illustrates the mind-set against Bettina in academic circles, as well as Bettina's penchant for mixing up the dates of her often undated letters almost 30 years after they were written. The editor had left out from the original edition of his book one of the three published in *Ilius*, but was contacted afterward by a collector living in a small town north of Berlin who had possession of the original and who showed it to the editor, causing him to write this:

> When I published the first comprehensive collection of the letters of Goethe's mother in 1904, of the three letters from her that Bettina . . . published in her *Ilius* book of 1848, I included only the first two, whose autographs I knew, but decided against including the third, which although appearing to have a grain of truth, seemed to me to resemble the style of Bettina's way of writing. . . . Now I have seen the lost version of the third . . . and although my reason [for excluding it] was correct, the blame lays on Bettina [who had dated it August 28, 1807]. In reality, the date should have been 28 August 1808 because [Bettina] wrote on it "the last letter in [Goethe's mother's] own hand before her death."[4]

LETTERS FROM GOETHE

Thirteen letters and two sonnets from Goethe to Bettina are reproduced verbatim in Walter Schmitz and Sibylle von Steinsdorff's edition of Bettina's works and correspondence published in 1992, which allows a word-by-word comparison of the letters as published in Bettina's *Goethe Correspondence* book with the found originals.[5] Table 11.1 provides a brief comparison of the original found letters from Goethe to Bettina for two sample years, 1809 and 1810, and the same letters as Bettina reproduced them in her *Goethe Correspondence* book. Of the 16 letters from Goethe in her book for those years, nine have been found and are reproduced in the 1992 Schmitz and Steinsdorff publication referred to above, while the remaining seven are missing. The fact that some are today missing does not mean they are inventions, as witness the discovery of one of the letters from Goethe's mother mentioned earlier in this chapter, originally believed by the editor of a publication of a collection of those letters to be an invention until it was shown to him by a private collector. Also, as shown in chapter 4, it is quite possible that Bettina destroyed two of her missing letters from Goethe that fell within the 1810 Letter Gap. Finally, any original letters from Goethe not destroyed by Bettina would over the course of more than 190 years have been in the possession of five generations of descendants of Bettina scattered across Germany, and may have been destroyed or lost as a result of wars, occupations by foreign armies, domicile changes, fires, possible thefts, and bombings.

Table 11.1. Sample Surviving Letters from Goethe to Bettina Compared to Versions in the *Goethe Correspondence* Book

Date of Letter in Goethe Correspondence *Book*	Date of Surviving Goethe Letter	Status
February 22, 1809	February 22, 1809	substantially unchanged
May 17, 1809	missing	likely reply to 2 surviving letters from Bettina
July 7, 1809	missing	specific reply to 2 lengthy surviving letters from Bettina
September 11, 1809	September 11, 1809	substantially unchanged
September 15, 1809	September 15, 1809	substantially unchanged
October 7, 1809	missing	short acknowledgment of receipt of letters from Bettina
November 3, 1809	November 3, 1809	substantially unchanged, paragraph added
February 5, 1810	February 5, 1810	changes in wording but not substance, sentences added
March 1, 1810	missing	very short, acknowledges receipt of Bettina's diary
March 19, 1810	missing	very short, expresses sympathy for Bettina's disappointment over outcome of Tyrol uprising
May 10, 1810	May 10, 1810	substantially unchanged
June 6, 1810	missing	within 1810 Letter Gap, has ring of truth
Undated, 1810	missing	within 1810 Letter Gap, has ring of truth
Undated, 1810	August 17, 1810	unchanged
October 25, 1810	October 25, 1810	unchanged
November 12, 1810	November 12, 1810	unchanged

The purpose of the table 11.1 comparison is to demonstrate that the letters from Goethe reproduced in the *Goethe Correspondence* book during the two sample but crucial years of 1809 and 1810 conform substantially to originals of those that have been found, and where there are differences, to show that the changes or additions made by Bettina to Goethe's words were largely to allow her to give expression to her own thoughts in her replies. As to the letters that are missing, the exercise shows that many pass the litmus test of having a ring of truth.

The analysis that follows does not deal with changes that Bettina may have made to her original letters to Goethe when she included them in her *Goethe Correspondence* book. They were, after all, *her* letters looked at by her after the passage of almost 30 years, so she was entitled to change them as she saw fit to better explain her own artistic and intellectual development refracted by the passage of time. Her book is *not* about letters *from* Goethe, but rather about her own thoughts and emotions as stimulated *by* Goethe and his letters. More than 90 percent of the words and pages of the letters in the *Goethe Correspondence* book for the two sample years are those of Bettina, not Goethe. Goethe's letters are relatively short and serve mainly as a platform for Bettina's responses in long and revealing letters of her own. Goethe is her straight man. I leave an analysis of changes made by Bettina to her original letters to others.

As noted in chapter 4, in her contemporary correspondence, Bettina did not pretend that her *Goethe Correspondence* book was simply an edited version of the originals. And as noted above, the reproduced letters were intended instead to give a record of Bettina's own evolving thoughts and emotions concerning life, art, music, politics, and nature in her rite of passage up to legal adulthood, which for women in those days was 25, starting as a naive 22-year-old who previously had been raised and educated for three years in a convent, then as a teenager had lived at the house of her grandmother, then had studied music in Frankfurt and near Munich. For the most part, the letters end in 1810 when she achieved the legal age of majority, although there are a few after the resumption of her correspondence with Goethe in 1817 after the death of his wife.

If there is fiction in the changes and additions made by Bettina to the Goethe letters that today survive, it arises mainly from politics. Bettina lived during the years 1809 and 1810 near Munich, in Bavaria, and many of the words that she added to the Goethe letters are responses by Goethe to political observations of Bettina about a complicated war at the time involving shifting alliances between Napoleonic France, Austria, and Bavaria, with the subplot of a Tyrolese uprising against Bavaria. Bettina took the side of the Tyrolese. Goethe's Weimar employer sided with the French and Bavaria. Open support of the Tyrolese insurgents in letters written by Bettina in Bavaria would likely have been censored, and could even have led to her arrest. The same would apply to letters of Goethe written by him in Weimar and would have cost him his job if not his freedom. Goethe's supposed comments on Bettina's stand are sympathetic but noncommittal. Bettina may have created those comments because of the views expressed by Goethe in his play *Egmont* (which Beethoven so admired), she believing Goethe would have supported her if his own thoughts could have been freely written.

Table 11.1 analyzes the 16 letters attributed to Goethe by Bettina in her *Goethe Correspondence* book for 1809 and 1810, years which I chose because they were probably the most significant in Bettina's life. The left-hand column lists the dates of all 16 letters from Goethe for those years as they appear in the *Goethe Correspondence* book. The middle column lists the nine that survive and their actual dates. The right-hand column notes whether the nine surviving letters were substantially the same or changed. Seven of the nine were unchanged or substantially unchanged, and the other two were slightly expanded. That a letter was unchanged or substantially unchanged means minor editorial changes of punctuation or language style have been ignored. As for the seven letters that are today missing, their subject matter is summarized in the right-hand column. Two lie within the 1810 Letter Gap referred to in chapter 4 and, as discussed there, were quite likely destroyed by Bettina.

ANALYSIS OF SAMPLE LETTERS

Seven of the letters attributed to Goethe in the *Goethe Correspondence* book for 1809 and 1810 were either unchanged or substantially the same as the nine surviving originals. The other two also were substantially the same but with some additions. The seven missing letters were quite possibly genuine, based on their contents. Many have the ring of truth. The reason they are today missing may be solely due to external causes, such as destruction by Bettina of letters within the 1810 Letter Gap. The fact that the Goethe letters were published in a book that was essentially a platform for Bettina's own literary, musical, political, social, and religious writings, and that she never pretended that it was simply a book of edited correspondence, may explain why she took liberties with those letters.

February 22, 1809: Letter Surviving. This letter is almost identical to the surviving original except Bettina added one sentence in which Goethe praises her ideas on music, one paragraph in which he asks her for more descriptions of his mother and describes a few memories of her, and another sentence in which he promises to write at more length with his reaction to her long letters and urges her to keep writing them.

May 17, 1809: Letter Missing. This letter appears to be a response to two surviving letters from Bettina dated February 1 and March 8, 1809. Goethe acknowledges receiving a parcel from Bettina that his employer, the duke, intercepted and was curious about. He also mentions that he discussed Bettina's views about the Tyrolean uprising with the duke, who regretted to learn that Bettina supported the opposing powers. Goethe also mentions that he knew a person involved in the uprising. The political parts of this letter may be fiction. Goethe writes about further memories of his mother stimulated by Bettina's descriptions in her letters.

July 7, 1809: Letter Missing. In this relatively short, four-paragraph letter, Goethe acknowledges receiving two long letters from Bettina, probably those of May 18 and June 16, both of which survive. He also adds fact-specific comments on what Bettina described in her found letters, including knowing a prominent Bavarian academic described by Bettina in her surviving letter of June 16. Finally, he encloses a copy of a poem Bettina apparently asked for.

September 11, 1809: Letter Surviving. This letter is relatively long and is identical to the surviving original except for a few insubstantial changes made to a short postscript in which Goethe apologizes for using a secretary to write the main body of the letter, including a sentence added by Bettina in which he mentions a new novel he is writing that will become the subject of comments by Bettina in her future surviving letters.

September 15, 1809: Letter Surviving. This letter is almost identical to the surviving original except that a sentence is added in which Goethe expresses interest in Bettina's descriptions of the war. He also says in an added sentence that his patron duke is sympathetic to her views but expects a tragic end. The additions are very likely fiction because they deal with politics and would have been censored if written.

October 7, 1809: Letter Missing. In this short, two-paragraph letter, Goethe acknowledges receipt of surviving letters from Bettina (probably the ones dated August 6 and September 13), accepts Bettina's reproach for using a secretary to write his September 11 letter to her, and asks her to keep writing.

November 3, 1809: Letter Surviving. This long letter is almost identical to the surviving original except that a paragraph is added in which Goethe describes initially mistaking for Bettina an unexpected visitor wearing a hooded coat. He nevertheless hopes he will see her in the spring. (Goethe related a similar incident in a surviving letter to his wife when Bettina in fact visited him in Teplitz the following summer.)

February 5, 1810: Letter Surviving. This short, two-paragraph letter, in which Goethe acknowledges receiving a parcel of gifts from Bettina, coincides for the most part with the surviving original, except that Bettina expands Goethe's description of the parcel's contents and adds some words explaining a little about his new novel. Bettina also leaves out a sentence referring to a painting she apparently sent to him, but adds a postscript acknowledging a parcel Bettina sent to Goethe's wife referred to in Bettina's surviving original.

March 1, 1810: Letter Missing. In this short, one-paragraph letter, Goethe acknowledges receiving Bettina's diary and asks her to keep writing.

March 19, 1810: Letter Missing. In this short, one-paragraph letter, Goethe acknowledges receipt of a missing letter from Bettina in which she described the tragic (for her) end of the Tyrolese uprising and the execution of one of its heroes. Goethe expresses sympathy over her disappointment but urges her to move on. Since letters from Bettina and Goethe about this would likely have been censored and resemble elements of his Egmont story, they are both likely fiction.

May 10, 1810: Letter Surviving. This short letter is identical to the original, except that a sentence is added in which Goethe states he does not know where Bettina is (she was traveling to Vienna at the time).

June 6, 1810: Letter Missing. This letter lies within the 1810 Letter Gap described in chapter 4. It is a response to Bettina's missing 1810 Beethoven Description letter, also within the 1810 Letter Gap. In it, Goethe suggests that he and Beethoven might meet next summer in Karlsbad where Goethe says he goes almost every summer. He also asks for copies of the two songs set to music by Beethoven (see chapter 10). The letter's contents have a ring of truth.

Undated Letter, Probably July or August 1810: Missing. In this missing letter that is within the 1810 Letter Gap, Goethe says that he is reading Bettina's diary, that he does not know where she is, asks for further reminiscences about his mother, and says that he hopes to see her sometime while he is in Bohemia that summer. It has a ring of truth.

LETTERS FROM BEETHOVEN

As shown in the analysis of sample letters above, Bettina's changes to Goethe's surviving letters were for the most part insubstantial when she modified them or added to them in her *Goethe Correspondence* book. Also, as noted in chapter 4, she never pretended that her book was simply an edited version of her correspondence with Goethe; rather, she presented it as a book akin in form to an epistolary novel. When she published it, she identified herself as its *author,* not its *editor.*

Nevertheless, as described in chapters 9 and 10, the liberties she took with her Goethe letters in the *Goethe Correspondence* book led those Beethoven scholars who were hostile to her to claim that she concocted the three letters from Beethoven that she published in 1839. For example, Adolph Marx claimed in his 1859 biography of Beethoven that they were concocted, citing as proof not only that the three letters had not then been verified, but that the language in the second letter (written in 1811) was "girl-like" and "unBeethovian." When the second letter was found in Nathusius's papers after his death in 1872, critics like Marx continued their attacks on the authenticity of the other two letters unabated. Those attacks continue to this day.

As noted in chapter 5, however, the forum for publication of the three Beethoven letters was completely different than that of the Goethe letters in her *Goethe Correspondence* book. The Beethoven letters were published without editorial comment in a literary and political journal whose editor certified to Thayer that he had reproduced them from the three originals he had had before him, and that he subsequently gave them back to Bettina.[6] Unlike the Goethe letters in the *Goethe Correspondence* book, the Beethoven letters were not platforms for Bettina to respond with her thoughts and ideas, and there was no response of any kind from Bettina by way of letters or otherwise in the literary and political journal. Further, in no case do the length, contents, and style of the three Beethoven letters bear any comparison to the length, contents, and style of the missing letters or additions to found letters attributed to Goethe in the *Goethe Correspondence* book. The distinction is apparent. Consider for example the text of the 1812 Teplitz Letter from Beethoven set out in appendix C. It is lengthy and rich in detail, and uses language that Romain Rolland believes would have required a "second Beethoven" to invent. In contrast and by way of example only, consider the length and contents of one of the missing letters from Goethe, the one dated March 1, 1810, summarized above. Assuming but without accepting that it was concocted by Bettina, it contains just five sentences, and responds to a letter from Bettina in which she asks Goethe if he received a diary that she had sent to him. Goethe apologizes for not acknowledging its receipt before and says he has read it and put it with all her many other letters which he rereads from time to time and finds stimulating.

In summary, the liberties Bettina took with the Goethe letters in the *Goethe Correspondence* book do not prove or even give a rational basis for contending that she did the same with or even concocted the Beethoven letters.

NOTES

1. Bruce G. Charlton, Editorial Preface to the English translation of Bettine von Arnim's *Goethe's Correspondence with a Child*, www.hedweb.com/bgcharlton/preface -bettina.html.

2. Charlton, Editorial Preface.

3. See, for example, Alessandra Comini, *The Changing Image of Beethoven* (New York: Rizzoli, 1987), 111–14; see also "A Virtuoso Muse," in *The Guardian*, August 23, 2003, www.guardian.co.uk.

4. Albert Köster, "Der Letze Brief von Goethes Mutter an Bettina Brentano," *Insel-Verlag Almanach 1918* (Leipzig: Leipzig Insel, 1918): 64–68.

5. Walter Schmitz and Sibylle von Steinsdorff, eds., *Bettine von Arnim Werke und Briefe*, 4 vols. (Frankfurt: Deutscher Klassiker Verlag, 1992), 2:575–753. For a version of Bettina's *Goethe Correspondence* book in original German, see Schmitz and Steinsdorff, 2:111–571.

6. Thayer English, 2:185.

· _12_ ·

The Antonie Theory

WHY ANTONIE BRENTANO COULD NOT
HAVE BEEN THE IMMORTAL BELOVED

_A_ consensus has developed over the past 75 years, as noted in chapter 1, that the letter to the Immortal Beloved was written by Beethoven in the Bohemian town of Teplitz in 1812 and was intended to be sent to the woman in the nearby spa town of Karlsbad. The eminent American musicologist Maynard Solomon thus reasoned that the woman must be Antonie Brentano, Bettina's sister-in-law, because she was the only woman closely connected to Beethoven in 1812 who was in Karlsbad when Beethoven wrote his letter.[1]

There are, however, a number of serious problems with his theory. In 1812 when Beethoven's letter to the Immortal Beloved was written, Antonie was the sickly mother of four young children and pregnant with her fifth. She and her husband, Franz, were good friends and financial supporters of Beethoven. Beethoven referred to them in a letter, according to his secretary Schindler, as "his best friends in the world."[2] He was like an uncle to their children and dedicated music to one of them, who sat in his lap when a child.

In his letter to the Immortal Beloved, Beethoven talked of their possibly living together. Would living together have been an option that Antonie and Beethoven realistically discussed, let alone mentioned in a letter intended to be sent to her in the small spa town of Karlsbad where she was staying with Franz and one of her children? After 1812, both Antonie and Franz, who by then had moved from Vienna to a town near Frankfurt, loaned money to Beethoven. In later years, Franz acted as Beethoven's financial agent and representative. In letters from Beethoven to Franz written after he and Antonie moved away from Vienna, Beethoven politely asked Franz to give his best regards to Antonie. For example, he ended an 1817 letter to Franz with the words "All my best greetings to my beloved friend Toni and to your dear children" [*alle schöne meiner Werthen Freundin Toni u. ihren lieben Kindern*], and he ended an 1821 letter with the words "With all my heart, I embrace you and ask you to remember me again to your excellent and especially lovely Toni. I remain, Sir, with kindest regards, your Beethoven" [*ich umarme Sie von Herzen, u. bitte mich noch ihrer ausgezeichneten einzig herrlichen Toni zu emphelen. Euer wohlgebohrn Hochachtungs Voll verharrender Beethoven*].[3]

Beethoven's letters to Antonie after she moved away from Vienna in 1812 clearly show a formal and polite respect. For example, he would begin those letters to her with words such as "My worthy friend," "Most honored friend," and "My honored friend" ("Meine werthe Freundin," "Verehrteste Freundin," and "Meine verehrte Freundin," respectively). He ended his other letters to her with the same formality, as in an 1816 letter which concluded with the words "With true and sincere regards, your admirer and friend, Ludwig van Beethoven" (*Mit wahrer inniger Hochachtung ihr verehrer u. Freund*).[4] In all of them, he addressed her in the formal German "Sie" form, not the intimate "du" form that he used in his 1812 letter to the Immortal Beloved. As noted elsewhere in this book, the use of "du" demonstrated a degree of intimacy between a German-speaking male and female not lightly bestowed by either of them, especially the woman. So far as is known, Beethoven never used "du" in any letter to a woman with whom he may have been romantically involved, except in the letter to the Immortal Beloved and one of his letters to Bettina. A change from "du" *back* to "Sie," although not unheard of,[5] would be rare. And while a change from "du" to "Sie" may be one thing, a change from the intimacy of a passionate love letter to the extreme respect and formality shown in Beethoven's letters to Antonie is another. One could try to explain it as an attempt at deception by Beethoven in case Franz intercepted the letters to Antonie, since Beethoven was writing to both of them, but deception was not one of Beethoven's faults.

As noted in chapter 1, Richard Specht, a distinguished Viennese musical critic and biographer, wrote in 1933 that "marriage meant for Beethoven a divine sacrament against which it would be a sacrilege to offend," and "he would have torn out his tongue rather than suffer it to utter words in the Immortal Beloved letter of such glowing passion and regret to another's wife."[6] This would be especially so given that Beethoven was a close friend to both the husband and wife, and was like an uncle to their children.

The principal reason Antonie must be ruled out as Beethoven's Immortal Beloved, however, stems from Beethoven's confession in 1816 overheard by Fanny Giannastasio del Rio, a young admirer, that he had met ("kennengelernt") a woman five years before who would have been his ideal life-mate and he still could not get her out of his mind.[7] Whoever that woman was, she is generally thought today to have been Beethoven's Immortal Beloved.[8] Beethoven's most definitive biographer, Alexander Thayer, whose biography of Beethoven first published in the 1870s remains one of the principal sources for Beethoven research, quoted a reliable source stating that Beethoven had known Antonie even before her marriage to Franz in 1798 as a result of Beethoven's visits to the house of her father before then.[9] That being so, Antonie could *not* be the woman Beethoven was referring to in 1816, and was therefore almost certainly not the Immortal Beloved. How Maynard Solomon attempted to discount Thayer's evidence in order to support his own theory will be dealt with in some detail below.

SOLOMON'S METHODOLOGY IN SUPPORT OF ANTONIE

That Antonie might be the Immortal Beloved was improbable, given the close relationship of Beethoven with Antonie and her husband Franz and their children, and Beethoven's idealization of the institution and sanctity of marriage. Nevertheless, Maynard Solomon developed a skilful but specious methodology to lend his theory an aura of factual certainty. Instead of arguing his case from the ground up as others had done with their candidates, he purported to establish, without identifying who the woman was, a group of "primary requirements" and another group of "secondary requirements" that he maintained any woman would have to satisfy in order to be the Immortal Beloved. Having set out these "requirements," he then deduced that the only woman who met all of them was Antonie. The flaw in this methodology was that he established requirements that he knew only his candidate could meet. They were therefore not independent objective requirements at all. What follows is an examination of the strength and validity of each of Solomon's requirements:

Requirement #1: The woman must have lived in Vienna.

Flaw: Beethoven in 1812 was quite well-known in Vienna and had a number of friends and acquaintances there. To have had romantic intimacy with a married woman who also lived there would likely have been noticed by his friends and acquaintances, if not by the husband. That the woman lived there is a possibility, not a requirement.

Requirement #2: The woman passed through Prague on her way to Karlsbad at the same time Beethoven was in Prague on his way to Teplitz, and they met while both were in Prague.

Flaw: This is pure speculation based on three feeble arguments: (1) Beethoven mentions writing the letter with the woman's pencil; (2) he also writes in the letter "today, yesterday, what tearful longings for you"; and (3) he describes events of the "last few days," that is, his travel misadventures in getting to Teplitz. As to the first argument, the ordinary manufactured lead pencil had only been invented in 1795, would still have been a novelty for travelers, and was seldom used by Beethoven in writing letters. In no way does Beethoven's use of the woman's pencil connect her to Prague. As to the second argument, the reference to tearful longings "today and yesterday" is more consistent with language referring in general terms to present and past, and has no connection to Prague. Even if one reads the word "yesterday" literally and accepts the speculation that Beethoven in fact met with the woman on July 3, the evening before he left Prague for Teplitz, those words in his letter were written on the following Tuesday, four days after his last evening in Prague. Finally, the description of events of the "past few days" (Beethoven's travel misadventures) does not mean that Beethoven must have met the woman in Prague, only that on the trip into Teplitz, his coach became stuck in the mud late at night. This was simply an adventure worth mentioning to someone Beethoven expected would be traveling around the same time to Karlsbad, a town in the vicinity of Teplitz. The Prague "requirement" is therefore merely speculation that might provide support for independent evidence establishing the woman's identity.

Requirement #3: Since the letter was to be mailed to the woman in Karlsbad, the woman must have been there when the letter was written.

Flaw: The fact that the letter was in Beethoven's possession when he died strongly supports the argument that he never mailed it, which works to support a candidate who first intended to go to Karlsbad but then traveled to Teplitz instead, as Bettina did.

Requirement #4: Beethoven confessed in 1816 that he had met the love of his life five years before.

Flaw: None. This is a valid independent, objective, and nonspeculative requirement. How Solomon attempted to deal with it is described in some detail later in this chapter

Requirement #5: The Immortal Beloved's name may have started with the letters "A," "T," or "M." Beethoven appears to have written these letters in his diary during the relevant years.

Flaw: There is no clear indication in the diary that they referred to the Immortal Beloved, and Beethoven did not write his uppercase "A" in the way it appears in his diary. Solomon specifically states that the Immortal Beloved did not need to have any or all of these initials, thus conceding that this "requirement" was not a requirement at all. It should be noted, however, that after Bettina's marriage in 1811 (a year before the letter to the Immortal Beloved was written), her last name (Arnim) began with an

"A." One commentator has speculated that whatever the letter was, it might possibly refer to the woman's husband.[10]

Requirement #6: In his letter, Beethoven said that he expected to see the Beloved "soon." If Beethoven did meet a woman soon after he wrote his letter, the identity of that woman would, in conjunction with other valid requirements, help verify that she was the Immortal Beloved.

Flaw. This is merely a statement of expectation by Beethoven. It cannot therefore be a probative requirement pointing to any one woman, although if the identity of the woman is established through other means (not necessarily Solomon's "requirements") and Beethoven did see her shortly after the letter was written, it would corroborate other evidence that firmly established the identity of the woman. It should be noted in this regard that Bettina arrived in Teplitz where Beethoven was several weeks after Beethoven wrote his letter. Had she gone to Karlsbad, she would likely have had to pass through Teplitz on her way back to Berlin.

What follows is a closer examination of Requirement #1, the Vienna connection; Requirement #2, the specious Prague connection; and Requirement #3, the Karlsbad connection.

THE VIENNA CONNECTION

As noted above, it would have been difficult for Beethoven to have had a romantic affair with Antonie (or for that matter, any other married woman in Vienna), without Antonie's husband, her children, and Beethoven's friends noticing it. And he surely would never have considered the possibility of living together, as suggested in the letter to the Immortal Beloved. As noted above, Antonie had four young children, was pregnant with her fifth, and was married to a wealthy and loyal husband who was a close friend to Beethoven when Beethoven's letter was written. One commentator has suggested that Beethoven's reference to "living together" was meant in a metaphorical, not literal sense, pointing out a possible distinction between the verb and preposition combination of "leben mit" (to live with) and "wohnen mit" (to dwell with), but "leben mit" clearly indicates co-habitation in the German language. Even Solomon makes it clear that co-habitation was the intention.[11]

In contrast, assume that Bettina in Berlin was writing to Beethoven in Vienna the same kinds of letters that she wrote to Goethe before Goethe ostracized her (see chapter 6). When she became depressed during her pregnancy and almost died at the birth of her first child (the child that her husband needed to gain control of his grandmother's estate and one of the main reasons for their marriage), it would have been natural for Bettina to rethink her decision to marry instead of remaining unmarried and devoting her life to music and politics, as she had told Achim von Arnim she wanted to do when he first proposed to her. If she did express these thoughts in her last despairing letter to Beethoven before he left for his summer interlude in Bohemia, it would have prompted Beethoven to write his comforting and hopeful letter to her, his Immortal Beloved, noting that she was "suffering" and tentatively ruminating about them living together if she joined him as his muse in a life of music.

Further, in his letter to the Immortal Beloved, Beethoven referred to his life "in V" as being "miserable." The reference to "V" is undoubtedly to Vienna,[12] where he then lived. This reference would have been unnecessary if the woman also lived there.

THE SPECIOUS PRAGUE CONNECTION

As noted above, the asserted Prague connection was based on three arguments that really had no apparent connection with Prague at all. For example, the writing of the Immortal Beloved letter with the woman's pencil did not mean she and Beethoven had met in Prague unless the pencil was established to have been made in Prague or came from an inn in which the Beloved stayed while there. However, it did superficially suggest that Beethoven had probably seen the woman recently. This is based on the modern perception of the pencil as being a cheap, mass-produced, and frequently used writing instrument. But in 1812, the manufactured lead (graphite) pencil had only been invented within the last two decades. At that time, correspondents almost always used quill and ink, which was available to travelers at all inns. But there were no fountain pens or other easily portable writing instruments. So for a reasonably well-to-do, "with-it" musician, writer, and artist on an extended trip across Europe, all of which applied to Bettina when she met Beethoven two years earlier, the pencil would have been a useful tool to take with her while walking in the outdoors and wanting to jot down artistic thoughts and sketches. The great bulk of Beethoven's letters and music sheets and sketchbooks up to the time he met Bettina were written with quill and ink. That Beethoven would have kept, treasured, and used when he traveled a very useful gift or writing tool that he had received or borrowed from Bettina two summers before is entirely plausible. In his single surviving 1811 letter to Bettina, he wrote that he carried the first letter she wrote to him around with him all summer and that it made him feel supremely happy. This clearly demonstrates that he treasured mementos from her. Of the 116 catalogued letters that Beethoven wrote after he met Bettina up to the time he wrote the letter to the Immortal Beloved, only four were written in pencil.[13] All of them were very short. The letter to the Immortal Beloved was very long.

Another argument used in support of the contention that Beethoven met the Beloved in Prague is that on Friday, July 3, the day before he left Prague for Teplitz, he was not able to meet that evening with a male acquaintance as he had originally intended. He wrote to the acquaintance after he arrived in Teplitz that something unexpected had occurred on his last evening in Prague but that he would explain all when they next met. Solomon suggests the unexpected occurrence was that Beethoven and Antonie met that evening and discussed significant issues about their relationship which prompted Beethoven to write to her as his Immortal Beloved.[14] The improbability of this theory becomes evident from the fact that Franz and Antonie, with their five-year-old daughter, only arrived in Prague that same Friday after an exhausting two-day coach journey from Vienna that began at 2 a.m. Tuesday morning. They stayed that evening at an inn which was some distance from the inn where Beethoven stayed, and left at 6 a.m. the next morning on the coach for Karlsbad.[15] A significant tryst in those circumstances? And if it were a pivotal meeting between the two as Solomon suggests, why would Beethoven write in a matter-of-fact way to the male acquaintance afterward that he would explain all about it when they next met?[16]

The Prague requirement is not a requirement at all. The fact that the two of them passed through the same city, a necessary start-off point for spa destinations in Bohemia by the many coach travelers from Vienna, was nothing more than a coincidence.

THE KARLSBAD CONNECTION

As noted above, the fact that the Immortal Beloved letter likely was not mailed works against, not for, Antonie's candidacy. In order to explain why the letter was in Beethoven's possession when he died 14 years later, Solomon suggested that perhaps Beethoven did mail it but Antonie gave it back and he kept it. Recognizing the improbability of that conjecture, Solomon alternatively suggested that the copy in Beethoven's possession when he died was merely a first draft, and that he wrote out a revised second letter and mailed it.[17] That conjecture is even more improbable, since Beethoven ended the letter with tender closing words and the initial of his first name. And if he did write a new letter, why would he keep his first draft? Of course if he did, it should be noted that the "new" letter never surfaced among Antonie's possessions after her death.

Also, why would Beethoven write such a long and intimate letter to Antonie, who came to Karlsbad with her husband and one of her children?

The risk of interception of the letter by the husband in that very small town would have been quite high, and Beethoven would only need to have waited until both he and Antonie returned to Vienna to give it to her or tell her about it if she were the Beloved.

WHEN BEETHOVEN MET ANTONIE

Only one of the six requirements asserted by Solomon is truly independent and objective: Beethoven's 1816 confession to the father of young Fanny Giannastasio that he had met the love of his life, almost certainly the Immortal Beloved, "five years before." Allowing a year's leeway on either side of this approximate time period, Beethoven must have met the woman between 1810 and 1812. Solomon contended that Antonie first met Beethoven at the same time as did Bettina when, in May of 1810, she accompanied Bettina to Beethoven's lodgings. However, Solomon was faced with a number of authoritative sources showing that Antonie as a child was known to Beethoven even before her marriage in 1798 as a result of visits of Beethoven to the house of her father. Antonie was born in 1780, sent for education to a convent when she was eight, then returned to live in her father's house from 1795 until 1798, when she married her husband, Franz, and moved to Frankfurt. She returned afterward for occasional visits to her father in Vienna from time to time, and finally for an extended period in late summer 1809 to care for him because he was ailing (he died in October of that year), but she and her husband remained in Vienna in her father's house until his effects were finally disposed of in 1812, when she and her husband moved back to Frankfurt.

In order to establish that Antonie did not meet Beethoven until 1810 and only then in company with Bettina, Solomon had to overcome two hurdles: (1) the sources that said Beethoven was a frequent visitor to the house of Antonie's father during her childhood, and (2) the sources that said she was known to Beethoven as a result of those visits even before her marriage in 1798.

BEETHOVEN AS A VISITOR TO THE
HOUSE OF ANTONIE'S FATHER

The fact that Beethoven was a frequent visitor to the house of Antonie's father does not of itself prove that Beethoven had come to know her as a result of his visits, but it was more than a remote possibility and so had to be dealt with by Solomon, especially because of Beethoven's reference to Antonie as "die Tonie" in Beethoven's found letter to Bettina.[18] This kind of diminutive nickname is often used in German when referring to someone who as a child was known to an adult, and is in marked contrast to the great formal respect Beethoven paid to Antonie in his letters to her when she had become an adult. For example, as noted earlier in the chapter, he ended letters to her with such words as "my most honoured friend."

Solomon contended, however, that it was not likely Beethoven even knew Antonie's father. He used as support for this theory the fact that the father was not among the subscribers to performances of Beethoven's trios, nor was he on the guest or gift list at Antonie's wedding in 1798. As for Beethoven coming to know the father after Antonie came to Vienna to care for him in late summer of 1809, Solomon suggested that it was improbable the father would have come to know Beethoven while he was "on his deathbed."[19]

A number of sources contradict Solomon's theory. For example, Anton Schindler, Beethoven's assistant and secretary, wrote in the revised 1860 edition of his biography of Beethoven that Beethoven had come to know Antonie's father and had been a visitor to his house since Beethoven's arrival in Vienna in 1792. Ludwig Nohl wrote in his biography of Beethoven published in 1867 that Beethoven was known in the house of Antonie's father since Beethoven's arrival in Vienna in 1792.[20] The 1884 edition of Adolph Marx's biography of Beethoven states that Beethoven already knew Antonie's father and Antonie's husband (and therefore Antonie) when Bettina came to visit the Brentanos in 1810.[21] Hans Tabarelli, in a book of Viennese "historical miniatures" published in 1947, wrote that Beethoven got to know Antonie's father shortly after Beethoven came to Vienna in 1792, and that the father had given Beethoven a key to his house's watchtower.[22] Klaus Günzel, in his 1993 book on the history of the Brentano family, wrote that Antonie had through her father known Beethoven from childhood.[23]

WHEN BEETHOVEN CAME TO KNOW "DIE TONIE"

As noted previously, if Beethoven knew Antonie since she was a child, she could not be the Immortal Beloved. This was Solomon's greatest hurdle. The issue as to when Beethoven came to know Antonie first came to light as a result of a statement in the original 1840 edition of Schindler's biography of Beethoven. There, Schindler stated that Antonie had first met Beethoven in the company of Bettina in 1810, as claimed by Solomon. In the 1860 edition, Schindler, who had since moved to Frankfurt and had presumably interviewed her or members of her family, retracted his earlier statement and instead stated Antonie had known Beethoven since a child in the house of her father.[24]

Solomon contended that Schindler was mistaken.[25] The only support for this contention came from a footnote in a book of Beethoven letters published by Nohl in 1867, where Nohl wrote:

> Beethoven was . . . *not* known in the house of [Antonie's father] since 1792 [as Schindler had written]. More than that, as the now 87-year-old [Antonie] has emphatically assured me, not until Spring of 1810 did [Antonie] become acquainted with Beethoven, and indeed that was a result of the visit of Bettina, who would not give up insisting until her sister-in-law [Antonie] accompanied her there.

Antonie added to Nohl that as a consequence of "her" resulting request [Bettina's, or possibly Antonie's, the meaning is not clear], Beethoven became a frequent informal guest at the house of the Brentanos, who although living in Frankfurt, were present in Vienna for a few years in connection with their inheritance [from Antonie's father].[26]

A number of points should be noted in considering Nohl's footnote. First, in an 1877 publication, 10 years after he published this footnote, Nohl wrote that Antonie's daughter Maxe, born in 1802, had sat on Beethoven's knee at the house of Antonie's father in 1808 (when she was six) during one of Antonie's visits to her father.[27] Second, in two publications made by Nohl after publication of the 1867 footnote upon which Solomon relied, Nohl stated that it was Bettina's sister Gunda, not Antonie, who accompanied Bettina to Beethoven's lodgings.[28] Third, on the question as to Beethoven's visits to the house of Antonie's father, Nohl's footnote does not deny that Beethoven was a visitor to the father's house, only that it was not as early as 1792 as Schindler had written.

Fourth, Antonie's emphasis when Nohl interviewed her was that Bettina persistently pressed Antonie to go with Bettina to Beethoven's lodgings, not her actual going with Bettina. When Antonie made her statement to Nohl, she was in her 80s, and the sequence of events some 50 years before may have become blurred in her mind. Bettina reported in a contemporaneous (1810) surviving letter to her friend Alois Bihler, "I very nearly did not see him at all, for no one wished to take me to meet him, not even those who called themselves his best friends [presumably Franz and Antonie] for fear of his melancholia, which so completely obsesses him that he takes no interest in anything and treats his friends with rudeness rather than civility."[29] She repeated essentially the same description in her missing letter to Goethe (see chapter 10).[30] Also, as noted later in this chapter, Franz was hosting a luncheon party that day, so it was unlikely that Antonie, as hostess, would be available to accompany Bettina.

Fifth, in the context of Antonie's statement to Nohl, it appears that it was Bettina who invited Beethoven to go back to the Brentano house, not

Antonie. Sixth, the fact that "the now 87-year-old" Antonie would openly discuss with Nohl her recollections of how she became a friend of Beethoven makes it unlikely that she and Beethoven would have had an illicit romantic connection many years earlier.

What appears most likely is that Beethoven would have known Antonie only casually as her father's daughter when he visited her father's house before and after her marriage, but that Antonie did not come to consider Beethoven as her own friend, as opposed to a friend of her father's, until after the time when Bettina brought him to her father's house in May 1810. Her father had died some seven months before Bettina brought him there. From Beethoven's perspective, Antonie would of course not be known to him as a friend, but rather as the child of his friend, her father. Accordingly she could not be the person he said in 1816 he had "met" ("kennengelernt") some five years before.

The revised statement by Schindler in his 1860 edition that Antonie had known Beethoven since she was a child and its inconsistency with Nohl's 1867 footnote led Alexander Thayer to try to settle the question once and for all. In 1872, he obtained through the American consul in Frankfurt a written statement from the then head of the Brentano family (Antonie had died in 1869). Thayer published the statement verbatim in German. Here is an English translation:

> The friendly relations of Beethoven with the Brentano family in Frankfurt/M [i.e., Antonie and her husband, Franz] originated in the friendly intercourse which had existed between Beethoven and Frau Brentano's father . . . already at the time when Frau Brentano visited her father in Vienna, where she went in 1809 for quite a long time with her older children, because her father had been seriously ill for some time. This friendly relationship [of Antonie and Franz with Beethoven] was continued after the death of [Antonie's father] on October 30, 1809, in Vienna and during the three years' stay of the Brentano family in Vienna.

Clearly, Antonie's friendship with Beethoven arose out of her father's friendship with Beethoven, which already existed when Antonie came to Vienna in 1809 to care for her father, and the friendship of Antonie and Franz with Beethoven continued after the death of Antonie's father in October 1809.[31] Thus Antonie and Franz knew Beethoven even in October 1809, well before Bettina came to visit them the following year. In addition to the family's statement, the American consul added in his communication to Thayer that he had independently ascertained that Antonie's father was a friend of Beethoven, that Beethoven was often in the father's house, and that Antonie and Beethoven knew one another even before her marriage to Franz in 1798.[32]

Solomon contended that the consul had "misread" the family statement and that the father's friendship with Beethoven only arose after Antonie came to Vienna to care for her father. Solomon then went on to contend that since the father was on his deathbed when Antonie came to care for him, it was unlikely that her father even knew Beethoven at all. This contention flew in the face of not only the family statement but also the many authorities referred to earlier in this chapter. Solomon also contended that the additional information from the American consul came from the consul's misreading of the family statement and therefore was wrong. However, the additional information contained in the consul's statement clearly did not come from the family statement but was supplemental to it, because the family statement made no mention of Antonie and Beethoven being acquainted before her marriage in 1798.

Based on Thayer's evidence and these other authorities, Antonie could not have been the love of Beethoven's life that he said in 1816 he had met five years before, and therefore could not have been Beethoven's Immortal Beloved.

BETTINA'S RECOLLECTION

There is no question that Bettina sought out and met Beethoven in 1810 while she was staying at the house of Antonie and Franz. What were Bettina's recollections? They are set out in four separate letters that she wrote to Goethe, Alois Bihler, Max Freyberg, and Prince Pückler-Muskau. Three of those letters survive, while the letter to Goethe, as described in chapter 10, is today missing. Three of the four, including the missing one to Goethe, were written contemporaneously in 1810 within a few weeks after she met Beethoven. However, as noted in chapter 10, the surviving portion of her letter to Goethe breaks off in midsentence just where she begins to describe her meeting with Beethoven, likely for the reasons explained in chapter 4. The missing portion was copied or re-created by Bettina in her *Goethe Correspondence* book. In the two surviving contemporaneous letters to her friends Bihler and Freyberg, both written in 1810, she also described essentially the same facts but with less detail.[33] The third surviving letter was written to Pückler-Muskau in 1832, 22 years later, when she was 47.

In Bettina's 1810 missing letter to Goethe, she wrote, "they were afraid to take me to him." In her surviving 1832 letter to Pückler-Muskau, she wrote, "no one cared to take me to him because of his eccentric disposition and unsociability." In the surviving contemporaneous letter to Bihler, she wrote, "I very nearly did not see him at all, for no one wished to take me to meet him, not even those who called themselves his best friends."[34] Those reluctant to take her to see Beethoven were probably Antonie and her husband, who, as established by Thayer, already knew him.

In one of the four letters, Bettina mentioned that "we" had to wait for half an hour because Beethoven was shaving at the time.[35] Who was with Bettina? As noted in chapter 7, one possibility was that Bettina was alone but was using the "royal we" in her letter, or that the other person was Beethoven's man-servant, whom she mentioned in another of the four letters as receiving her and chatting with her while they waited.[36] If she was not alone, it is likely that she was accompanied by her married sister Gunda, who was accompanying Bettina in her travels through Europe that year. This was the view of Nohl in publications of his dated after he published the footnote on which Solomon relied.

Thayer interviewed Bettina several times from 1849 to 1855, asking about her recollections of meeting Beethoven as she had described in her missing 1810 Goethe letter and her surviving 1832 letter to Pückler-Muskau, which were the only two published at the time. In his 1877 biography of Beethoven, Thayer wrote, "The present writer had the honour of an interview with Mme. von Arnim in 1849–50, and heard the story [of meeting Beethoven] from her lips; in 1854–5, it was his good fortune to meet her often in two charming family circles—her own and that of the brothers Grimm. Thus at an interval of five years he had the opportunity of comparing her statements, of questioning her freely and of convincing himself, up to this point, of her simple honesty and truth." Of Bettina's accounts in the two letters that had then been published, Thayer wrote, "The two accounts differ, but they do not contradict, they only supplement each other."[37] (Part of Thayer's account of his interviews with Bettina describing her visit to Beethoven's lodgings is set out in chapter 7.) In none of the four letters is there any mention of Antonie, except that Bettina brought Beethoven back to a luncheon party being held at her house that day.

Bettina's account is also corroborated by specific details about their meeting, such as Beethoven playing and singing for her his setting of a poem by Goethe about Mignon (a fictional character with whom she identified, as described in chapter 2), her insistence that he put on a better coat to accompany her back to the party at Antonie's house, and their reception at that party.[38] "Everyone was surprised to see me enter a company of more than forty persons, sitting at the table, hand in hand with the unsociable Beethoven."[39] Later in the same letter, Bettina wrote that a lady at the party played a sonata by Beethoven in his honor, and that he then played it himself. This indicates clearly that the party was a mixed gathering and makes it virtually certain that Antonie would have been the hostess and would not have accompanied Bettina when she went to meet Beethoven.

MORE WEAKNESSES IN THE ANTONIE THEORY

Beethoven wrote many songs between 1809 and 1811, one of them entitled "To the Distant Beloveds" and another entitled "To the Beloved." The first was dedicated to a Viennese princess who certainly was not the Immortal Beloved, but he never dedicated the second. However, a manuscript of the second bears unsigned handwritten words in the upper corner: "requested by me from the author, March 2, 1812." The handwriting is not Beethoven's but is possibly Antonie's. Solomon suggests that the song was written by Beethoven for Antonie, and Solomon used the inscription as evidence that Antonie was the Immortal Beloved. Even if we assume the handwriting is Antonie's, however, the inscription is not a dedication by Beethoven. As noted previously, Antonie was a friend, admirer, and financial supporter of Beethoven, and the words are hardly words of passion referring to a secret lover but rather an acknowledgment that she received the manuscript from Beethoven.[40]

Found with the letter to the Immortal Beloved after Beethoven's death were two miniature portraits in ivory, apparently of two different women. One of them is generally thought to be a woman who certainly was not the Immortal Beloved. As to the other, Thayer thought it was likely Therese von Brunsvik.[41] Solomon thought it was likely Antonie,[42] while proponents of different candidates thought it was likely their candidate.[43] However, there is no evidence that the woman in the miniature was in fact the Immortal Beloved.

In addition to the flaws in Solomon's theory outlined earlier in this chapter, the reader should consider as well the emotional outpouring of Beethoven in his 1812 letter to the Immortal Beloved as contrasted with the polite, formal letter exchanges between Beethoven, Antonie, and Antonie's husband in their surviving correspondence. Unless Beethoven and Antonie were both deceptive, it does not make any sense that those surviving letters could involve the same person as the Immortal Beloved. Compare them with the emotional content of the one surviving 1811 letter from Beethoven to Bettina (see appendix B), a letter that shows his grief at her marriage and his almost obsessive love for her. It has also been established beyond any reasonable doubt by the facts shown in chapter 2 that Beethoven and Bettina were corresponding in the months between 1811 and the time he wrote his letter to the Immortal Beloved.

Finally, the reader should consider whether it makes experiential sense that Beethoven could have had a passionate connection with a woman with four children who was expecting another and was married to a man who subsequently became a financial supporter and respected friend of Beethoven. Why would Beethoven risk sending a long, passionate letter to the small town of Karlsbad where Antonie was vacationing with her husband and one of their children, when all he had to do was wait until they both returned to Vienna? I submit that it does not make experiential sense, let alone evidentiary sense.

In the 1990s, the British writer Susan Lund, an ardent believer in the Antonie theory, visited the ancestral home near Frankfurt of Antonie and Franz, where they lived after they moved from Vienna in 1812. Lund was hoping to find mementos, letters, portraits, or other relics of Beethoven in Antonie's remaining effects or somewhere in her household, but she found none. Contrast this with the finding in Bettina's possessions after her death of a plaster relief of Beethoven, likely a gift from him to Bettina as described in chapter 2. Consider also Bettina's well-known reverence throughout her life for Beethoven and his music, even as musical fashions changed, as described in chapter 3. Finally, consider the pressed foliage and flowers from Beethoven's grave found in the possessions of one of Bettina's daughters, quite likely passed down to her by her mother.[44]

NOTES

1. Solomon, *Beethoven*, 207–46.
2. Schindler, *Beethoven*, 259. If Schindler was referring to Beethoven's letter to him of January 23, 1823, the actual words Beethoven used were "meiner einzigen Freunde in der Welt," or "my only [true] friends in the world." See Brandenburg, Letter No. 1524.
3. Anderson, Letter No. 758; Brandenburg, Letter No. 1083; and Anderson, Letter No. 1064; Brandenburg, Letter No. 1451.
4. Anderson, Letter No. 607; Brandenburg, Letter No. 897.
5. Kopitz, "Antonie Brentano in Wien," 144.
6. Richard Specht, *Beethoven as He Lived*, trans. Alfred Kalisch (London: Macmillan, 1933), 177–80.
7. Thayer Forbes, 646.
8. Solomon, *Beethoven*, 220.
9. Thayer German, 3:216. An abbreviated version of the information supplied to Thayer by the American consul may be found in Thayer English, 2:180.
10. Rita Steblin, "'Auf diese Art mit A geht alles zu Grunde': A New Look at Beethoven's Diary Entry and the 'Immortal Beloved,'" *Bonner Beethoven Studien* 6 (Bonn: Beethoven Haus Verlag, 2007), 153.
11. Solomon, *Beethoven*, 241.
12. Thayer Forbes, 534.
13. Brandenburg, Letter Nos. 450, 460, 547, and 575. The first found pencil-written pocket sketchbook of Beethoven was written in 1811 and contains only 20 small pages. The next found pocket sketchbook was written by him in 1815. See Barry Cooper, *Beethoven and the Creative Process* (Oxford: Clarendon, 1990), 3; and for a more detailed analysis, see *The Beethoven Sketchbooks*, ed. Douglas Johnson, Alan

Tyson, and Robert Winter (Berkeley: University of California Press, 1983), 81–4 and accompanying explanatory charts.

14. Solomon, *Beethoven*, 241, 245.

15. Kopitz, "Antonie Brentano in Wien," 137.

16. Kopitz, "Antonie Brentano in Wien," 137–8.

17. Solomon, *Beethoven*, 243–4.

18. Brandenburg, Letter No. 485. Beethoven referred to Antonie, in his respectful letters to her husband, Franz, as "Toni," not "die Tonie" as he did in this surviving letter to Bettina. I believe the difference to be significant, as he did not refer to her as if she were still a child in letters to her husband but did so to Bettina.

19. Solomon, *Essays*, 175–6.

20. Ludwig Nohl, *Beethovens Leben*, 3 vols. (Leipzig: E. J. Günter, 1867 and 1877), 2:318.

21. Adolph Bernhard Marx, *Ludwig van Beethoven: Leben und Schaffen*, in 2 parts (Berlin: Verlag Otto Janke, 1884), 2:293.

22. Hans Tabarelli, *Altwiener Scherenschnitte* (Vienna: Paul Neff Verlag, 1947), 154.

23. Klaus Günzel, *Die Brentanos: Eine deutsche Familiengeschichte* (Munich: Artemis and Winkler, 1993), 83–86.

24. Schindler, *Beethoven*, 259. The statement of Schindler in his first 1840 edition is quoted verbatim by Thayer in Thayer German, 3:215.

25. Solomon, *Essays*, 175.

26. Ludwig Nohl, *Neue Briefe Beethovens* (Stuttgart: Verlag Cotta, 1867), 53. The principal part of the footnote reads: "Beethoven war . . . nicht bereits wie Schindler angegeben hat, seit 1792 in seinem [Antonie's father's] Hause bekannt; vielmehr ward er, wie mir die jezt 87 jährige Frau Brentano [Antonie] in Frankfurt selbst ausdrücklich versichert hat, erst im Frühjahr 1810 mit dieser seiner Tochter bekannt und zwar in Folge des Besuches von Bettina, die eben nicht nachgelassen hatte als bis ihre Schwägerin sie dorthin begleitet hatte. Ihre Aufforderung folgend war dann Beethoven häufig ungenirter Gast bei Brentanos, die für gewöhnlich in Frankfurt lebend, eben jezt wegen Regulirung der [family] Erbschaft für einige Jahre in Wien anwesend waren."

27. Ludwig Nohl, *Beethovens Leben*, 3 vols. (Leipzig: E. J. Günther, 1867 and 1877), 3:275. Vol. 3, with the description of Antonie's daughter Maxe sitting on Beethoven's lap in 1808, was published in 1877, 10 years after publication of Nohl's footnote on which Solomon relied. Because Thayer in his 1877 biography of Beethoven pointed out the inconsistencies (see Thayer English, 2:180), Nohl added a qualifying endnote in an appendix to his 1877 publication in which he stated that Antonie's daughter Maxe must have sat on Beethoven's lap in 1810 [when she was eight], "or even later"(3.2:873). In the 2nd edition of Nohl's biography (published in 1913), the year in which Maxe sat on Beethoven's lap was changed to 1809 (before Bettina's visit to Beethoven), and Nohl's qualifying endnote was deleted (3:80).

28. Ludwig Nohl, *Beethoven Depicted by His Contemporaries*, trans. Emily Hill (London: Reeves Fleet Street, 1880), 86. Nohl's dedication of this book was dated "Heidelberg, October, 1876," nine years after his publication of the book containing the footnote on which Solomon relied. Also see Nohl, *Musiker-Biographien, Beethoven* (Leipzig: Verlag Reclam, 1917), 66.

29. Sonneck, *Impressions*, 76.

30. Sonneck, *Impressions*, 80.

31. For the original German text of the Brentano family statement, see Thayer German, 3:216. It is set out below, as well as the text of the supplemental statement from the consul.

> Die freundschaftlichen Beziehungen Beethovens zu der Familie Brentano in Frankfurt a/M, resp. zu Frau Antonie Brentano . . . und ihrem Gatten Herrn Franz Brentano . . . entsprangen aus dem freundschaftlichen Verkehr, in welchem Beethoven zu dem Vater der Frau Brentano, dem Kaiserlichen Hofrath Johann Melchior von Birkenstock . . . schon zur Zeit gestanden hatte, in welcher Frau Brentano ihren Vater in Wien besuchte, wohin sie sich im Jahre 1809 mit ihrem älteren Kindern für längere Zeit begab, weil ihr Vater, Hofrath von Birkenstock, schon seit einiger Zeit in ernster Weise kränkelte. Dieser freundschaftliche Umgang wurde auch nach dem am 30 Octob., 1809 in Wien erfolgten Tode des Hofrath von Birkenstock und während des dreijährigen Verbleibens in Wien der Familie Brentano fortgesezt.

The supplemental statement from the consul dated October 18, 1872, reads as follows:

> Ich erfuhr, dass Hofrath Birkenstock ein Freund Beethovens war; dass Beethoven sehr oft im Birkenstockischen Hause war; und dass die Bekanntschaft der Tochter mit ihm vor ihrer Heirath mit Hrn. Brentano begann.

Solomon's incorrect translation of the family statement (Solomon, *Essays*, 175) reads as follows:

> The friendly relations with the Brentano family of Frankfurt [i.e., Antonie and Franz] . . . had their origin in the friendly intercourse between Beethoven and Frau Brentano's father which had existed since the time when Frau Brentano . . . visited Vienna in 1809. . . . This friendly association [i.e., of Antonie and Franz] was maintained after the death of [Antonie's father] on 30 October 1809.

Solomon's phrase "had existed since the time when" should read "already existed at the time when."

It should also be noted that even Solomon's incorrect translation states that the relationship of Antonie and her husband with Beethoven was maintained after the death of Antonie's father in October 1809. That means it existed almost seven months before Bettina came to Vienna and visited Beethoven, which is when Solomon contends Antonie first met Beethoven.

32. Thayer German, 3:216. This additional communication to Thayer from the American consul in Frankfurt to the effect that Antonie was acquainted with Beethoven even before her marriage was not included in Thayer English, 2:180.

33. For letters to Bihler, Goethe (partial text only), and Pückler-Muskau, see Sonneck, *Impressions*, 76–79, 79–82, and 84–88. The complete text of the letter to Goethe may be found in the *Goethe Correspondence* book, 283–8. For the letter to Freyberg, see Steinsdorff, *Briefwechsel Freyberg*, 68–71. Bettina dated the missing Goethe letter May 28, 1810. The surviving letters were dated June 8, 1810 (Freyberg), July 9, 1810 (Bihler), and March, 1832 (Pückler-Muskau).

34. Sonneck, *Impressions*, 76.

35. Sonneck, *Impressions*, 77.

36. Sonneck, *Impressions*, 84.

37. Thayer English, 2:181.

38. Thayer English, 2:186. It was translated as a "dinner party" in Thayer English, but in the original German edition, it was called "Mittagsmahl," a luncheon party. See Thayer German, 3:217.

39. For the letter to Pückler-Muskau, see Sonneck, *Impressions*, 84–88.

40. Solomon, *Beethoven*, 229.

41. Thayer Forbes, 1052.

42. Solomon, *Beethoven*, 230–1.

43. For an overview of the various theories about the two portraits, see Sieghard Brandenburg, *Beethoven: Der Brief an die Unsterbliche Geliebte* (Bonn: Beethoven Haus Verlag, 2001), 54–55.

44. Susan Lund, "The Visit That Beethoven Did Not Make—A Journey to the Brentanohaus in Winkel Germany," *Beethoven Journal* 13, no. 1 (1998): 24–30.

· *13* ·

Synopsis and Conclusion

SUMMARY OF THE NARRATIVE

$\mathscr{P}$resented here is a summary of the narrative contained in chapters 2 and 3 establishing that Bettina Brentano was Beethoven's Immortal Beloved. Following it is a summary of the sources corroborating the facts leading up to this conclusion.

1. Bettina Brentano, a German of Italian descent, age 25, traveled to Vienna in 1810, where she looked up the 39-year-old musical genius Ludwig van Beethoven and spent almost a week in his company, attending concerts, strolling through palace gardens, and attending social functions with him.

2. Bettina, who studied music, played the guitar, sang in choirs and as a soloist, and wrote music that is still performed, was fascinated with genius and especially music. Three years earlier, she had similarly looked up the famous German writer Goethe, 35 years older than she and married, resulting in a lifetime correspondence with him. In one surviving letter to him written in 1810, the same year she met Beethoven, and two years before Beethoven wrote his letter to the Immortal Beloved in which he acknowledged that the Immortal Beloved loved him, she told Goethe emphatically how much she loved him and promised physical intimacy with him as a reward for what his artistic genius had brought to her.

3. Several weeks after Bettina met Beethoven, her future husband, Achim von Arnim, proposed marriage. He needed at least one legitimate child to be able to inherit control over his wealthy grandmother's estate, and he told Bettina he considered her the ideal woman for this purpose. To his astonishment, Bettina initially declined, saying she was contemplating forgoing marriage and devoting her life to a career in music and politics.

120

4. After receiving Arnim's marriage proposal, Bettina wrote a long letter to Goethe asking his advice, and she ultimately traveled to meet him to ask his advice in person. She also wrote two letters to Beethoven.

5. Bettina finally decided to accept Arnim's marriage proposal and married him in a private and secret ceremony in early spring 1811.

6. After the marriage, Bettina continued to write to Goethe and Beethoven, and in midsummer, while on a belated honeymoon, she visited Goethe and his wife. Bettina and Goethe's wife quarreled, and Goethe's wife forbade any further communication between Bettina and Goethe. Goethe acquiesced. Bettina had by then become pregnant.

7. During her pregnancy, Bettina became ill and depressed. She wrote later that a woman finds it difficult not to hate the man who caused her pregnancy. She nearly died at the birth of her child in the spring of 1812. Her doctor prescribed a rest cure for her, so her husband planned to take her to the Bohemian spa town of Karlsbad, where his brother was spending the summer. In the meantime, Bettina continued to write to Beethoven, telling him that having given her husband the child he needed, she considered marriage to have been a mistake, and suggesting and finally promising she would join him in Vienna as his apprentice and muse. She also told him of her husband's plans to take her to Karlsbad, and that if Beethoven went to nearby Teplitz, they could meet in one town or the other, when she would announce her decision to her husband.

8. Beethoven traveled to Teplitz, arriving there in the middle of the night on July 5, 1812. He wrote his letter to Bettina, his Immortal Beloved, over the next several days, intending to send it to her and believing she was by then in Karlsbad. In it, he noted that she was "suffering" and hesitatingly hinted that perhaps they might be able to live together if she came to Vienna.

9. Bettina's departure for Karlsbad had been delayed due to her illness. She induced her sister, who was to travel with Bettina, Arnim, and the baby, to press Arnim not to go to Karlsbad but instead to Teplitz, where both Beethoven and Goethe were. Bettina wrote to Beethoven in Teplitz of her trip's delay and change of destinations, which caused him not to send his letter to the Immortal Beloved. He kept it instead.

10. When Bettina arrived in Teplitz on July 23, Beethoven was overjoyed and wrote immediately to his publisher to send to him in Teplitz as quickly as possible the manuscript of Bettina's favorite song that he had played and sung for her when they met in Vienna two years before. He therefore expected to stay in Teplitz for some time.

11. Bettina and Beethoven met the day after she arrived. Her husband described in a surviving letter Beethoven's "friendly smiles" but noted that the composer was growing increasingly deaf.

12. When Bettina and Beethoven met, she told him that she had changed her mind and would not leave her husband and child to join Beethoven in Vienna.

13. Beethoven was shattered and disoriented. He left Teplitz soon after, neglecting to take with him even his travel papers. In leaving, he handed Bettina a letter in which he wrote that "even minds can love one another," begged her to keep writing to him, and ended with the words "God, how I love you!"

14. Bettina and Beethoven continued to secretly write to one another after Teplitz. Bettina confided to a friend in her old age that Beethoven had loved her until he died.

15. Except for the one letter from Beethoven that Bettina gave away to a young literary disciple in her middle years, no others from him to her survive nor any letters from her to him. This leads to the inference that he agreed to destroy her letters to him before his death to protect her marriage and family, and that she did the same with his letters to her before her death. But she could not destroy the single letter from him that she had given away.

SUMMARY OF THE CORROBORATING SOURCES

This section reviews the sources corroborating the narrative summarized above. No sources are given for facts in the narrative that are generally accepted. Where facts stated in the narrative do not have direct corroborating sources but are reasonable inferences from them, the corroborating sources from which the inferences were drawn are cited. Where facts in the narrative are speculative and have no corroborating sources, such as the contents of letters between Beethoven and Bettina in the interval between his surviving 1811 letter to her and his letter to the Immortal Beloved, the narrative identifies the facts as speculation. The sequence of the corroborating sources generally follows the sequence of the narrative.

1. Bettina's 1810 letter to the 60-year-old married Goethe telling him of her deep love for him and promising physical intimacy as a reward for what his genius had brought to her. See surviving letter from Bettina to Goethe dated January 8, 1810.[1]

2. Time spent by Bettina with Beethoven in Vienna, 1810. See surviving letters from Bettina to Freyburg, Bihler, and Pückler-Muskau[2] and the missing letter to Goethe about Beethoven contained in Bettina's *Goethe Correspondence* book.[3] Critics contend that Bettina exaggerated the number of days she spent with Beethoven in Vienna in her *Goethe Correspondence* book. However, as shown in chapter 7, their contention is wrong.

3. The economic reasons behind Achim von Arnim's marriage proposal to Bettina. See surviving letter from Arnim to Bettina.[4]

4. Bettina initially declining Arnim's marriage proposal for the possibility of a career in music and politics. See surviving letter from Arnim to Bettina.[5]

5. Bettina seeking Goethe's advice about marriage or a music career. This is an inference drawn from (1) the fact that Bettina made a detour to the Bohemian spa town where Goethe was vacationing about nine weeks after she left Beethoven in Vienna and about seven weeks after she received Arnim's marriage proposal; (2) Goethe's surviving letter to his wife written shortly after Bettina left him in which he says that it was quite certain that Bettina had decided to marry[6]; (3) the fact that Bettina's 1810 letters to Goethe, beginning in the middle of a surviving letter just where she started to describe what happened between her and Beethoven and extending up to the time she made her detour to see Goethe, are missing; they did exist, however, because they were referred to in surviving letters from Goethe to her[7]; (4) the fact that Bettina mentioned in a missing letter to Goethe falling within the 1810 Letter Gap (referred to in chapter 4), but rewritten or recreated in her *Goethe Correspondence* book, that she gave several of her songs to Beethoven, who had praised them and suggested that if she were to devote herself to music, she had great musical potential[8]; (5) Bettina's confession in a surviving letter to a young literary disciple many years later that she had broken a promise she made to Beethoven.[9]

6. Bettina's depression during pregnancy and her near death during childbirth. See two surviving letters from Bettina to Arnim and one surviving letter to one of her children.[10]

7. Bettina's correspondence with Beethoven during pregnancy and after childbirth. This is a reasonable inference based on (1) Beethoven's surviving letter to her of February 1811 in which he acknowledges already receiving two letters from her, recognizes her marriage, and begs her nevertheless to write to him again "soon and often"; and (2) the sonnet Beethoven wrote for Bettina that she later gave to Joachim. The contents of her letters to him are unknown, but it is a reasonable inference that she confided in Beethoven her depression, pregnancy, and near death at the birth of her child. It is also a reasonable inference that having been cut off from writing to Goethe, she wrote in a similar vein to Beethoven, admitting a spiritual love for Beethoven and lapsing occasionally into hints of physical longing as she had done previously in her surviving letters to Goethe.[11]

8. Change of plans of the Arnims to go to Teplitz instead of Karlsbad. See surviving letter from Arnim to his brother-in-law Clemens.[12]

9. Beethoven's excitement when Bettina arrived in Teplitz. See surviving letter from Beethoven to his publisher dated July 24, 1812.[13]

10. Beethoven and Bettina meet in Teplitz in 1812. See surviving letter from Arnim to his brother-in-law Savigny commenting on Beethoven's "friendly smiles" and growing deafness.[14]

11. What Bettina told Beethoven when they met in Teplitz. This is a reasonable inference based on (1) Bettina's surviving letter to a young literary disciple written many years later in which she gave him the one letter to her from Beethoven that survives and confessed that she had broken a promise to Beethoven[15]; (2) Beethoven's Teplitz Letter handed to Bettina as he hurriedly left town.

12. Authenticity of Beethoven's Teplitz Letter. This missing letter, written only several weeks after the letter to the Immortal Beloved, proves conclusively that Bettina was that woman. Bettina's editor-publisher certified to Thayer that he had seen and copied it from the original,[16] and its authenticity was also publicly confirmed by a prominent Berlin professor and writer, who stated that he had seen the original and urged its publication by Bettina for political reasons.[17] See chapter 5 for additional evidence proving its authenticity.

13. Beethoven's hurried and unexpected departure from Teplitz. See the surviving July 27 letter from Goethe to his wife that Beethoven had already left Teplitz to go to Karlsbad.[18] There is also the Karlsbad registration of Beethoven on July 30 (there were several days of grace before registration was mandatory), noting that he had left his passport in Teplitz but that he should produce it in a few days.[19] Consider also the fact that Beethoven did not return to Teplitz until the second week of September, around the time when Bettina's original registration there showed she was to leave.

14. Secret correspondence between Bettina and Beethoven after their 1812 meeting in Teplitz. This is a reasonable inference arising from (1) Beethoven's plea in the Teplitz Letter asking Bettina to continue to write to him despite his devastation by her decision[20]; (2) Beethoven's confession in 1816 overheard by a young admirer that the relationship with Beethoven's beloved was the same then as at its beginning five years before (i.e., "a chimera")[21]; (3) Bettina's admission to a close friend shortly before Bettina's death that Beethoven loved her until he died (how would she know if she had not been corresponding with him?)[22]; (4) Bettina asserting facts about Beethoven and Goethe in her surviving letter to a friend in 1832 that she could not have learned during her 1812 sojourn in Teplitz.[23]

15. Destruction of correspondence between Bettina and Beethoven. Bettina carefully preserved letters to her from others, and she actively reclaimed and preserved her own letters to others, as described in chapter 4. But missing are the most significant letters from her to Goethe during the 1810 Letter Gap, starting just where she began to describe what happened between her and Beethoven in Vienna. That they existed is corroborated by Goethe's reference

to them in his surviving letters to her; he called them the most interesting that she had sent to him up to then. We know that by the time of her marriage, Bettina had already written two letters to Beethoven, and Beethoven had written to her at least once before (they are referred to in his surviving letter to her). We know that in the surviving letter from Beethoven to Bettina and in the Teplitz Letter, Beethoven begged her to write to him soon and often.[24] We know that Bettina was a compulsive letter writer (surviving letters from her number in the hundreds). We also know that Bettina refused to discuss her correspondence with Beethoven when asked about it by Schindler when he visited her in 1843. [25] All of this leads to an inference that letters to Bettina from Beethoven were destroyed by Bettina, likely for the reasons discussed in chapter 4. As to the letters from Bettina to Beethoven, we know that two certainly existed and that many others likely existed, yet none were found in his estate. But they were important to him because in his surviving letter to Bettina, he wrote that he carried her first letter around with him all summer. This leads to an inference that either she got them back from Beethoven and destroyed them herself as she had done with some of her Goethe letters, or that Beethoven destroyed them himself, possibly at her request.

CONCLUSION

The purpose of this book has been to show not only that Bettina was Beethoven's Immortal Beloved, but also that (1) she was an extraordinarily musical, literary, artistic and talented woman, worthy of Beethoven's adoration and love; (2) her descriptions of Beethoven are not "richly embroidered" or even concocted as some contend, but are rather the most accurate descriptions we have of this great musical genius, of far greater importance than other accounts of him in his later life by other firsthand witnesses such as Schindler; (3) what she reported he said to her is totally truthful and gives the most penetrating insights into his beliefs and psyche that we have; and (4) throughout her long life, she never betrayed Beethoven or his image, or flaunted her intimacy with him, but in fact tried to hide it, and she also remained an ardent advocate of his music throughout her life even as musical fashions changed.

From a contemporary witness's letter, Nobel Prize laureate Romain Rolland extracted a description of Bettina as she was when she met Beethoven. The writer of the letter, says Rolland, "could not sufficiently idolize and admire this charming girl—the riches of her mind, the bountiful spring of her fancy, her poetical passion, her natural grace, and the kindness of her heart. She was then 25, but appeared to be only 18 or 20 at the most; there was in her nothing false, nothing mean; she displayed a generosity without limit, of both mind and heart, and spontaneity without compare."[26]

As Bettina grew older and married, she became not only a musical composer and performer, but a writer of poetry and literature, an artist, and a political activist who publicly sympathized with the liberal reforms which were the foundations of the 1848 European uprisings. She also advocated expansion of Jewish rights. She spoke her mind to but was nevertheless tolerated and respected by the king of Prussia in the face of her pleas to him to establish a constitutional democratic monarchy. She became prominent in musical and literary circles. The Grimm brothers were close friends. Brahms, Schumann, and Joachim dedicated music to her; Franz Liszt was a friend; and Beethoven would have dedicated one of his masses to her had she not married.[27] Alexander Thayer, the great biographer of Beethoven and a meticulous scholar, met with Bettina repeatedly from 1849 to 1855 and thus, as he stated, "had the opportunity of comparing her statements [about her letters describing Beethoven], of questioning her freely and of convincing himself . . . of her simple honesty and truth."[28]

However, after publication of her *Goethe Correspondence* book in 1835 and of three letters to her from Beethoven in a political journal in 1839, accusations began to be made that she had concocted the letters she claimed to have received from Goethe and Beethoven. Thayer was convinced of the authenticity of the Beethoven letters and defended them vigorously in a periodical and also in the text of his biography of Beethoven. He quarreled with his own German translator, Hermann Deiters, about them, noted that persons who did not know Bettina as he did were wrongly attacking her credibility, and that she ought to have refuted them but "then it was too late—she lay on her death-bed. Her silence under the attacks made upon her veracity is therefore no evidence against her."[29]

After Bettina's death, her detractors began to gain the upper hand, while supporters who knew and admired her, such as Thayer, Carrière, and Nohl, died off. A whole new generation of academics who did not know her, but possibly were biased because of her politics or gender, began to pile calumny after calumny upon her. She was sometimes called "hysterical." Max Unger called her a "phantastin," and Oscar Fambach accused her of forgery (a few of their most blatant academic blunders in their efforts to discredit Bettina are detailed in chapters 9 and 10). When Romain Rolland continued to defend her, he was dismissed by Unger as a Frenchman not capable of understanding Beethoven.[30] Rolland, one of Bettina's last defenders, died in 1944.

So now we have a whole new generation of academics who accept the views of Unger, Fambach, Riemann, and Deiters as akin to absolute truth. They ignore evidence such as that detailed in chapter 11, that the letters from Goethe in her *Goethe Correspondence* book adhered substantially to the originals. As shown in that chapter, the main changes Bettina made to a sample group of them were additions to create a sequential narrative, as well as words she attributed to Goethe supporting the cause of Tyrolean insurgents similar to the thoughts he expressed in *Egmont*. He could not do this in his letters to Bettina because his Weimar employer was part of a political alliance with Bavaria that was suppressing the Tyrolean insurgency.

The academics of the new generation also ignore the evidence obtained by Thayer as to the authenticity of the three Beethoven letters she published,[31] and dismiss as unimportant the fact that one of those survives (the one Bettina gave away), and more importantly, that it is *identical* to what she published. They also ignore the fact that the forum for publication of the Beethoven letters (a literary and political journal) was very different from the forum for publication of her *Goethe Correspondence* book, which she considered an epic of her own personal and artistic development, not simply an edited version of her correspondence with Goethe. As for her description of Beethoven, her critics contend that Beethoven's image has been distorted by what they believe to be overblown accounts of him. But again to quote Rolland:

> Her picture of Beethoven is as true as that famous painting by Claude Lorrain of the Roman Campagna. Scrupulous realism could not reproduce more faithfully the plains of Rome and the brilliance of the light. Thus with the Beethoven whom Bettina saw and painted. No other eye has fathomed the depth of his genius so deeply as hers; feminine intuition absorbed his secret thoughts even before Beethoven himself had a clear conception of them. It is a plunge into the fiery furnace of the Cyclops. Bettina listened, just as Beethoven spoke, in a *raptus*, and that is why she perceived what ponderous intellectuals, who know nothing of the lightning which illuminates the soul, are unable to grasp.[32]

NOTES

1. *Goethe Correspondence* book (German), 671–3.
2. Sonneck, *Impressions*, 76 and 84; and Steinsdorff, *Briefwechsel Freyberg*, 68.
3. Sonneck, *Impressions*, 79–82.
4. Otto Betz and Veronika Straub, eds., *Bettine und Arnim: Briefe der Freundschaft und Liebe*, 2 vols. (Frankfurt: Verlag Josef Knecht, 1986), 2:358. For a condensed English translation of this remarkable letter from Arnim to Bettina, see Helps and Howard, *Bettina*, 71–72.
5. Helps and Howard, *Bettina*, 72; and Betz and Straub, *Bettina*, 2:359.
6. Fritz Böttger, *Bettina von Arnim: Ihr Leben, ihre Begegnungen, ihre Zeit* (Munich: Scherz, 1990), 108; Heinz Härtl, *Bettina von Arnim 1785–1859: Eine Chronik* (Wiepersdorf, Germany: Stiftung Kulturfonds Kuenstlerheim Bettina von Arnim, n.d.), 17; Ingeborg Drewitz, *Bettine von Arnim* (Munich: Goldmann Verlag, 1989), 79.

7. See the chapter 4 discussion of the 1810 Letter Gap. For the text of Goethe's surviving letters, see *Goethe Correspondence* book (German), 2:575–753.

8. *Goethe Correspondence* book, 291.

9. *Ilius*, 2:623. See chapter 3 for a translation of the part of that letter in which Bettina mentions breaking a promise she made to Beethoven.

10. Helps and Howard, *Bettina*, 143; Böttger, *Bettina*, 118; Wolfgang Bunzel and Ulrike Landfester, eds., *Bettine von Arnims Briefwechsel mit ihren Sohnen* (Göttingen: Wallstein, 1999), 1:85; and Steinsdorff, *Briefwechsel Freyberg*, 224–5.

11. *Goethe Correspondence* book (German); 2:671–3.

12. Reinhold Steig and Herman Grimm, eds., *Achim von Arnim und die ihm nahe standen*, 3 vols. (Bern: Herbert Lang, 1970), 1:302–3.

13. Anderson, Letter No. 379.

14. Wilhelm Schellberg and Friedrich Fuchs, eds., *Die Andacht zum Menschenbild: Unbekannte Briefe von Bettine Brentano* (Bern: Herbert Lang, 1970), 178.

15. *Ilius*, 2:623. See chapter 3 for a translation into English of the key part of that letter.

16. Thayer English, 2:185.

17. Thayer English: 2:185.

18. Thayer Forbes, 537.

19. Kopitz, "Antonie Brentano in Wien," 142.

20. Teplitz Letter (for a translation into English of this remarkable letter, see appendix C).

21. Thayer Forbes, 646; Harry Goldschmidt, *Um die Unsterbliche Geliebt: Ein Beethoven Buch* (Leipzig: Rogner and Bernhard, 1977), 100, 472.

22. Rolf Strube, ed., *Sie Sassen und Tranken am Teetisch: Anfänge und Blütezeit der Berliner Salons, 1789–1871* (Munich: Piper Verlag, 1991), 191, quoting Karoline Bauer, a well-known Berlin actress.

23. See the 1832 letter from Bettina to Pückler-Muskau in Sonneck, *Impressions*, 84–8. It is possible Bettina learned details about Goethe and Beethoven in her brief and emotional meeting with Beethoven in Teplitz, but unlikely. See chapter 3.

24. For the text in English of the 1811 found letter from Beethoven to Bettina, see Anderson, Letter No. 296. An independent translation into English of the 1812 Teplitz Letter from Beethoven to Bettina is included in appendix C.

25. Schindler, *Beethoven*, 158.

26. Rolland, *Goethe and Beethoven*, 9.

27. Anderson, Letter No. 325; Brandenburg, Letter No. 523. Beethoven wrote in the letter, "As to the Mass, the dedication might be altered. The lady is now married, so the dedication would have to be changed accordingly." It is a reasonable assumption that given the date of the letter (October 1811), he was referring to Bettina, although the original letter to his publisher naming Bettina has not been found.

28. Thayer English, 2:181.

29. Thayer English, 2:183.

30. Unger, "Romain Rolland als Beethoven-Forscher," *Deutsche Musiker-Zeitung* 60 (May 1929): 440.

31. Thayer English, 2:185.

32. Rolland, *Goethe and Beethoven*, 21.

Appendix A: English Translation of Beethoven's Letter to the Immortal Beloved

Translated by Virginia Beahrs, in "My Angel, My All, My Self: A Literal Translation of Beethoven's Letter to the Immortal Beloved," *Beethoven Newsletter* 5, no. 2 (1990): 29. Courtesy of the *Beethoven Journal*.

PAGE 1

July 6
In the morning.—
    My angel, my all, my self.—only a few words today, and indeed with pencil (with yours)—only tomorrow is my lodging positively fixed, what a worthless waste of time on such—why this deep grief, where necessity speaks—Can our love exist but by sacrifices, by not demanding everything, can you change it, that you not completely mine, I am not completely yours—Oh God

PAGE 2

look upon beautiful nature and calm your soul over what must be—love demands everything and completely with good reason, so it is for me with you, for you with me—only you forget so easily, that I must live for myself and for you [words in italics underlined by Beethoven], were we wholly united, you would feel this painfulness just as little as I—my trip was frightful, I arrived here only at 4 o'clock yesterday morning, because they lacked horses, the postal service chose another route, but what a

PAGE 3

horrible way, at the next to the last station they warned me about travel-ing at night, made me afraid of a forest, but this only provoked me—and I was mistaken, the coach had to break down on the terrible route, a mere bottomless country road without 2 such postillions as I had, I would have been stranded on the way. Esterhazy on the other customary route here had the same fate with 8 horses, as I with four—still I had some pleasure again,

PAGE 4

as always, whenever I fortunately survive something—now quickly to inte-rior from exterior, we will probably see each other soon, even today I cannot convey to you observations, which I made during these last few days about my life—were our hearts always close together, I would of course make none of the sort my heart is full of much to tell you—Oh—there are still moments when I find that speech is nothing at all—cheer up—remain my faithful only treasure, my all, as I for you the rest of the gods must send, what must and should be for us—your faithful ludwig

PAGE 5

Monday evening on July 6—

   You are suffering you my dearest creature—just now I notice that let-ters must be posted very early in the morning Mondays—Thursdays—the only days on which mail goes from here to K.

   —you are suffering—Oh, wherever I am, you are with me, I talk to myself and to you—

   —arrange that I can live with you, what a life!!!! as it is!!!! without you—Persecuted by the kindness of people here and there, which I think—I want to deserve just as little as I deserve it—Humility of man to man—it pains me—and when I regard myself

PAGE 6

in the framework of the universe, what am I and what is he—whom one calls the Greatest—and yet—herein is again the divine spark of man—I weep when I think that you will probably not receive the first news of me until Saturday—as much as you love me—I love you even more deeply but—but never hide yourself from

PAGE 7

me—good night—as one bathing I must go to sleep—Oh god—so near! So far! Is not our love a true heavenly edifice—but also firm, like the firmament— good morning on July 7—while still in bed my thoughts thrust themselves toward you my Immortal Beloved now and then happy, then again sad, awaiting fate, if it will grant us a favorable hearing—I can only live either wholly with you or not at all

PAGE 8

yes I have resolved to stray about in the distance, until I can fly into your arms, and can call myself entirely at home with you, can send my soul embraced by you into the realm of spirits—yes unfortunately it must be— you will compose yourself all the more, since you know my faithfulness to you, never can another own my heart, never—never—O God why have to separate oneself, what one loves so and yet my life in V as it is now is a miserable life—Your love makes me the most happy and the most unhappy at once—at my age I would need some conformity regularity of life—can

PAGE 9

this exist in our relationship?—Angel, right now I hear that the mail goes every day—and I must therefore close, so that you will receive the L[etter] immediately—be calm, only through quiet contemplation of our existence can we reach our goal to live together—be patient—love me—today—yesterday—What longing with tears for you—you—you—my

PAGE 10

love—my all—farewell—o continue to love me—never misjudge the most faithful heart of your beloved
>   *L.*
>   *forever yours*
>   *forever mine*
>   *forever us*

Appendix B: English Translation of Beethoven's Surviving 1811 Letter to Bettina

Vienna, Feb 10, 1811

Dear, Dear Bettine

I have already received two letters from you, and see from your letter to "die Tonie" [Bettina's sister-in-law Antonie] that you still think of me, and far too favorably at that. I carried with me your first letter all summer long, and it has often made me very happy . . . ; although if I haven't written to you often, and although you don't see anything of me at all, in thought I write to you a thousand letters a thousand times. Even though you haven't written to me about it, I can imagine how you have to put up in Berlin with those "worldly" good-for-nothings—much chatter about art but no action!!!! The best description of this can be found in Schiller's poem "die Flüsse," where the Spree River [in Berlin] is imagined to speak about it—you are getting married, dear Bettine, or maybe it has already happened, yet I haven't even been able to see you beforehand; nevertheless may all blessings that marriage offers stream down upon you and your husband; What can I say about myself? "Pity my fate!" I exclaim with poor Johanna [referring to Johanna Sebus, in a poem by Goethe]. If I am granted a few more years of life, I shall thank the all-embracing almighty for it, whether those years be ones of contentment or pain.

If you write to Goethe about me, try to use words that will convey to him my most profound respect and admiration for him. I am just about to write to him myself about Egmont which I have set to music, quite literally out of love for his poetry, which makes me very happy; but who can thank enough a great poet, the most precious jewel that a nation can possess? And now I must close, dear good B. I did not get back home until 4 this morning from a drunken party that made me laugh heartily, and for which I am now

tempted to cry nearly as much. Uproarious jollity often drives me back into myself. Many thanks to Clemens [Bettina's brother] for his kind interest; as for the Cantata the topic is not important enough for us here; it's otherwise in Berlin—as for affection, the sister has such a large part of it that not much is left over for the brother; will he be satisfied with that? And now goodbye, dear, dear B., I kiss you [the words "with pain," so mit Schmerzen!, *are written, then struck out] on the forehead, and thus press on it as with my seal all my thoughts for you [N.B. this entire sentence is written in the intimate German "du" form]. Write soon, soon and often to your friend*
    Beethoven

Illustration 7 is a photocopy of this found letter, reproduced with the kind permission of Sotheby's London from its 1990 Salzer catalogue.

Appendix C: English Translation of Beethoven's Missing 1812 Teplitz Letter to Bettina

$\mathcal{T}$he authenticity of this letter is disputed because the original does not survive. See chapter 5 for a defense of its authenticity. Here is its text.

Dear good Bettine

Kings and princes can indeed make professors and privy councilors, and can hang upon them ribbons of titles and orders, but they cannot make great men, spirits that rise above the world's rabble. That is beyond them, so such great must be held in respect. When two men like Goethe and me come together, then these great gentlemen [kings and princes] should discern what real greatness means in men like ourselves [Goethe and me].

On the way home yesterday we met the entire imperial family. From far away we saw them coming towards us and Goethe slipped away from me to stand to one side; and whatever I said, could not convince him to advance a step further. I pulled my hat down on my head, buttoned my overcoat, and with folded arms pushed through the most crowded part of the group. Princes and hangers-on moved aside into a line; Duke Rudolph took off his hat; the Empress was the first to greet me. Persons of rank know me. To my great amusement, I saw the procession file past Goethe; who hat in hand stood at the side, bowing deeply. Afterwards I criticized him thoroughly, showed him no mercy and reproached him for all his weaknesses, especially relating to you, dearest Bettine. We had just been talking about you. God! Had I been able to spend as much time with you as he has, I know I would have produced many, many more great works. A musician is like a poet; and by a pair of eyes he can feel himself suddenly transported into a lovelier world where mighty spirits join with him to give him daunting challenges.

All kinds of ideas came into my mind when I got to know you in the little observatory during the splendid May rain that excited me as much as you. Then the most beautiful themes came from your eyes into my heart, themes that will enchant the world when Beethoven will no longer be there to conduct them.

If God will only spare me a few more years, I must see you again, dear dear Bettine; so calls within me the voice that must be obeyed and never errs. Even minds can love one another, and I shall always court yours. Your praise is dearer to me than that of the rest of the whole world. I gave Goethe my opinion of how praise should affect people like ourselves—and that we wish to be listened to in the intellects of our equals; forgive me for saying this, but emotion is only for women; but for a man, music must strike fire in his mind. Oh dearest girl! I have known for so long that we are of one mind about everything!!!

The important thing is to possess a beautiful, kind spirit that is shown through every act and in the presence of which nothing need be hidden. One must be somebody special if one wants to be so recognized; the world must recognize him, and it is not always wrong. To me, however, that is of no importance, for I have an even higher aim.

I hope to find a letter from you when I get back to Vienna. Write soon, soon—a long letter. I will be there in a week; the court leaves tomorrow, and there is one more performance today. The empress rehearsed her role with him. He and his duke want me to perform some of my music. I have refused them both. They are both mad about Chinese porcelain so there is need for indulgence, since common sense has taken a back seat. I shall not conform to their silly whims; I shall not take part in absurdities at public cost with princes who never themselves have pay those costs.

Farewell, farewell, darling. Your last letter lay for a whole night on my heart and comforted me there. Musicians are permitted to take those kinds of liberties.

God, how I love you!
Your most faithful friend and deaf brother.
Teplitz, August 1812
Beethoven

As first published in the *Athenaeum* in 1839, the place and date "Teplitz, August 1812" appears at the left-hand margin above and across from Beethoven's signature, which was at the right-hand margin. These words were probably in Bettina's handwriting on the autograph copy loaned to the editor of the *Athenaeum*, a political and literary journal. The letter bore no date or place of writing in the usual place at its head, unlike the other two letters from Beethoven published in the same journal (including the surviving 1811 letter). Edouard Duboc (pen name Waldmüller), who must have been shown the letter by Bettina (see chapter 8), confirms that the letter was undated (see Waldmüller, 228). In Bettina's handwritten copy of the letter in her *Ilius* manuscript (see chapter 5), the date appears below the replication of Beethoven's signature and reads "Teplitz, August 15, 1812."

Bibliography

ABBREVIATED REFERENCES FREQUENTLY CITED

"Anderson." Emily Anderson, ed. and trans., *The Letters of Beethoven*, 3 vols. (London: Macmillan, 1961). This is the most recent collection of Beethoven letters translated into English.

"Brandenburg." Sieghard Brandenburg, ed., *Ludwig van Beethoven: Briefwechsel Gesamt Ausgabe*, 7 vols. (Munich: G. Henle Verlag, 1996).

"*Goethe Correspondence* book." English translation of Bettina von Arnim, *Goethe's Correspondence with a Child* (Boston: Ticknor and Fields, 1859). This is the only English version of the book published in North America. It is out of print and very rare. Thanks to Bruce Charlton of Newcastle University, U.K., it may be found online at www.hedweb.com/bgcharlton/bettina-goethe.html.

"*Goethe Correspondence* book (German)." Original German version of Bettine von Arnim, *Goethes Briefwechsel mit einem Kinde*, vol. 2 of *Bettine von Arnim Werke und Briefe*, 4 vols., ed. Walter Schmitz and Sibylle von Steinsdorff (Frankfurt: Deutscher Klassiker Verlag, 1992).

"*Ilius*." Bettina von Arnim, *Ilius Pamphilius und die Ambrosia*, vol. 2 of *Bettina von Arnim Werke und Briefe*, 5 vols., ed. Gustav Konrad (Darmstadt: Frecken Verlag, Wissenschaftliche Buchgesellschaft, 1959).

"Thayer English." Alexander Wheelock Thayer, *The Life of Ludwig van Beethoven*, 3 vols., ed., trans., and completed by Henry Krehbiel (New York: Beethoven Association, 1921).

"Thayer Forbes." Elliot Forbes, ed. and rev., *Thayer's Life of Beethoven* (Princeton, N.J.: Princeton University Press, 1989).

"Thayer German." Alexander Wheelock Thayer, *Ludwig van Beethovens Leben*, 5 vols., ed. and enlarged by Hermann Deiters and Hugo Riemann (Leipzig: Breitkopf and Härtel, 1923).

OTHER FREQUENTLY CITED REFERENCES

Theodore Albrecht, ed. and trans., *Letters to Beethoven*, 3 vols. (Lincoln: University of Nebraska Press, 1996).

Arthur Helps and Elizabeth Howard, *Bettina: A Portrait* (London: Chatto and Windus, 1957).

Klaus Martin Kopitz, "Antonie Brentano in Wien, 1809–12," *Bonner Beethoven Studien* 2 (Bonn: Beethoven Haus Verlag, 2001).

Ludwig Nohl, *Beethovens Leben*, 3 vols. (Leipzig: E. J. Guenther, 1867 and 1877).

Romain Rolland, *Goethe and Beethoven*, trans. G. A. Pfister and E. S. Kemp (New York: Harper, 1931).

Anton Felix Schindler, *Beethoven As I Knew Him*, ed. Donald MacArdle, trans. Constance Jolly (New York: Norton, 1972).

Maynard Solomon, *Beethoven Essays* (Cambridge, Mass.: Harvard University Press, 1988).

Maynard Solomon, *Beethoven*, 2nd ed. (New York: Schirmer, 1998).

O. G. Sonneck, ed., *Beethoven: Impressions by His Contemporaries* (New York: Dover, 1967).

Sibylle von Steinsdorff, ed., *Der Briefwechsel zwischen Bettine Brentano und Max Prokop von Freyberg* (Berlin: Walter de Gruyter, 1972).

Max Unger, "Auf Spüren von Beethovens Unsterblichen Geliebten," *Musikalisches Magazin* 37 (Langensalza, 1910).

Max Unger, "Neue Liebe, Neues Leben," *Zeitschrift für Musik* 9 (September 1936).

Robert Waldmüller (Edouard Duboc), *WanderStudien: Italien, Griechenland, und daheim*, 2 vols. (Leipzig: Theodor Thomas, 1861). This book is very rare. I located a copy in the Staats und Universitätsbibliothek in Dresden with the sonnet facsimile intact. Since then, Google.de has reproduced the book online, but half the sonnet is cut or blocked out.

Index

About the Author

Edward Walden was born near Toronto, Canada. He obtained a degree in honors history from the University of Western Ontario in London, Ontario, in 1956, a diploma in European philosophy from the University of Vienna in 1957, and a Dr. Juris from York University in Toronto in 1960. Before his retirement in 2001, he practiced law with one of Canada's largest law firms. He has four grown children, one teaching philosophy at New York University in the United States. His interest in Bettina and Beethoven was stimulated by his passion for music, mystery, history, and romance.